n in Charolles, F.ar   , in 19 1.

n Bray, Berkshire, which has held three   s

     won countless awards and w..tten ma   and
       .ks, which have sold over one million copies w   e. In
    e was awarded the OBE.

Praise for *Life is a Menu*

'As an account of what a life wholeheartedly dedicated to the cause of gastronomy actually entails, Roux's memoir is remarkable.'   *New Statesman*

'One of the world's leading gastronomic stars portrays his life in the form of a menu, his reminisences punctuated with an array of fabulous dishes and witty anecdotes.'   *Publishing News*

'Entertaining and instructive reading. You can almost smell the baking, feel the flour on your hands, and taste the mouth-watering delicacies on every page.'   *Living France*

MICHEL ROUX
Life is a Menu

Reminiscences of
a Master Chef

ROBINSON
London

Constable & Robinson Ltd
3 The Lanchesters
162 Fulham Palace Road
London W6 9ER
www.constablerobinson.com

First published in hardback in the UK by Constable,
an imprint of Constable & Robinson Ltd 2000

This paperback edition published in the UK by Robinson,
an imprint of Constable & Robinson Ltd 2003

ISBN 1-84119-242-2 (HBK)
ISBN 1-84119-673-8 (PBK)

Printed and bound in the EU

10 9 8 7 6 5 4 3 2 1

To Mother,

who devoted her life to her four children
and taught me everything.

Acknowledgements

There is only space to mention a few of the many friends, clients and colleagues who have helped me in my life's work.

First and foremost among them all is my wife, Robyn, the great joy of my life. I thank her for making me a nicer person (at least that is what all my friends from the trade say!); for trying to slow me down in my endless need to achieve more; for cooking the most delicious food; and for keeping me young and smiling.

It was Leigh Herbert who telephoned me one morning and arranged for me to meet Robyn. He was once a young apprentice at The Waterside Inn and a very fast learner, especially when in *patisserie*.

In my own early days as a chef, I tended to see the front of the house as second to the kitchen. Over the years, I realised how wrong I was. Silvano Giraldin and Diego Masciaga have been crucial to the success of Le Gavroche and The Waterside Inn. They are among the best *maîtres de maison* in the world.

Pam Keogh is equally inseparable from my memory of Roux Restaurants, having been with us for over twenty years. Whatever happened, however often we brothers changed our minds, she always kept her sense of humour and her smile. She was the perfect representative of the Roux spirit: the first to arrive, the last to leave, always happy to help… and she makes the best cup of tea I have ever tasted!

There are many others who helped us behind the scenes. Michael von Clemm, Jan Bailey and Michael Racher were among the first to invest in Le Gavroche and inspired others to follow. If John Brackenbury had not bent some rather big rules, the business would have folded six months after the opening. His continued loyalty, friendship and advice have been a constant in our lives. Bill Pilgrim had unending patience in teaching me financial skills. And Chris Sellors, who was a young boy of less than twenty when he joined me at The Waterside Inn, worked alongside me for fifteen years on all my books, promotions, demonstrations and consultancies. He is like a spiritual son to me.

For over three decades Andrew Grima has offered me his friendship, wisdom and support as well as continuous inspiration.

Ramon Pajares is the epitome of a great hotelier with fantastic vision. He supported and encouraged the Roux Scholarship since its inception in 1984. We are lucky to work in a generous industry. Around the world, chefs, patissiers, charcutiers, winemakers and hoteliers have welcomed me, all sharing a passion for their craft. In Britain, Richard Shepherd stands out for his boundless generosity. I consider him and Brian Turner to be two of the greatest English chefs of the '70s and '80s, and I am delighted to count them as friends.

In the two biggest consultancy contracts I have held, I was blessed to work with two men who ensured standards to carry my name in the air and at sea. It is not surprising that they were both chefs, Kurt Hafner and Alfred Goldinger.

And how could I fail to mention the thousands of clients who have spoilt me by visiting time after time, and by telling me when things were wrong as well as right. They allow me to do what I most love, which is to make them happy.

In putting together this book, I have had the invaluable support of Julian Nundy, who took time out from his full-time career to visit me regularly, encouraging me to delve deeper into my memory and assisting me in producing the text.

Edmond Oger and Jacques Delfontaine helped me relive the time we worked together for Melle Cécile. The photographs they were kind enough to pass on took me straight back to our Rothschild period. Michael and Sylvia Jay were enormously generous in welcoming me back to the British Embassy in Paris so that I could research my past. Their open-hearted warmth made me feel as if I had never left. Yvon Castel was my soulmate during my army experience in the Sahara with conversation and silence.

Claude Grant, my loyal secretary for the past sixteen years, has supported me through every crisis, big and small. She has typed the manuscripts of all my books with her nimble fingers, often in the quieter hours of her personal time. She has also kept the archives that have been so essential in ensuring the accuracy of these memoirs.

It has been both a pleasure and an inspiration working with my publisher and editor, Carol O'Brien, who is a doyenne of her profession. My thanks are also due to Susan Fleming for her careful editing and to Glynn Boyd-Harte for his fine illustrations.

Finally, I would like to thank my literary agent, Andrew Nurnberg, for his patience, knowledge, love of cooking, and unfailing sense of humour. He is a valued friend who has guided me through the maze of writing this autobiography.

To all these, and the many others I have no space to mention here: I thank you from the bottom of my heart.

Contents

Introduction

From *la France profonde* to rural Berkshire

DURING the Olympic Games in Atlanta in 1996, I was talking to Nadia Comaneci, the legendary Romanian multiple gold-medallist, and her American husband, Bart Conner, himself a dual gold-medallist at the 1984 Los Angeles Olympics. We discussed how some athletes are champions for just a day and then disappear forever from public view. Others, whose success is less ephemeral, have the stamina and skills to hold on to their world and Olympic titles over a period of time. And there are those who build on their sporting triumphs and go on to successful careers in other domains.

Conner asked me what made a three-star Michelin chef. He knew from our conversation that my most prized award, that of *Meilleur Ouvrier de France,* or 'best French craftsman', was awarded in a contest that, like the Olympics, is held every few years. He asked what it took not just to win cuisine's most respected rating but then to keep it year in, year out. How much was it a question of innate gifts, and how much a matter of will and drive? I replied that, in my view, it took about 40 per cent talent and 60 per cent determination, discipline and hard work day after day. 'Just like athletes,' Conner replied.

In the Beginning

I WAS BORN in the small town of Charolles, after which the most famous French beef cattle, the Charolais, are named, on 19 April 1941, ten months after France's Second World War defeat by Germany. Years later, my mother told me I was born in the same bed as my paternal grandfather. She said I was so small and thin that, when she looked at me for the first time, she cried out, 'My God, how ugly he is! He looks like a scalded cat!' I was the third child in the family, following Liliane, who was seven, and Albert, five.

We lived at 3 Place de l'Eglise over the *charcuterie* which belonged to that same grandfather, Benoît Roux. Before I was born, he had retired and

1

handed over the business to Francis Chevalier, his best apprentice, as my father, Henri, although a *charcutier* by training, had been considered too inexperienced to take over the business. As the German occupation began, my father started working as a woodcutter in nearby forests and had to leave home before dawn. This had the advantage of keeping him out of sight of the Germans, and he thus avoided being sent off to Germany, as many young Frenchmen were, to work in the place of Germans called up into the armed forces.

From a very early age I knew the days of the week, not by their Monday-to-Friday names, but by what Francis was making in the *charcuterie*. I could tell where we were on my own internal calendar by the smells of *boudin,* black pudding, on the Monday, *andouillettes*, chitterling sausages, on Tuesday, and so on throughout the week. The wonderful smell of pâtés, terrines, and of curing ham or bacon came wafting up the stairs and swirling through the open windows. Francis, who shared the third floor of the building with us, used to sell us his wares at knock-down prices, helping my mother vary our menus in those difficult wartime days.

At the beginning of 1944, fearing the German troops whose presence was becoming more and more overbearing and menacing, we moved a few miles from Charolles to live over the stables on a friend's farm in the village of Prizy. We swapped the odours of *charcuterie* for the more earthy smells of hay, animals and cow-dung, and ran around in fields which filled with mushrooms in August. Half a dozen rabbits living in a hutch and a hen that followed my mother everywhere made up the rest of our community. During our stay there, I was baptised. My godfather, Jeannot Pinot, described as a cousin by my father, was in reality, I later learned, my half-brother...

I have no recollection of the meal that followed my christening but I imagine it was rabbit with wild mushrooms and some of the wonderful fresh vegetables that my mother grew in her kitchen garden. It would no doubt have been followed by some of the juicy pears that were to be had from a pear tree a little way from the farmhouse.

My mother, Albert and I returned to Prizy in 1992. The farmhouse was abandoned and in ruins and the pear tree had gone. Though Mother refused to go in, because of all the memories this would evoke, we went and bought a picnic of pâtés and a knuckle of ham from Grandfather Benoît's old shop.

My grandfather had died in 1950 at the age of eighty-four. I remember him as an upright, hard-working man who was respected by everyone in that very rural part of *la France profonde,* deepest France. My recollections of him, of course, are very faint, but I do remember a sensation of calm and well-being on the occasions he put me on his knee.

The Move to Paris

AFTER spending the last year of the war in Prizy, we went back to our home in Charolles where we stayed another two years. Then, in 1946, the family moved to Saint-Mandé, on the eastern edge of Paris. Our new flat had two rooms and a tiny kitchen but no bathroom. The only luxury was a private lavatory (many modest Paris households then had communal toilet facilities). Shortly after we moved in, my mother gave birth to another sister, Martine, adding a baby's cries to already difficult living conditions. I shared a double bed with Albert. The other room served as dining-room and bedroom for my parents. Liliane slept there too on a sofa-bed, and Martine had a cot. Sardines, in my view, have a better deal: at least they have oil in their tins to stop them chafing against one another!

My father went into business the following year with a partner who had opened a *charcuterie* nearby in Vincennes. My father was talented and hard-working, and quickly attracted a good clientele. No one could make better *boudins,* black or white, liver pâté or veal's head pâté than my father. Just recalling the tastes and smells makes my mouth water. He was not, however, a reliable man. He gambled away his inheritance from his own father on horse-racing, and what he earned from day to day never lasted long. Then my mother found out that he had a mistress. The business started to go down-hill and, finally, the shop was closed to stave off bankruptcy.

My father spent less and less time at home. He found a job in a *charcuterie* near the Place d'Italie in the south of Paris then changed jobs again and again, only rarely giving my mother any money. His absence disturbed me and I transferred all my affection to my mother who had started taking cleaning jobs to feed and clothe us. By the time I was eight, my sister Liliane was fifteen and had left school to work in a *charcuterie* herself. Albert and I were at the local Paul Bert primary school. Fortunately, Liliane helped out with the household chores. That Christmas, Liliane built us a manger from brown packing paper decorated with snow made from cotton wool. On Christmas Eve, she found a candle somewhere that she put next to the Three Kings. The flickering flame seemed to bring the little plaster figures to life. On Christmas morning, Albert and I found by the manger two large balls wrapped in silver paper taken from a chocolate packet. Inside were two oranges. That was the first orange I had ever eaten, and we shared them out with great ceremony.

Every 1 May gave me an opportunity to raise a little money for the family. On that day, French law allows the sale of *muguet,* lily of the valley, picked in the wild. It is a traditional way for children to raise some pocket money. I used to go to the Sénart forest, pick as many flowers as I could carry and bring them back home. I put them in water and wrapped individual sprigs in cellophane. On the May Day holiday, I stood outside the local *métro* station and usually sold out within a couple of hours. I always kept the last sprig for my mother.

My mother attached huge importance to our diet. Her cooking was designed mainly to nourish us, but even after her hard-working days, she did it with great care, using the post-war ration tickets to vary the ingredients whenever she could. When she made a *blanquette* of veal, I would beat the two or three egg yolks in a bowl with a fork while she poured in the stock from the dish. I was fascinated by the transformation as the stock thickened and turned into a creamy sauce. I even enjoyed peeling and mashing potatoes and, when my mother took the vegetable mill from the cupboard, I was there like a shot, frantically turning the handle. The steam rose into my face and I loved inhaling that potato smell. When the job was done, I added a little knob of butter, something that could not be done lightly on our budget, and a drop of boiling milk. I would then taste the result with my finger, once, twice and perhaps a third time, until I heard my mother sharply telling me to 'Think of the others'.

My mother made her vinaigrette with just the right quantities of mustard, vinegar and oil, and left me to mix the salads, particularly the dandelion salad with diced bacon. I adored the appetising smell it produced. My fascination for cooking grew naturally by my mother's side, but I was as much attracted to the world of sugar as I was to the world of salt. I helped make flans that we called *caberons,* and fruit *clafoutis*, tarts and pancakes. I used to delight in flipping *crêpes* in the pan and soon became a virtuoso.

One summer, I went to the Alps to a children's *colonie de vacances*, organised by Mademoiselle Baudron, a social worker at our local town hall. We children, either excited by the adventure (as I was), or anguished by separation from our families, travelled from the Gare de Lyon to Annecy by night train, our sleep broken by the whistles and loudspeaker announcements at stops along the way. The Vignaults, the couple who ran the camp near La Clusaz, adored children. They had several of their own and did all they could to make our stay comfortable and fun. I adored the tranquillity and the clean air of the mountains, the icy water we found in troughs and the sightings of a dormouse, red squirrel or fox. On day-long hikes, we used to pick bilberries, raspberries and wild strawberries. At those heights, their smell and taste had an intensity that I have never found elsewhere.

From mid-August on, after some rain, we began to find cep or chanterelle mushrooms that we took back to add new flavours to our meals. When the rain lasted for several days, we were rewarded by the appearance of snails that were also destined to find their way to our plates. Raw hams were made in nearby villages, as were Reblochon and Tomme de Savoie cheeses, and we occasionally enjoyed them with a local bread which had a slightly sour taste. At the end of many a day, I would watch the cows coming back to their byres and the farmer would often give me a glass of smooth, fresh milk.

Later in the summer, my mother took us to the Atlantic coast, to Saint-Gilles-Croix-de-Vie where we exchanged the mountain air for the iodine of the sea, collecting fresh milk every evening from another farm, cooking sardines on a barbecue and picking mulberries that stained our fingers like ink. This fruit was turned instantly into jam. We carried it back in jars like trophies to Saint-Mandé for the winter months.

In the school yard, the boisterous pushing and shoving that often degenerated into fighting never bothered me. Albert, my brother, was never far away and I was under his protection until the day he left school. The same could not be said of life at home. Our bedroom was heated by a boiler made by the Godin company. One evening when I particularly annoyed him, Albert lifted me up and sat me down bare-bottomed on the stove. My screams brought my mother running, and she lifted me off to find the word 'Godin' branded in reverse on my backside!

When Albert finally left school, he broke with the family *charcuterie* tradition to become an apprentice in a *pâtisserie*. Since his shop was on the road between home and school, I often dropped in at the back door, the door of the '*laboratoire*' where the food was prepared. I only had to open my mouth and Albert would pop something he had just made into it. My favourite was the *religieuse* with a pastry cream that seemed to explode in my mouth.

I had a wonderful teacher for my last two years of elementary schooling, M Guignard, a man who had the gift of understanding each child and of deciding whether he or she was really a dunce or just stubborn. Thanks to him, I obtained my one and only academic diploma, my school-leaving certificate.

After school, I always went straight home to help my mother. I would go to the market on the Avenue de Paris on Thursdays and Sundays, either very early or very late to avoid the crowds, when the stallholders would take greater care of me. At the end of the day, prices used to tumble. I began to understand how to find the best cheese or identify good-quality meat. A pork wholesaler near the market, called Chandon, employed several butchers whose job it was to unload whole pigs from wooden carts. Lumps of pork fat would get left behind which I was often given, good for frying that evening's potatoes. On the way home, I stopped at the baker's for a 'polka' or 'restaurant' loaf, seeking well-cooked bread with a good thick crust. My mother used to say bread was earned with the sweat of her brow and she never failed to make the sign of the cross with the point of her bread knife before slicing it.

I have few fond memories of my father and, when I was about ten, he finally disappeared. I remember him with his ear pressed up against a crackling radio following one of his two passions: horse-racing or the constant succession of prime ministers, some of whom often lasted no more than a day or two. My father was fascinated by France's political instability. He was jubilant when the Communists or Socialists came up with magic solutions to make the people prosper. He dreamed of the pre-war Popular Front. From that, I suppose, came my own aversion to left-wing political parties and to the promises and lies that so resembled those my father used to make to my mother. Evening meals when he was there were usually sad and silent affairs. He sat in silence and his presence struck the rest of us dumb as well.

As I prepared for my first communion in our local church, the priest recruited me for the choir. My voice was much admired and I enjoyed singing, but Mass bored me to tears. It was then that I entered my first competition – as a singer – but in secret so that no-one would know if I failed. The contest was organised at the local Le Rex cinema one Thursday afternoon, and there were about twenty of us, both boys and girls. When my turn came, I sang *'Mon Petit Bonheur'* by Félix Leclerc. I didn't keep time with the pianist very well – the stress of the moment made me pump out the words too quickly – but when they announced the *'Titi Roi des Gosses de Paris'* (The Little King of the Kids of Paris), my name was called. I ran home to show my certificate to my mother. I had won my first competition!

A Pâtissier's *Apprentice*

I DECIDED to become a *pâtissier* like Albert and, in June 1956 when I finished my schooling, I found a place at Camille Loyal's *pâtisserie* in Belleville in northern Paris. Loyal, stocky with a greying moustache, was a taciturn and imposing man who told my mother that my small wage showed how times had changed. In his day, his parents had had to pay for his apprenticeship. He offered me a three-year contract and, despite his suggestion that I should think things over for a few days, I accepted on the spot.

I started my new job at six forty-five on 1 September after the summer holidays. I changed into my new *pâtissier's* overalls, put on my *calot*, the white *pâtissiers'* cap, and entered the shop's *'laboratoire'* where all the preparation was done. I greeted Loyal and Guy, another apprentice, somewhat shyly and began my first day's work by Loyal's side. I was to help him prepare puff pastry. The rolling pin slipped from my hands at first, but I soon had it under control. During that day, although my mother refused to believe it when I told her in the evening, I formed the basic puff-pastry dough into a smooth ball, cut a cross in the top and, on a lightly floured surface, rolled out the dough from the middle of the cross in four places, leaving a raised platform in the centre, like four ears surrounding a small head. I put chilled butter on the head, folded over the four ears to enclose it completely, making sure that the butter could not ooze out. Immediately I did this, Loyal took it away to complete the lengthy rolling, turning, layering and chilling process that the finest puff-pastry demands.

At around nine o'clock, we had a large bowl of coffee with some warmed-up croissants from the day before, and buttered *tartines* made from *baguettes*. Mme Loyal and Maryse the *vendeuse*, a pretty brunette aged about thirty, joined us for breakfast. The coffee break lasted fifteen minutes and Loyal was in total charge – of its length, the subject of conversation and whether or not we too might get a word in. He was from Alsace. He was disciplined, meticulous, hard-working, an artist, an excellent manager and very talented at making all sorts of gâteaux, desserts, ice-creams and chocolates. I felt secure in his presence and this helped me do my best. In less than a year, I could make about three-quarters of the goods that he sold to his regular and faithful clientele. Sunday, when many people would make the trip from the suburbs – such was Loyal's reputation – was our busiest day.

I got my first pay on the last Sunday of the month. I was hugely proud and put it in the purse Albert had given me before he left home to do his military service. Around five o'clock I rushed to the Bois de Vincennes to find my mother sitting on our usual bench by the lake. It was a pleasure to be able to hand her my hard-earned money.

A few months later, I bought myself a Solex moped so that I could get to work every Sunday morning, when the *métro* opened later than usual, by five sharp. My boss would not tolerate lateness, even just a few minutes. I often arrived early enough to go to the La Veilleuse café near the Belleville *métro* station to drink black coffee with two buttered *ficelles* of bread on the zinc bar counter. Paris was just beginning to wake up but some of the other customers were already on their first *ballon* of red wine. Sundays were my favourite day for two reasons: the working week was drawing to a close and the shop was filled with different and savoury odours. Many customers brought their Sunday roasts – legs of lamb, beef, ducks or chickens, surrounded by vegetables – to cook in the Loyals' ovens. As the junior apprentice, it was my job to watch over the cooking, turning the vegetables and basting the meat.

The Loyals had a house in the country outside Paris where they spent Mondays when the shop was closed. They would often arrive the next day with fruit from their garden – apricots, cherries, nectarines and apples – to be used in tarts. I particularly disliked the apples that arrived by the caseful in October, all different shapes and sizes, some shrivelled, some with worms in. We had to stay on after the usual ten- to twelve-hour working day to peel and chop them. They were then turned into a *compôte* with which we used to fill tarts throughout the winter.

Holiday times were very busy. Epiphany was the first of the year, when the French eat the traditional *galette des rois*, a golden flat marzipan-filled piece of puff pastry with a *fève* hidden inside. The person who finds the lucky charm in their piece is designated king or queen of the holiday. From my second year, I was in charge of the oven and cooked more than 600 *galettes* in three days. Then came Valentine's Day with a rush on treats for lovers, Easter with its eggs as well as hundreds of kilograms of tiny chocolate pieces, and then Mother's Day when children would order a special dessert, sometimes weeks in advance. There were also huge *croquembouche* pieces for first communions. I would have to deliver all these in a wicker basket on foot, sometimes several miles from the shop and often up several floors in buildings with no lifts. Summer brought its own surge in work when we made all kinds and flavours of ice-cream. These had to be churned several times a day in the cellar until our fingers cracked and grew sore with the cold.

Nothing, however, compared with December when we opened every single day and worked non-stop. We had to make literally thousands of *bûches,* yule logs big and small, chocolate or coffee-flavoured, with or without praline. From 20 December until the morning of Christmas Eve, Guy and I slept on sacking by the ovens, getting up, aching all over, at three in the morning after only four hours' sleep to start the day's work. During the night, fat, glistening cockroaches that nested between the ovens used to emerge, sometimes jolting me out of my sleep as they ran across my hand. On Christmas Day, Loyal sent out to the local café at lunch time for our *apéritif.* This could be a lemon-flavoured *Picon Citron*, a *fond de culotte,* a 'knicker bottom', of Suze with blackcurrant syrup, or a Dubonnet. Mme Loyal and Maryse always left the shop and joined us back in the laboratory for this little celebration. It was a moment to take stock of what we had accomplished. As Loyal used to say, a good job takes no longer than a bad one and it has the added bonus of being immensely satisfying.

I spent most of my time off, on Mondays, cooking at home, making madeleines and tarts, and prepared parcels of pastry and cakes to send out to Albert in Algeria. When my mother came home after work, I would give her what I called my *'douceur pour toi',* 'a sweet for you'. Then I set about cleaning the coal stove and the working surfaces in the kitchen until they all shone. Once a week, I went to evening classes to work towards my diploma as a pastry-cook. I was especially enthusiastic about the decorative and artistic aspects of the trade and fascinated by the forms I could make with sugar.

Of those three years of my life, I retain a strong memory of intense physical fatigue, especially when there were deliveries of dozens of sacks of flour or sugar. As the youngest apprentice, it was my job to take them to the store on the fifth floor of the building, up a tortuous narrow staircase. Some of the sacks weighed as much as I did. At eight o'clock every Tuesday morning, come rain or shine, I had to clean the main shop window. I had twenty minutes in which to do it and, for material, I had only old newspapers and a vinegar and water solution. Mme Loyal would watch me over her spectacles from inside the shop as I worked. It was also a time of sexual awakening. Maryse used to rub her breasts against me as she came down the stairs to where Guy and I dressed and undressed. At first, I did not know how to react. After a few months, her black skirt often carried the floury marks of my hands. Guy explained to me that she was just a tease.

Over those years, I faithfully wrote down all the recipes we used, and this was to become my bible, still with me now, over forty years later. It is now marked throughout with buttery fingerprints, and smudges of sugar and chocolate, proof of its usefulness and vitality. *Pâtisserie*, as taught by Loyal, instilled in me a sense of discipline, organisation, love of a job well done, and a respect for the raw materials of my chosen trade.

On Her Britannic Majesty's Service

MY apprenticeship nearing its end, Albert, by now *sous-chef* in the kitchens of the British Embassy in Paris, suggested I apply for the position of pastry-cook there. I was taken on, which delighted me, as the Embassy was famous for the high quality of its food and its elegant receptions, rivalled only by the nearby American Embassy. M. Loyal gave me a glowing reference and, as I left, paid me the compliment: 'You are the first apprentice I've not had to kick in the arse.'

The change of district from the working-class Belleville for the elegant rue du Faubourg Saint Honoré was a real culture shock. There was no more dancing in the streets to the sounds of an accordion on Bastille Day, 14 July. Instead there was the calm of luxury boutiques, the Elysée Palace, the Rothschilds' magnificent *hôtel particulier*, and of the British Embassy itself, originally purchased by the Duke of Wellington. On 1 February 1959, I walked into number 39, and was put into the care of Emile Rouault, the chef.

- Biarritz : 250 gr de beurre, 500 gr de sucre glacé 6 œufs, 300 gr de farine, 150 gr de fecule, Vanille.

- Brioche : 1 l de farine, 15 gr de levure, 15 gr de sel 6 œufs, 30 gr de sucre, 350 gr de beurre a mettre en dernier avec le sucre un fois la pâte corsée.

Batons salés : 1/4 d'eau chaude, 25 gr de sel, 15 gr de levure, 375 gr de beurre, 25 gr de sucre, farine 1 kg (Parmesan)

- Biscuit cuillère : 20 jaunes montés avec 300 gr de sucre 20 blancs montés avec 200 gr de sucre, 600 gr de farine melanger les deux appareil.

- Bavaroise : 1/4 de lait, 4 jaunes, 1/4 de sucre, 4 feuilles de gelatine, crème fraîche fouettée.

- Bombe : 150 gr de sucre, 3 jaune d'œuf, 1 longua de crème fraîche, 1/2 quart de lait, melanger le tout a froid porter a ébullition laisser refroidir passer et ajouter 1 litre de crème fouettée.

- Bombe Bellegarde : chantilly chocolater mouler avec des cerises au sirop, 3 heures de Freezer. Demouler et servir avec petit gateau.

Barquette : en pâte sablé garnie crème au beurre à l'Anglaise, glacer fondent decorer d'un petit mimosa ou boule Argent servir bien frais.

Bananes Alibust : Soufflé Vanille avec bananes cuite et confiture abricot cuire dans plat de terrine. poudrer au sucre glace.

Brioche : melanger a peine le tout laisser pousser 2 Heures rompre puis une autre pousse 2 Heures et mettre au Frigidaire (proportion d'un recette normale)

Biscuit Roulé au beurre : 6 œufs - 190 de sucre - 150 gr farine 9 gr beurre -

*Mostly I only listed the ingredients, since once I had
made something I remembered the method.*

11

Life is a Menu

The British Embassy kitchen was huge. It had a cold part for storage, a separate pastry section (where I was to spend my time), and a central coal-fired oven in front of which Albert and three *commis* chefs worked. As soon as I finished preparing my desserts, I used to go to Albert's side to learn about savoury and other aspects of cooking, and soon I became part of the team.

The lunch-time service lasted three hours. First, we fed the Embassy domestic staff, of whom there were about twenty, then we made up trays for the secretaries and Colonel Andrew G. Graham, a typical Englishman, with a back as straight as a rod, a weatherbeaten face (no doubt a result of many overseas campaigns), a carefully groomed moustache and pink cheeks that one could easily imagine turning red at times of anger. He was in charge of the day-to-day running of the Embassy. We then devoted ourselves to the ambassador, Lord Gladwyn Jebb, and his guests. Usually, there were just a few, four to eight people, when the menu was simple and classic, roast or grilled lamb, always with mint sauce. This was new to me, and I felt it drowned the taste of the meat. Or there might be chicken with bread sauce, which I came to like in time. In the evenings, there were numerous cocktail receptions, for which we made hot and cold canapés, among them little cheese pastries and baked chipolatas with honey and prunes wrapped in bacon.

I was also amazed by the splendour of the big dinners, which might be attended by as many as 140 guests. For these, Rouault used to bring in chefs from outside. I particularly remember two brothers, Daniel and Edmond Pinaudier. Edmond was about sixty, his brother ten years older. Both possessed uncommon skills and I watched their every movement. They often told anecdotes drawn from their long careers. Daniel, whom I particularly liked, had worked in a number of aristocratic homes and had been the Duke of Windsor's chef during the Second World War. Apart from tales of celebrities he had known and of his travels, he taught me about herbs, warning me against using them to excess.

Foie gras, caviar and smoked salmon were often served at those dinners. We would work for days beforehand preparing thousands of baked château potatoes or hundreds of artichoke bottoms. Podding peas for 140 people, taking care to keep only the smallest, was not a mind-expanding task. In addition, huge patience was needed to decorate some of the cold dishes, like salmon, sea bass or chicken, with aspic. However, through this, I learned to arrange tarragon leaves, hard-boiled egg-whites cut to look like

12

lily of the valley, or small pieces of truffle on dozens of pieces of fish or meat. This required amazing concentration, and the whole process delighted me. During the game season, roast pheasants were served with their plumage as decoration. Roast beef was pre-carved and formed on bases made of decorated, fried bread.

Some thirty minutes before the first dish left the kitchen, Rouault would call all the cooks round him. A small man, he would climb on a stool and count to make sure that all sixteen or eighteen of us were there. There would be complete silence as he gave his last-minute instructions. Behind him, on the hot-plates, there would invariably be a battery of copper pans containing vegetables and sauces: inside the ovens, there might be hindquarters of lambs, loins of veal, phalanxes of pheasants or farm hens.

The service in the dining-room was no less theatrical and spectacular. The food was arranged beautifully on solid silver trays, and butlers and valets in tail-coats and white gloves took them without a sound from the kitchen into the magnificent dining room. I was proud to play a role in those great dinners, and not a single day of my fifteen months in the Embassy was boring or ordinary. Six months into my time there though, our lives were to change. Albert left to become the personal chef of the horse-trainer Major Peter Cazalet at Fairlawne in Kent which, although we didn't recognise it at the time, was the true beginning of our British adventure.

However, as if practising for the future, I was learning about British food at the Embassy. I discovered the glories of Stilton cheese, which we served in a white napkin accompanied by a vintage port. When three-quarters of the Stilton had been eaten, we poured in a little port and then scooped the cheese out on to chunks of celery or little squares of toast to make canapés. In winter, I made orange marmalade and Christmas puddings for the following year, two British favourites utterly alien to me at first. Every day, I would spend hours making Melba toast, especially before a big dinner. I had to master scones and orange cakes for tea. We also had to prick hundreds of bitter oranges with cloves to fill the air of the Embassy salons with their fresh, musky scent. One of the rare things that upset me was the use of margarine rather than butter in *pâtisserie*. Rouault used to say this was not just for reasons of cost but because margarine was better, particularly in puff pastry. I was in total disagreement.

The darling of the kitchen staff was Stella Jebb, the ambassador's daughter. She was smiling, beautiful, young and very kind. She worked for *Vogue* and would sometimes be out until very late which caused her to miss regular meals. Often her head would suddenly appear in the serving hatch, asking for a meal tray. Occasionally, to our great pleasure, she came into the kitchen. During my time there she married, and about 1,000 guests came to her reception in the Embassy. It fell to me to make the seven-tier wedding cake, my first ever.

From my bedroom on the second floor of the Embassy, I could see the workshops of the Lise fashion house where a number of young seamstresses worked. For the feast of Sainte Catherine on 25 November 1959, they organised a dance in the workshop and, by sign language, invited me over. I arranged an evening off, and found myself surrounded by charming girls. I struck up a conversation with Françoise Becquet, a girl of my age who was shy and sweet, with a disarming smile. We danced a *slow* then a twist. Three years later, we married.

I left the Embassy on the last day of April 1960. On the recommendation of Emile Rouault, I had taken a post as *commis* in the kitchen of Cécile de Rothschild, five doors down the street. I was to be mainly responsible for preparing meals for the fifteen or so staff.

It was less the immense Rothschild fortune that impressed me about my new employers than the family's reputation for having one of the most refined tables in Paris. They wanted quality above all and did nothing for show. My boss, Armand Jonard, the chef, was an elegant, tall man with white hair, who spoke little and then only about work. Although dedicated, he disliked being subjected to the whims of his employers who created and dictated the menus for every meal. When Marcel Muet, the butler, would tell him at the end of a day's work to wait until Cécile de Rothschild handed him the order book for the next day, he would show his displeasure with a short epithet or angry wave of the hand.

After a few weeks, on days when there were not many guests for dinner, and Jonard had a day off, I was left to handle all the cooking. Before taking any holiday, Jonard would stock up with as much food as possible, and leave instructions that staff meals should not cost more than seven to eight *francs* per person while those of Cécile de Rothschild and her guests could run to fourteen *francs*. Quickly, the lady of the house began to put me to the test, suddenly inviting six or eight people and asking me to prepare a soup of vegetables of the season, a farm hen with tarragon and an *omelette Rothschild* for dessert. To my surprise, she would not hesitate to come into the small but well-equipped kitchen to check on how things were going. She was nearing fifty, and tall, slim and naturally elegant. Even dressed in a potato sack, she would have looked smart. Her personality commanded respect, and her deep, rather masculine voice, induced perhaps by incessant smoking, only added to her aura. I must have passed some sort of test fairly early on, as I assumed many more responsibilities as time went by.

Although this first interlude with the Rothschilds was to be a short one – I was called up for my military service after ten months – it was highly fruitful. Jonard was impressed by my skills with sugar and encouraged me to develop and to enter competitions. When I obtained my first bronze medal at the age of nineteen, Jonard made sure that Cécile de Rothschild knew. She congratulated me but told me that, in the future, I was expected to come back with the first prize.

Occasionally, when there were guests at the Rothschild house at Noisy-sur-Oise, north of Paris, Jonard and I would go there to help Madeleine, the regular cook. On one occasion, Cécile de Rothschild took me alone and, dispensing also with the services of the chauffeur, drove her Bentley herself. After what seemed like an interminable silence, she began to talk as she drove and questioned me closely about myself and my work. When she heard that I was going into the army, she asked for my call-up order and made the right contacts to ensure that I went into specialised and privileged units. Once my induction courses were over, I was back cooking again, this time for the military.

Desert Cuisine

I BECAME a soldier in 1961, when France was bogged down in its long war in Algeria. Albert had spent three years in military service, two of them in Algeria, and the death in combat of some of his army friends was to affect him for several years thereafter.

Joining the 93rd Infantry Regiment at Frileuse in Picardy, I was moved to Satory near Versailles. My high point in that first year was writing to my mother and Françoise to tell them not to miss the 14 July Bastille Day parade on the avenue des Champ-Elysées. I was to be one of the 4,000 soldiers marching past and saluting Charles de Gaulle. That was a rare moment of variety in otherwise monotonous months. In Satory, I and four other conscripts, all cooks in civilian life, cooked for about 100 people every day. Nobody recognised our talents and, although I tried to raise the quality of the products used and dishes prepared, I quickly realised that this was futile.

One positive piece of news was the ceasefire that ended the Algerian war in March 1962, but with the nationalist OAS fighting to keep Algeria French, and some Algerian factions insisting on France's immediate departure, the following months were destined to remain tense. The French army had the official mission of maintaining order. On 19 April, my twenty-first birthday, I left Marseilles by ship for Algeria, then travelled by a train worthy of a Western to Béni-Ounif, an oasis on the frontier with Morocco, and on to an army research base, B-2 Namous. There were just a handful of conscripts there. Other parts of the base housed an ever-changing contingent of around thirty soldiers of the Foreign Legion, given a rest from the front line with a spell overseeing security at the camp.

Life there, like the dull, low buildings that made up the camp, was monotonous. The summer temperatures could go as high as fifty degrees centigrade, and a bright red cloud rising above the horizon heralded the beginning of a suffocating sand storm which covered the once white walls of the base with ochre dust. Vegetation was practically non-existent, with just a few dried up tufts here and there. Animal life was mainly hostile consisting of snakes (which often found their way into the showers or latrines), scorpions and tarantulas, forcing us to remain permanently alert for danger. Fortunately, Yvon Castel, our Breton corporal and medical orderly in charge of an impressive collection of antidotes, was there to reassure us. After a while, we learned to catch and kill the snakes and preserve them to take back to France to impress our families, friends and girlfriends. At night, we would hear the cackle of hyenas and Yvon, who was also the base meteorologist, sometimes saw the reflections of the eyes of jackals when, with his torch, he went out before dawn to take his first measurements.

Every six weeks, we were taken back to the Béni-Ounif oasis for a few days of rest, a diet of old films and, most important of all, really good sweet dates for breakfast, which came straight from the oasis palm-trees. Every three months, Madame Viviane's mobile brothel brought girls to ease the monotony, an event that aroused no desire in me at all. I took solace, however, in the natural beauty of the desert and used to contemplate the horizon until, suddenly, I could see a cluster of vivid green palm trees . . . a mirage.

Every afternoon at five o'clock, after our siesta, I would make a pot of the highly scented tea Albert sent me from England, to share with Yvon, who has remained a friend to this day. With my dog Fanfan at our feet, waiting for some crumbs, Yvon served *galettes*, Breton biscuits. He told me about the books he was reading and passed them on to me once he had finished. I told him of my plans to go into business with my brother and open a high-quality restaurant near Dover, to benefit from the trade that the Channel Tunnel would surely bring. Little did I imagine then that it would take another thirty years for the tunnel to become reality!

Helped by Chougui, an Algerian civilian, I spent my time preparing food for the seven of us who were not legionnaires. It was Chougui who taught me to make a North African *couscous*. The menus needed a good deal of ingenuity since there was not much in the way of raw materials. Once a week, a truck brought us some fruit and vegetables that arrived in a fairly limp state, and once a month we received a hind-quarter of frozen beef. Under that burning sun, I opted for a Mediterranean style of cuisine, with *ratatouille*, tomatoes slowly stewed in olive oil with dried herbs (dried because fresh were unavailable in the middle of nowhere!), grilled aubergines, and *couscous* garnished with courgettes, carrots and tomatoes. For meat to accompany the *couscous,* we had either the beef or gazelle killed on hunting trips into the desert. Sometimes, I made a *daube à la provençale* stew. I kept the gazelle livers and hearts for kebabs with peppers, to be served with a sauce using the local strong *harissa* spice. For dessert, I made fruit tarts or an *île flottante* with dates for special occasions.

At lunch time we accompanied our meal with a salt tablet to stem the loss of fluids from our bodies. The afternoons were given over to a siesta since it was impossible to move around or work in the desert heat. We would drink from three to four litres of water each afternoon. We kept the water in bottles wrapped in jute, with a lining of wheat or rice grains soaked in water to keep the water inside the bottle cool. Dinner was served at seven o'clock with another salt tablet for *apéritif.* Sometimes, we would drink local Algerian beer and play *boules* or cards with the legionnaires.

Life is a Menu

In December 1962, I took a merchant ship to Marseilles and, a few days later, handed my uniform back to the *gendarmerie* in Saint-Mandé. I took a few weeks' rest and spent Christmas and New Year with Françoise before heading to seek a new position in civilian life. By pure luck and without any planning or premeditation, my search was to take me straight back to Cécile de Rothschild.

The 'Rothschilds University'

ARMAND Jonard, my first boss at the Rothschilds', had encouraged me to join the *Société des Cuisiniers Français*, through which I remained in touch with the profession. At the beginning of 1963, I headed to its offices on the Avenue Victor Hugo to find a new job. At that time, the society had some 400 members, all working in the kitchens of the wealthy. Sadly, by 1999, there were only eighty left, many of whom were now employed by big companies to prepare business lunches. When I arrived, a young woman began looking through the list of possibilities and, half-joking, mentioned that Jonard had recently retired and Cécile de Rothschild was unhappy with his replacement. Immediately, I decided to head off to make contact with Marcel Muet, the butler. When Marcel saw me, he nervously asked me to wait in his office. I suddenly heard that unmistakeable voice: 'Well then, send him to see me.'

I found Cécile de Rothschild standing, rolling her hair between her fingers, a sure sign that she was worried. She asked me to sit down, asked after my health and for news of my family. Abruptly, she said *'Mon chef'* had left her two months before. There was a silence and she said she had not been able to get on with his successor. She stared at me for a few seconds and offered me the post: 'I know you will be able to do the job *con brio* – right?'

I replied instantly: 'If Mademoiselle thinks so, I am sure she is right.' Not yet twenty-two, I became the youngest chef ever employed by the Rothschilds. I knew that success depended on discretion, diplomacy and patience as well as faultless professionalism, good management and creativity.

One of the first things I did was go and see my suppliers. On the rue des Belles Feuilles was Herrier the fishmonger whose wife, Elvire, was the real boss. There was also Le Poulet de Bresse, run by a family from the south-west, where I bought my poultry, game and *foie gras*. This shop supplied around four-fifths of the great households of Paris at the time, as well as many starred restaurants. From early morning, the shop was filled with some of the city's most illustrious chefs exchanging gossip or recipes and heading off to take a coffee together in the Le Gavroche café next door. At the covered market at La Madeleine, my butcher was Daumain, a huge man who sold only Charolais beef and milk-fed veal. Otherwise, Fauchon at La Madeleine provided fruit and vegetables while its neighbour Hédiard had exotic foods and spices. A *charcutier* at the nearby Cité Berryer had the breadcrumbed knuckles of ham that Cécile de Rothschild adored. My suppliers were all people that I trusted totally and they never let me down.

I was sent to the Banque Rothschild at 21 rue Lafitte to collect an advance from the personal secretary of Baron Elie de Rothschild. She gave me an account book and a sheaf of crisp new notes. I did not have the courage to count the sum in front of her. Wishing me long service with the Rothschilds, she asked me to give her a few days' warning when I needed more money. Each time, I handed her my book detailing my expenses and she gave me more funds.

For shopping, I used a moped to avoid the traffic, filling up two large saddle bags. If the volume of food was too great, I had it delivered. Shortly after, I bought my first car, a Renault 4, but I used this only for holidays or for visiting Françoise's parents in Ognon in Picardy. Françoise and I were discussing our future life together, and I had told her of my intention to head off for Britain to work with Albert. Françoise, by this time working for Givenchy, seemed happy with this project and we married on 2 February 1963, the month after my return to the Rothschilds'. As we did not have much money, Cécile de Rothschild helped us find an inexpensive flat. She was always generous. At the end of that year, Christine, my first daughter, was born.

In the Rothschilds' kitchen, when things were going well, I would sing. Edmond Oger, the chauffeur, spoke about my voice to his father-in-law, who had been a professional singer. He came to the kitchen one day, persuaded me to take lessons with him, and tried to lure me into changing careers. But it was too late, it was cooking that had become my passion.

Everyday life, in any case, had all the melodrama of an operetta. There would be a sudden change in the number of guests invited for a meal. Marcel could never tell me when a lunch might be served. Suddenly, he would rush into the kitchen to announce that 'Mademoiselle has decided to eat now. She's in a hurry.' On other days, when the meal was nearly ready, he would tell me that Mademoiselle would not be there for another couple of hours.

I have kept the order books with the details of the menus I served during those years, with annotations made by Cécile de Rothschild, with changes or even little sketches explaining her wishes. Some of them are reproduced throughout this book. Thanks to her high standards and impeccable taste, I learned to be a gourmet, an essential quality for a chef. And I shall never forget her advice or her instincts about food and its quality. For example, she only ever wanted to eat hen pheasants. Her *entrecôte* steaks had to come from a three-year-old heifer since they were tastier and more tender than those from a bull; a leg of lamb from a ewe was more succulent and delicate in taste than that from a ram. Tomato salads could only be served in Provence, where the tomatoes would have been picked well ripened and were used immediately. The little spray of watercress decorating a piece of meat should have several drops of lemon on it to sharpen its taste. Lobsters should be small, around 375 grams, and from Brittany.

She loved the Château d'Yquem served at most of her big dinners to be so chilled in the freezer that little needles of ice floated in the bottle. Ice-cream and sorbets had to be freshly churned at the beginning of a meal. She would telephone me to give her choice of flavour as late as six in the evening. I would process the ripest fruit to a purée, add a dash of syrup and lemon juice, and it was then up to my *commis* to turn the handle of the antique hand-operated *sorbetière,* until the sorbet or ice-cream had the desired consistency, a task that could take over half an hour.

Cécile de Rothschild wanted her soufflés to be '*convivial*', that is, served in one dish and not in individual portions. They had to be as upright as a chef's hat, runny in the centre, tender on the sides and never overcooked. She liked them in all flavours, but savoury were her favourite. She preferred goose *foie gras* saying that ducks' livers were not delicate enough. She liked offal, brains, tongue, sweetbreads, calf's liver and *boudin* blood sausages. In winter, *sauerkraut,* a *cassoulet* or even a cottage pie made with the leftovers of a leg of lamb or of roast veal were among her favourites. She particularly relished fillets of hare 'German-style', which had to be cooked

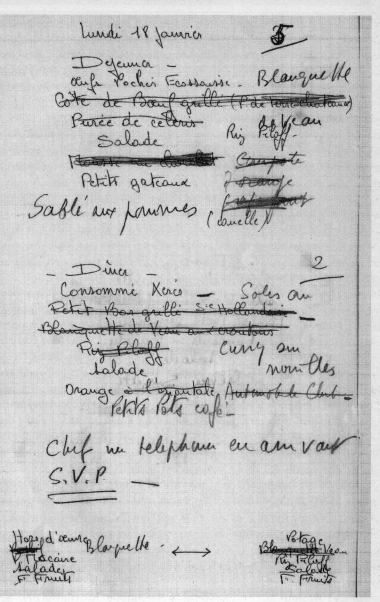

A strict order: 'Telephone as soon as you arrive'.

pink and served on a bed of fresh pasta. Because she adored chocolate, I created a *roulé marquis au chocolat* dessert especially for her.

In the evening, when the kitchen was closed, she would sometimes make a little inspection tour to ensure that everything was properly cleaned and stacked away. Habitually, she took out the cheese that we put in the refrigerator reserved for vegetables. In the morning, I would find a note saying 'The cheese is too cold'.

Her generosity towards her guests made her extremely popular among her friends. She knew their tastes and tried to choose dishes and wines that would please them. Her friends included people from the theatre, the cinema, the business and banking worlds, and the aristocracy. An Indian maharajah once repaid her kindness with jute sacks filled with long-grain rice that had a smell of mould. It was oily to touch and had been been harvested some years before. It was, in a sense, a vintage rice. Cooked, it was sublime and its flavour compared with no other rice I had ever eaten. Another regular visitor was Giovanni Agnelli and, a fan of cars, she always had a Fiat in her small fleet of vehicles.

Cécile de Rothschild was an encyclopedia of taste and knowledge about food. She always made the right comments and liked doing so out loud. 'Remember,' she said, 'a dish must be good to look at but it is better for it to look less good if, that way, it tastes better.' When she had been unimpressed by a meal she had eaten away from home, she would tell me: 'It wasn't worth a rabbit's fart, Chef.' I heard from Marcel that, after an evening spent at one of the great Paris three-star restaurants, she would praise the food she had there to the skies and yet, when my dishes arrived on the table for the next meal, she would tell those around her that there was no place like home. As a result, life as Cécile de Rothschild's chef suited me. Passing through corridors where highly valuable paintings were stacked on the floor (since there was simply no more room on the walls), I began to appreciate art. I tasted my first great wines. I picked up management skills and learned to pander to the tastes of a boss who liked all food from the simple to the elaborate. For me, the Rothschild school was the school of perfection.

At the beginning of 1964, I decided to change my *commis* who was not really to my liking, and I took on a young man of eighteen, Jacques Delfontaine, who stayed until he was called up to do his military service. I could count on Jacques 100 per cent and, when his time came, I told Cécile de Rothschild that he wanted to do his national service in the navy. Her response was typical: she invited an admiral to dinner, called Jacques in to meet him, and his wish was granted.

One evening, Baron Elie de Rothschild, her brother whom she adored and who was her closest confidant, decided, as he often did, to pop in for an *apéritif*. After his third vodka, he opted to stay for dinner. Cécile de Rothschild asked me to add *crêpes soufflées au Parmesan* to the menu. The diners, three in all, sat down to dinner at a quarter past eight and the *crêpes soufflées* were served ten minutes later. Suddenly, the hatch of the serving lift linking my kitchen to Marcel's office began slamming brutally. I was trying to understand what was going on when I heard Baron Elie shout, 'There's no more cheese in your *crêpes* than there is in my arse, Chef!' One vodka too many had plainly neutralised the baron's tastebuds. I was furious, and began taking off my apron to leave on the spot. Marcel grabbed me by my chef's jacket to stop me and, very quickly, he went to the dining room and returned with the baron's apologies. When her brother had gone, Cécile de Rothschild apologised again for his remarks, and I told her I would leave if something similar were to recur. On another occasion, Marcel's head appeared in the hatch and he hissed, 'Send it up quickly, Chef, the baron is sounding off.' At this, Baron Elie, who had crept up just behind him, shouted, 'Maybe I sound off, but remember, I'm the one that pays!'

In July 1964 I made my first trip to the Côte d'Azur, where Cécile de Rothschild was spending some of the summer in her house, Villa Suveret, at Valescure, just above Saint Raphaël. This, like Cannes, was considered one of the better-class resorts, and it contained hundreds of luxurious villas. Cécile de Rothschild – as usual, thinking of everything – asked me to take things that were difficult to find on the Riviera, like saffron, jars of truffles, vanilla pods and other *pâtisserie* ingredients. The journey by sleeper with dinner in the restaurant car was extremely agreeable and Edmond, the chauffeur, was waiting at the station in the morning. The Villa Suveret was just next door to the Golf Hotel where Lord Mountbatten and the Duke and Duchess of Windsor often stayed. They were occasionally invited to meals with Cécile de Rothschild.

In the mornings, I was wakened by the sound of crickets and would head off to market at seven to buy seafood, fruit and vegetables. The local shops had produce that was as good as at Fauchon in Paris, but they have all since sadly disappeared. Depending on what my boss wanted, I served Marmande tomatoes in a salad, French beans, juicy melons, lots of grilled fish like red mullet or bass, or fresh pasta with snipped herbs. These dishes were often cooked in a local olive oil. I was enchanted by the colourful array of fruit and vegetables Provence offered, and I arranged them in my dishes as if I were designing a flower-bed.

Cécile de Rothschild was a good golfer and, after a morning's play, she would bring others in her party back to a late lunch served on the terrace with its superb view of the Mediterranean. She sometimes went away for the day, and the staff took advantage of this to go out as well. On one occasion she lent us the Bentley and told us to go to Saint Tropez to eat at the Club 55 at her expense. Edmond was delighted to drive without his cap and his grey uniform, and Marcel, the butler, who had left his bulldog-like wife in Paris, became a different man. We marvelled at the bamboo huts on Tahiti Plage, and took a look at the first nudist beaches which were just then welcoming a few intrepid devotees. We washed down our meal at the Club 55 with an excellent Provencal rosé. On our way home, we stopped at a famous seafood shop and chose some crayfish for Cécile de Rothschild's lunch the next day. This was our treat for her, to thank her for our day out.

One of the most arduous tasks I had was to load up my Fiat 1100, or the Citroën 2CV allocated to me, to go to the country house at Noisy on a Friday afternoon or a Saturday morning. The number of guests and the menus were rarely communicated to me before I took the wheel. My *commis* and I simply had to make a guess and prepare for all possibilities. This infuriated me and, on several occasions, I considered resigning since I hated being treated this way. Cécile de Rothschild would sense when I was in a bad mood and come to the kitchen in Noisy, cracking jokes and trying to make up for being difficult. I would take full advantage of these all-too-brief moments of contrition, slamming down saucepan lids and dropping hints about there being too many people in the kitchen. . .

The Noisy house had ten guest bedrooms that allowed Cécile de Rothschild to entertain up to twenty people for a weekend. However, there were rarely more than a dozen. As soon as I arrived, I would take a walk in the garden with its wonderful views over the Oise valley. I liked to stop by the century-old chestnut tree where guests enjoyed *apéritifs* in summer. The garden boasted many varieties of roses and trees rarely seen outside a botanical garden. Fruit trees gave me the raw material for tarts or sorbets, and the kitchen garden supplied me with fresh vegetables and herbs for that day's dinner. The chief gardener came to me every morning to find out what I needed, and advised me on what was best.

There were times when Cécile de Rothschild left Paris for several weeks or even months on travels abroad. These absences gave me time to enter culinary competitions, and to work in other houses as an extra or to replace a sick chef. At one home on the quai de New York, I had the run of a huge and well-equipped kitchen where I was assisted night after night by two *commis* to make dinner for just two people. They sat yards apart at each end of a long table, the lady of the house dressed in Dior and her husband in a maroon dinner jacket. At Cécile de Rothschild's suggestion, I also worked alongside chefs employed by other Rothschilds to vary my experience and learn new techniques.

On her return, she would always ask how I had spent my time and I took the opportunity to try out new dishes on her. She loved macaroons, for example, and during one of her lengthy absences, I experimented with a multitude of new flavours. She told Marcel that my macaroons were the best to be had in Paris, 'But don't tell him I said so.'

Once, a modicum of jealousy surfaced. Greta Garbo came to stay in August 1966, for two weeks, and was on a diet that rather cramped my style. She only ate grilled fish, with castor oil served separately in a little flask, and steamed vegetables. After dinner one night, my boss called me in to discuss what menus we could dream up for the actress. As we talked, Greta Garbo removed her dark glasses and stared right at me. 'What beautiful blue eyes you have, Chef,' she said. Cécile de Rothschild sent me the most withering glance, and I took this as a signal to get out of the room and fast. She didn't like me receiving compliments about anything other than my food.

From 1964 on, Françoise and I went to Kent every summer to visit Albert and his wife, Monique. On occasion, we would go to London restaurants, like the Empress, Le Coq d'Or, La Belle Meunière or Prunier, and they confirmed our prejudices. The food was poor and the service worse, all of which strengthened our resolve to set up in Britain.

Albert, who was still working for Peter Cazalet, and I exchanged a host of letters, describing our work and menus and putting the finishing touches to our project. I have kept them all. Albert began buying silver at good prices in auctions, and he stored this in his garage. He visited restaurants that were for sale in London or in the countryside around, and kept me abreast of details like the prevailing interest rates for bank loans. I usually replied by return and, if I did not, he would telephone me to make sure none of the letters had gone astray. In June 1966, we set up our own company, Roux Restaurants Ltd, and I transferred my savings of 50,000 *francs* at the highly unfavourable rate of 13.60 *francs* to the pound as my contribution to the capital.

At the end of that year, I asked to see Cécile de Rothschild. She put off the interview for two weeks, plainly guessing the reason. When she did, she heard me out, twisting a strand of her hair, just as she had done the day she took me on. She made no comment on my plans. On 31 March 1967, after I had served out my three months' notice, Cécile de Rothschild wished me *'Bonne chance'*.

Crossing the Channel

AND thus began my life in England, which shall be detailed in the following chapters of my life's menu. On 3 April I landed in Dover, revealing for the customs officer my work permit, number 727468, twelve chefs' jackets, six pairs of white trousers and several *toques*.

The final departure from France had been hard. Nobody understood my decision. But I had weighed up the pros and cons for some time. Britain then had the highest standard of living in Europe, and the pound was strong. The total cost of setting up a restaurant in London was half that of Paris, and we could take out bank loans for which we were not personally liable, as we would have been in France. Above all, it was still the culinary Stone Age, and we wanted to pioneer a change in the eating habits of the British.

The beginnings were to be anything but easy, though Françoise and I had decided to live separately at first, with her staying in Paris. Our two daughters were then aged three and eighteen months. I hugged them all with a heavy heart as I set off in my overloaded Renault 4. I also had with me an oil painting of a Parisian *'gavroche'*, or urchin, which I had found in

Montmartre. It was to become our symbol. I was also worried about the effect the move to London would have on Françoise. Our financial situation was not going to be rosy; we had had two good salaries in Paris, and we could expect to wait several years before attaining the same level in London. Other complications included the fact that I spoke no English and that neither Albert nor I, however accomplished we were as chefs, had ever worked in a real restaurant. We were jumping in at the deep end, and there was no time for trial and error.

My first sight of Le Gavroche, on the corner of Lower Sloane Street, enchanted me. A team of builders and decorators had been at work for two weeks, and the restaurant was taking shape. The decoration was in the hands of David Mlinaric who popped in during my first visit. He was elegantly dressed and smiling, his long hair giving him a slight look of Mick Jagger. He juggled colours with ease, installed lighting that could be dimmed at will – a technique new at the time – and introduced shades of ochre and tinted mirrors that resulted in a warm, comfortable and beautiful dining-room. Albert translated for me and I began to understand how dependent I would be on him to begin with.

The opening was in three weeks and, since invitations had been sent out, there was no question of any delay. We had retained the services of Antonio Battistella, the manager of the former Canova Italian restaurant which had been on the same spot. This was a master-stroke since Tony turned out to be a master of the art of running a restaurant, as well as being loyal and gutsy. Tony in turn took on five Italian waiters and a wine waiter-cum-barman. Albert had found one other cook, and I recruited a former *commis* who had worked for Cécile de Rothschild. As soon as the building work ended, the furniture began to arrive, and we organised the menus and wine-lists, the bill-pads, wine and, not least, the food.

When the day came, etchings that I had chosen in London were in place. The Lumley-Cazalet Gallery, partly owned by the daughter-in-law of Albert's former employer, had generously lent us some paintings too, meaning that Chagall, Miró and Dali among others were jostling for space on our walls. The Cazalets, who had invested in our company, had helped organise the guest-list of 150. The afternoon was spent preparing the buffet, and the guests began arriving about eight o'clock. An hour later, the restaurant was packed. I was struck by the difference between the elegance of the women and the often creased and slightly shabby suits of some of the men, something that would be inconceivable in France.

Rolls-Royces were double-parked outside, and guests who had intended to stay for just thirty minutes were still there two hours later. One of the last to leave was Christopher Soames, soon to be British Ambassador in Paris. In fluent French, he predicted a radiant future for Le Gavroche. I was a little disappointed to notice that the Rothschilds were among the few who did not turn up. After a few months, however, when the reputation of Le Gavroche was made, they became customers. When the restaurant finally emptied, we noticed that not a crumb of our buffet was left. And we opened more champagne, this time for the staff.

The next day, after just six hours' sleep, Albert and I were unlocking the service door at the back of the restaurant. The telephone was already ringing and didn't stop. Before we had properly changed into our working clothes, we already had a full house of around sixty customers for that night.

Our first menu was a short one and was printed only in French with no English translation. There were about thirty items, comprising soups, *hors d'oeuvres*, fish and shellfish, meat and poultry, vegetables and the desserts that were to make our reputation. We charged around six shillings for the soups, sixteen shillings for the *hors d'oeuvres* and fish courses, twenty-three shillings for the main course and twelve shillings for the desserts. Other renowned London restaurants, like Prunier or the Savoy Grill, offered around sixty items, many of which, like smoked salmon, potted shrimps or the ubiquitous prawn cocktail, required little skill on the part of the cooks.

As the evening approached, Albert changed into his dinner jacket to take orders in the dining-room. I began to suffer from anxiety. I was afraid I would not be able to cope in this completely unfamiliar, new world. The service bell rang and my first order chit which, weighted by a clothes-peg, dropped into the basket by the washing-up area. I called the order out aloud, and the first course left the kitchen less than ten minutes later. Other orders followed, all far too quickly for my taste. I was used to households where the food was the same for everyone, but I had no time to think, I had to run the kitchen and cook at the same time. I instructed the others to prepare a duck and send it to the dumb-waiter, to beat the egg whites for a *soufflé suissesse*; I checked the progress of other dishes; made sure a silver tray was ready for an *omelette Rothschild* dessert. Then, suddenly, I began to feel a certain satisfaction. My anxiety had gone.

Around half-past nine, the rhythm began to slow down. Albert told me by intercom that another ten clients were expected after the theatre, and the last orders arrived before midnight. By all accounts, the customers were happy and seduced by the cooking of the 'Roux Brothers'.

The following day, Albert passed on customers' comments. Some were complaining that the portions were too small. I replied that we were offering a gastronomic cuisine, and we should be prepared to accept criticism even insults, since we were introducing a culture shock to a London dominated by mediocre Italian restaurants and Lyons Corner Shops. Having just turned twenty-six and cooking in a restaurant for the first time, I realised that I was going to need great strength to rise above the mediocrity around me.

Soon after Le Gavroche opened, when I had found a small house in Tooting Bec, Françoise and the children crossed the Channel. We put Christine into a nearby nursery school with some concern, fearing that she would be lost amongst English children. However, within days, she had picked up her first words and was soon fully operational in English.

In mid-September, I finally put on my own dinner jacket to make direct contact with the customers, something I had hesitated to do earlier because of my linguistic shortcomings. I delighted the first table with a welcoming and hearty 'Good night', and quickly experienced an anxiety similar to that of my first evening in the kitchen. I had problems writing down the orders and explaining the dishes, so Tony Battistella began to take some orders to ease the pressure on me. After that, Albert and I alternated weekly, with one of us serving in the dining-room for six nights while the other stayed in the kitchen. This formula greatly amused some customers, who often asked what the configuration would be when they reserved. However, it seemed to make no difference since we had a constant full house.

The following March, my son Alain was born and I attended the birth of one of my children for the first time. I hoped this would strengthen relations between Françoise and myself. Françoise was having a hard time adapting to life in Britain, and she seemed to resent a professional success in which she had played no part. I was getting home at two in the morning and she was suspicious about the reasons. And when it came to choosing a name, there was a minor dilemma. Albert had named his son 'Michel' after me, but we found 'Albert' a bit old-fashioned, and compromised by finding a name beginning with the same syllable.

Life is a Menu

By this time Le Gavroche had become famous, and expansion was on the cards. Our board decided that we should open a *charcuterie* as one of the first steps towards increasing our 'hold' on London food. This, Le Cochon Rose, or 'the pink pig', opened shortly thereafter in Sloane Street. Then we opened another restaurant in the City, Le Poulbot, as many of our existing customers worked in the City and were eager for higher quality business lunches. After Le Poulbot received the Egon Ronay Golden Plate for the best restaurant of the year, we started looking around for a second restaurant in the City, and in 1970 opened La Brasserie Benoît, named after our paternal grandfather. However, about a year later, we changed the name to Le Gamin (lad), and this also became the base for our catering operations. As you can imagine, at that time I seemed to be making do with only four or five hours' sleep a night!

But by 1972 we were ready for a fresh adventure. I was exhausted all the time, but I was also a little bored. We thought we should like to bring the Roux London touch to the country and started looking around in the Thames Valley for a suitable property – exploring villages and towns like Beaconsfield, Henley and Marlow. It was actually François Merlozzi, a co-director, who discovered the Waterside Inn in Bray. As soon as I saw it, with its 100-year-old willow tree and its wonderful river frontage, I knew it was the perfect place. It was a nice pub, but had a grotty dining-room. After buying the lease from the tenant (the pub actually belonged to Whitbreads), we borrowed as much money as we could from the bank in order to revamp the entire place, particularly the dining-room overlooking the river.

We brought in a very gifted young chef, Pierre Koffmann, and his wife Anne became the manageress, an arrangement that worked beautifully. For at least three years, the weekends were fantastically busy and weekdays dead as a dodo. Thanking God that we had all our other restaurants to keep us going, Albert and I would go to the Waterside every alternate weekend. I think at that time, because we were rushing so much from one restaurant to another, that our cars held more chefs' jackets than anything else!

The reputation of the restaurant grew very quickly, and our first visitors' book reads like a *Who's Who* of the talented and famous. At the end of 1973 Egon Ronay, in an article in the *Telegraph*, predicted that one day the Waterside would be the best restaurant in Britain – something indeed to work towards! In 1990 I bought the freehold from Whitbreads, which has enabled me to expand and refurbish, and to offer rooms as well as food, earning me membership of *Relais & Châteaux* as well as *Relais Gourmands.* I've also expanded within Bray itself, buying the cottage next door to the Waterside, where I have my private dining-room. My own house, where Robyn and I now live, is on the river a few hundred metres away. . .

Robyn, who used to work in theatre, likens the theatre to the restaurant. One has a script, the other a menu; one has an audience, the other customers; one has a cast, the other chefs and waiters. I never have time to go to the theatre, I must admit, but it's only because I'm performing in my own play every day and night in front of my own audience, following my own personal script. My life has indeed been, and still is, dominated by the menu.

Markets

A GOOD MARKET is the essence of a good menu. And a good menu should always be market-led. It is far more gratifying to pick up what is on offer and what is seasonal than to go shopping with fixed ideas. The end result will be better for the palate and more satisfying for all concerned. The unexpected appearance of an unusual seafood in the market, for example, can determine the choice of a first course; similarly the arrival of game can give ideas for a more original main dish than the one the buyer may first have had in mind.

Most tourists, when they arrive in a foreign country, head for their hotel information desks to ask about museums, art galleries and local landmarks. For myself, when on holiday, I seek out the hotel chef and ask him for directions to the food market. The next day, at dawn, I am on my way to experience the unique blend of odours, colours and noises that each market has. For I have always been fascinated by the fact that no two markets the world over are alike. They are reflections of national and regional heritage and culture. For me, therefore, they are just as much in need of preservation as architectural monuments.

My first experience of markets was obviously in France. In the first months of my apprenticeship, Camille Loyal, my boss, took me to Les Halles at six in the morning, from Belleville to the Rambuteau *métro* station, to buy scallops and other ingredients for our *bouchées à la reine* and other savoury specialities. He taught me how to pick the best cream-coloured mushrooms in huge baskets, the scallops and mussels, with their shells firmly closed, which we bought in twenty-kilogram sacks. Returning to the *pâtisserie* was less easy as we heaved our load on to trains already packed with commuters. Seawater from our shellfish dripped on our fellow passengers' shoes, drawing a series of insults. Loyal looked me straight in the eye and muttered 'Let them sing'. Thereafter, I would often go to Les Halles, known as the 'belly of Paris', by myself, to watch food being unloaded and then sold, just for the pleasure of the spectacle. In the 1970s, the market was moved to Rungis, south of Paris, to a site the size of a small town.

Now, I actively seek out markets wherever I am in the world, be it Hong Kong, Bangkok or Sydney. On holiday in the south of France, I take special pleasure in looking at the different kinds of Mediterranean fish and Provençal vegetables to be had at the small markets dotted around the region. My fear is that these may disappear now that European legislation obliges stallholders to put some produce in refrigerated display containers – costing an average 30,000 *francs* or £3,000 – and to wrap everything, which stops customers from touching or smelling the goods to determine their quality.

In Britain, Albert and I decided to take a look at London's markets with a view to seeing what we could find there as opposed to the goods provided by our usual wholesalers. Very quickly, we decided to cover the markets ourselves. The quality of the meat and fish at Smithfield and Billingsgate markets was excellent, and the prices were sometimes as much as thirty per cent lower than those of our wholesale suppliers. The fruit and vegetables at Covent Garden were, by contrast, limited and of poor quality. This prompted us to buy some of our vegetables in France, especially the young spring produce that is so essential to many delicate French dishes.

We decided to visit the London markets three times a week. On one of my trips to Paris, I bought the perfect buyer's garment: a long white overall, with deep pockets that would have made any poacher envious. To set this off, I had a leather bag on a strap round my neck with compartments for notes of big and small value, coins, receipts and invoices.

It was nonetheless Albert who set off alone to inaugurate our new policy in mid-1969. After about two weeks, he then called me in to show me the ropes in the early hours of the morning, a sure sign that he was beginning to feel the strain. He took a special delight in showing me round places he had only just got to know himself. We probably made rather a strange spectacle. Albert, small and lively, led the way from stall to stall, limping slightly as the result of a road accident, and I, taller, followed behind, straining my neck so as not to lose him from view in the crowds. The vendors, attracted by our exchanges in French, soon found names for the 'Frenchies': 'Mike and Bert.'

On days when I did the markets, I realised that man can get used to most things, even going without sleep. Just four hours or so after leaving the Gavroche kitchens, I would call, first at our office on the Wandsworth Road where I listened to the late-night messages left by our cooks on the answering machine with details of what was lacking. They were often partially obscured by background kitchen noises and I would have to guess at what was needed. From there, I drove along south of the Thames, in our Ford Transit, usually with the window wound down to keep me awake, with only a few courageous joggers to keep me company. I always felt a thrill at seeing the Houses of Parliament and Big Ben rise out of the darkness as I crossed the river.

Shortly after, I was at Covent Garden. The narrow streets around were blocked by lorries and vans of all shapes and sizes. Porters and buyers rushed here and there pushing clattering trolleys stacked with wooden cases over the roadway. The overall impression, however, was a sad one. The wholesalers went about their business without enthusiasm; they seemed lazy with little interest in trade. The vegetables – carrots, cabbages, leeks, potatoes and Jerusalem artichokes – were enormous and lifeless. I looked in vain for little blue turnips and tiny crisp artichokes, for the large misshapen succulence of Marmande tomatoes and for the young carrots with bright green leaves attesting to their freshness, all of which I knew in France. Courgettes were considered a luxury, even exotic and were therefore unavailable, as were extra-fine beans, little button mushrooms and tiny onions. Everything suggested to me that neither the producers nor the traders were really interested in the customer. Only one wholesaler, by the name of Poupart, made any effort. Sometimes he could get hold of vegetables I wanted. I noticed that his display was quickly empty, that other alert buyers went straight to him. As for all the others, I used to think that, with their humourless fixed expressions, they had missed their vocation. They would have made good undertakers.

As soon as I had made my purchases, I would leave, irritated at the insipid nature of it all, load up my van and put it into first gear, happy in the knowledge that in fifteen minutes, I would be at Billingsgate. There, in complete contrast, I was greeted by the fresh smells of the sea, the damp, slippery ground, gulls flying overhead, and the loud, lively banter of the traders, buyers and porters. The scene was a welcoming one and it warmed my heart. The first time I got there in my special market-buyer's garb, I was greeted by a crescendo of whistles, jeers, catcalls and applause. My strange appearance was soon forgotten, however, and the traders started looking out for me, to advertise loudly the merits of their monkfish, salmon, sole, turbot, bass, eels and carp. I touched the flesh of each fish to see how firm it was, turned back the fins, favouring those that were stiff, with pink or red gills and with bright, full eyes (another sign of freshness).

The merchants shouted the prices before I asked. I often told one of them, Alex Howe, that my success and inspiration depended on the variety, quality and freshness of my raw materials and that I needed his help. Often he would put a case or two of out-of-the-ordinary fish to one side for me, like red mullet or sardines that he could have sold 100 times before I got there. I used to tell him how I liked to prepare red mullet: how I would sponge it with a cloth, never washing it under water since this would make it lose its taste, substance and colour. After frying it lightly in olive oil, never cooking it too long, so that the flesh remained pink on the bone, I would serve it with the *sauce vierge* that I had made so often for the Rothschilds at Saint Raphaël, with basil, tomatoes, olive oil, coriander and lemon juice.

Sardines would be boned and then cooked under the salamander grill for just a few seconds. They were served with a mustard sauce heightened by a little lemon juice and a few leaves of quickly fried spinach. Alex was all ears and he listened to every detail. With his eyes wide open, he could not resist throwing a proud glance at his little fish.

George, the best shellfish merchant, was at the back of the market. He had a huge choice of crustaceans – crabs and scallops that were tightly shut and still filled with seawater, a testament to their freshness. The crabs' claws were immobilised by elastic bands and kept in wicker baskets. (George walked slightly sideways, just like his crabs!) Next to his display, George had an enormous cauldron over a gas ring filled with permanently boiling water. Into this he threw the crabs that had already died. He sold the result, at a knockdown price, to cafés and pubs to go in sandwiches and salads. Sometimes, if he was on the point of trying to give me a tired-looking crab, I would tell him it was one for the pot, and throw it myself into the boiling water. On occasion, George kept for me one or two spider crabs that had made their way by accident into a fisherman's net. All the prices were much below those of France, as the British did not seem to have the same yearning for shellfish as the French. The domestic demand was so small indeed that many of these excellent 'home-grown' products were destined for the Continent.

The good humour of Billingsgate was contagious. Everyone joked and smiled whatever the weather, whether it rained or snowed. Even in bitterly cold temperatures, the vendors plunged their hands into the ice to pull out a few kilograms of sole or turbot so that I could better examine them. The scene was further enlivened by the uniform of the porters, in waterproofs and boots like fishermen. Many of them had rigid flat hats. At the end of my rounds, one would offer his services. He took the heavy cases on a trolley and the lighter ones piled on his hat. I was entranced by the skill, the moral and physical strength and, most of all, by the smiles of these porters.

It was at this point that I would begin to feel pangs of hunger. Opposite the market was an excellent café which served good English breakfasts. As I went in, the smell of bacon, and even toast covered in salted butter, caressed my nostrils. (Not many people are aware of the fact that at the beginning of the day your sense of smell is very much more alert – one reason why wine-tastings are generally held in the morning.) The café looked unremarkable from the outside, but was always clean and full to bursting. It was run by an Italian with slicked-down dark hair. I ordered a tea, toast, two eggs, bacon and sausages. As soon as a metal stool became free, I was on it, and the boss would bring over my plate and tea when they were ready. Like any good Frenchman, I then wiped my plate clean with a piece of toast. The mug of tea served a dual purpose: to warm my stomach and comfort my chapped hands.

Over the years, I found that other markets have their breakfast traditions. In 1981, Albert and I were in negotiation to open a Gavroche at the Pierre Hotel in New York. The enormous variety of excellent fish and seafood available in the city convinced us it should be a fish restaurant. For among the many fish on sale at the huge Fulton fish market, we saw black sea bass, red snappers, blue-fin tuna, swordfish, pompano from Florida, excellent cod and exceptional scallops. The arrangement finally fell through, sadly, although we had drawn up our menus and started engaging staff. Despite our disappointment at not being able to set up in the Big Apple, we did discover New York's answer to my favourite breakfast bacon-and-egg café near Billingsgate – a series of little fish restaurants open from five in the morning with queues lining up to eat one delicious local speciality that I had not known until then: clam chowder.

On my London rounds, my next stop after Billingsgate was Smithfield. From afar, I could see Charlie, in the long coat that he wore winter and summer. I sounded the horn and flashed my headlights to let him know I was arriving. Charlie took pride in finding me a place to park, as he did for some fifty other buyers. He would bare his teeth in what passed for a smile and put out his hand for his half-a-crown fee. My load was always in good hands; a Dobermann could not have done better.

I walked quickly around the three pavilions of the market to gain an overall view of what was on offer, to study the quality of the poultry, beef, lamb, game and offal. After that, I went back to the displays that had attracted me and began negotiating prices. I looked at the skin of the chickens to make sure it was smooth, as well as the pliability of the beaks and wings as a gauge of their youthfulness. Sometimes I would come across a case of plump squab pigeons that had got there by some miracle. Often the vendor did not have a clue as to the price he should ask. I could already see them in the pot, cooking with little mushrooms and chunks of bacon and some *parisienne* potatoes, set off by a sprig of thyme. Discoveries of the unexpected like this made my day.

The best wholesaler was called Gutteridge whose display groaned under saddles, racks and barons of lamb, hindquarters, forequarters and legs of beef. Among the dozen salesmen, two in particular used to look out for me. Paul, a little stocky man who wore the traditional white butcher's cap, would tug at my sleeve and say, 'I've kept a little treasure back for you.' I would follow him through the rows of lamb hanging from rails on the ceiling. Then he would run his hand over the neck of a lamb and pronounce it 'a champion'. Its pale pink flesh, pure white fat and short legs proved it was young and of good quality. I would nod and Paul would pull a wooden spike from a pocket and plant this in the sheep's backside to show it was sold. His colleague, Ronnie, would then repeat the performance, taking me to see an excellent sirloin of beef. I could already see this on my butcher's slab and me cutting off a sliver to eat raw with a few grains of coarse sea salt. Both these men inundated me with information about where the meat had come from. They were experts and anxious to share their professional knowledge.

Only at the offal counters was I disappointed. I was looking for good sweetbreads but they were often shrivelled. I used to buy lamb or beef tongues. Veal kidneys were difficult to come by, and those I saw were often a blackish grey in colour, with the fat that should have enveloped them hanging down limply. After many attempts, I would sometimes get a vendor to keep back a jerrycan of pig's blood that he had saved from the abattoir so that the Cochon Rose could make *boudin* or blood sausage. Often the blood was unusable since the addition of vinegar and swift whipping it needed to stop its coagulation had not been carried out just after slaughter. Gradually, thanks to our strict requirements, some of the wholesalers began to compete to provide the best possible. A wink or a pat on the shoulder was all the reward they wanted.

A permanent problem was watching out for Smithfield porters. They would pull carts with 400 or 500 kilograms of meat along at breakneck speed, unable to stop or change course. By the time you heard their 'Mind your backs!' it could be too late. I sometimes tried to take my purchases to my van myself, lifting the load on to my shoulders, an intense physical effort that was actually to my liking. The alternative was to find a porter at the place called the Bell. I would queue for about fifteen minutes and then hand the porter all my bills. He would go round all the wholesalers to pick up the meat while I waited in the Transit. It was less tiring but took longer, depending on the speed and goodwill of the porter.

Once the buying was over, it was time to deliver. I stopped first at Le Poulbot because it was the closest of our restaurants to Smithfield. The pub was just opening for breakfast when I got there at eight. I knocked down a double espresso to give me a little kick and set off for Le Gavroche, usually through heavy traffic. I finished at Le Cochon Rose, just before opening at nine. Liliane, my sister, would be arranging her displays, and she always tried to tempt me into conversation, but I would cut this short and head off back to the Wandsworth office. The van was empty and I felt as though I was flying. At the office, I opened the post and put the market bills into order.

Albert and I kept up this strenuous rhythm for about twelve years. However, as our activities grew, we took on several young cooks and trained them in 'doing the market'. One who stood out in particular was Gérard Pommier, from the Charente Maritime department on the Atlantic coast. He was twenty-one when he first arrived as a *charcutier* at Le Cochon Rose in 1970. He was honest, ambitious and devoted to a job well done. Albert and I decided to train him as a buyer at the end of that year, and took him under our wing. After a few months, he was doing the market alone, proud to have our trust.

Suddenly, however, he fell ill with cancer and we sent him for an operation in a private clinic. To this day, I am sure that he owes his survival both to his own iron determination and to our paternal support. Now married (we hosted his wedding party at the Waterside Inn), he is back in

France, where he has qualified as an auditor and heads his own accounting firm. He is a prime example of someone who came from nothing, with that drive and will to achieve and live, that often is better in life than luck.

My best memories of the London markets are perhaps of the times I went there with Albert. A complicity and friendship developed between us and the wholesalers and their employees, who would all call out to us as we passed. Once, at Smithfield, I lost sight of Albert for a good ten minutes. I went back to the van but he was not there. I looked up and down the alleys to no avail. Suddenly, in the middle of the crowds, a quarter of beef appeared, moving at ground level and heading straight towards me. Suddenly, I heard an exhausted voice plead, 'Help me, for God's sake!' Albert was bent double under this enormous piece of meat that weighed more than 100 kilograms. I quickly opened the van doors and grabbed the beef to help Albert get it off his back. He was proud of his exploit but I was relieved to see him straighten up.

On his own Albert tended to let himself be carried away. He could not keep to the agreed buying list and, on more than one occasion, he swamped our restaurants with an exaggerated quantity of lamb or salmon, justifying himself by claiming it was a bargain he could not pass up. This annoyed our chefs who did not want to waste anything. The younger cooks sent to the market kept to what was required.

My own discovery of London markets opened up for me the joys of markets everywhere. When I started travelling around the world, I used markets to discover about the people of the country, about their wealth or their poverty through the abundance or the paucity of the goods on offer. A market represents a unique insight into the heart of a country.

THE MENU

Champagne and Canapés

DURING THE WATERSIDE Inn's annual winter closure in 1985, I flew to join my wife Robyn on holiday in Australia. When I arrived in Sydney in the evening, I found Robyn in a state of some agitation. Michelin had called from London and wanted me to call back as soon as I could. They insisted on talking only to me and would not leave any other message. We got home and I paced the floor before returning the call from Derek Brown, who then headed the *Guide Michelin*'s operations in Britain. Finally, for better or for worse, I took the plunge and dialled the number. According to Robyn, my neck started to go red and a rash rose up my face as the conversation got under way. I became speechless.

Derek confirmed the rumours rife in the food world – that the Waterside Inn had been awarded the coveted three Michelin stars, the world's greatest and most respected gastronomic accolade. I was both overwhelmed by the honour and daunted by the new pressure that I knew this would put on me. Not only had I worked hard to earn it, I knew I would now have to keep working just as hard to keep it.

My immediate desire – as Derek Brown sought reassurances that renovation of the Waterside Inn's kitchen would not delay its re-opening – was to share this news with my colleagues, those who had earned the three stars with me. This was impossible, though, since they, like me, were all away on holiday. And as Michelin had now given three stars to both the Roux Brothers, I regretted that Albert, who gained his in 1982, could not celebrate this with me.

When Christopher, my brother-in-law, heard me whoop for joy, he shouted, 'I've got just the thing!' He came straight in with a bottle of vintage 1979 Krug champagne that had been chilled in expectation.

If only one champagne were to survive, I would want it to be Krug. This is not to say, although I love Krug, that it is the only one I drink. There are twenty-four major champagne houses, or *grandes marques*, and, outside the big names, there are many small growers whose cheaper brands allow the consumer to buy champagne for more general consumption. For there is a champagne for each moment in life – one for drinking on the lawn in summer, one for the fireside in winter, one as an *apéritif* after a hunting trip – just as there is a wine for every occasion. So it would be a heresy to say I have only one champagne, just as it would be a heresy for me to single out one person whom I should like to cook for me. As I would not want to entrust my palate and my stomach to a single cook but to several, I would not want to taste only one champagne for the rest of my life.

There are three grapes used in making champagne, the Chardonnay, the Pinot Noir and the Pinot Meunier. The latter is the least used. *Blanc de Blancs* champagne is made just from the Chardonnay grape. In total, more than 5,000 growers cultivate the grapes in Champagne for a total of 261 houses. An indication of quality lies in the fineness of the bubbles and in the regularity of their rise to the surface. The smaller they are, the finer the champagne. Although I have never personally checked this detail, experts say a bottle of champagne contains some 250 million bubbles. For me what makes a good champagne is its complexity and aroma. I am never at ease with the use of complicated words and elaborate phrases about the fragrances to be found in any wine. Such formulae give me headaches.

When my brother Albert and I worked together at Le Gavroche, we had a little daily ritual. Whoever was working in the kitchen in the evening prepared a dinner plate for the one in the dining room once service was finished. The one, who had been serving in the restaurant brought a glass of champagne. This gave us a little kick and helped us end each day on a festive note.

I like all wines: whites, reds, both dry and sweet. I adore wine in general in the same way that I adore food in general. However, champagne, drunk from a flute, a *coupe,* an ordinary wine glass or a silver goblet, is in a category of its own. Champagne is the only wine that you can drink at any time of day. You can drink it when you wake up, during the day, in the evening, at night and before, during and after making love. Champagne is the king of *apéritifs,* a wine of joy and happiness, one that warms the heart. If it were up to me, the Champagne region would be declared one of the wonders of the world.

My personal discovery of champagne came when I worked for Cécile de Rothschild. The Rothschild family had an affinity for and a friendship with Pol Roger, so that was the champagne they drank. When there was a reception or some other occasion at which champagne was served, Marcel would pour me a glass as we wound up the day.

On my first visit to Champagne in the early 1970s, I met the Krug family: Paul Krug, then the head of the family and an imposing personality; Henri, who was in charge of *vinification,* the actual wine-making; and Rémy, *l'ami,* the friend, the happy, joyful *bon vivant* who sells the wine and who has struck up close relationships with many starred chefs.

I once had the privilege of tasting a 1911 Charles Heidsieck, from one of the best-ever champagne years. However, a 1928 Krug in a magnum, which the Krugs shared with me when it was nearly fifty years old, was a real revelation. Like trying to do justice in words to a great work of art, it is difficult to describe that 1928 Krug. It had a slightly golden colour, bearing witness to its age, and a coloured foam. Everything else about it was youthful. It danced in the glass and was still perfectly fresh. It had fine bubbles that, half a century after they were first imprisoned, celebrated their release with all the vigour of a young vintage. It showed absolutely no signs of maderisation. That champagne really left its mark on me.

My preference is always for a magnum, which is the ideal size for the development of flavour and proper ageing of a champagne or most other great wines. When there is a greater volume of something, there is a better harmonisation – just as a stew for eight will always be better than one for four. I always have magnums of champagne in my personal cellar. I like champagne that is at least ten years old since this is not a wine that should be drunk too young as the French tend to think. I also like it *brut,* low in sugar. It was in London that I began to understand this, in the same way that I learned a lot about wine in general from Britain's highly qualified wine professionals.

Champagne is not, however, the world's only *apéritif.* When I am in my house at Gassin near Saint Tropez in summer it's a case of *'Bonjour, pastis!'* I put some ice cubes in a glass, and listen to them crackle as I pour in my yellow *pastis*, then water (more than most people, since I prefer it quite dilute). Rather than well-known brands like Pernod or Ricard, I always buy from Bardouin, a small manufacturer. In winter, when I am not really thirsty but have had a long, hard and perhaps frustrating day, then I like a whisky, a single malt, neat or with just a little still water. This happens probably about ten times a year. With the gulls' eggs I serve during Ascot Week in June, I prefer a glass of white wine, like a Muscat d'Alsace on a hot day.

The perfect accompaniment to an *apéritif* is the canapé. Cécile de Rothschild had the nasty habit of ordering me to rustle up some canapés at around six-thirty in the evening. This was not very convenient for me, but a good ruse on her part: she could guarantee her canapés would be absolutely fresh. She would say she needed a few appetisers in half an hour. 'I want them crunchy with a gooey and fresh filling, Chef.'

Cécile de Rothschild taught me that canapés, which also go by the names of *amuse-gueules* or *amuse-bouches* in France, were intended 'to arouse the appetite, not to send it to sleep. I want them to awaken my tastebuds.' Her favourites were made with fresh vegetables, like asparagus tips or tomato slices that had just been cooked and were not yet cold, on toast with a tiny drop of olive oil. Very simple, with a twist of the peppermill. She also liked cherry tomatoes, centres scooped out and filled with a spiced tomato sorbet. Preparing and freezing a sorbet was quite some task when I had just half an hour to get things ready…

She adored Roquefort cheese. She liked little sticks of celery with a Roquefort butter and she wanted this to contain a few specks of the cheese itself. 'If you don't put some in, I can't taste the Roquefort. I need just a little cushion of Roquefort butter to make up for the tartness of the celery.'

Cécile de Rothschild also liked fresh vegetables with a dip, especially when weekending in Noisy-sur-Oise, at her house north of Paris. The dip might be just a mayonnaise or a mayonnaise-based sauce, lightly flavoured with tomato and a drop of cognac. As many of the vegetables as possible came from the garden, like little cauliflower florets or asparagus tips, or I might buy some mushrooms. The most important consideration was seasonality. She adored radishes and asked me to keep the tops on. 'They help the digestion and are the clothing of the radish,' she said. 'Without them, the radish is naked.'

When preparing canapés, it must be remembered that they are not part of the meal and should therefore never be heavy. The seasoning must always be sharper and higher than is usual for other dishes, something contrary to my usual principles since I prefer to under- rather than over-season a main dish. Paprika, cayenne pepper and a good sprinkling of salt inspire the palate.

When we opened Le Gavroche in 1967, we offered canapés to our customers, a custom we introduced to Britain. We made them, as I'd done at the Rothschilds', at the last moment. We never tried to offer a huge choice, just two or three with the *apéritif*, but they had to be of high quality. Even those who do not want an *apéritif* are offered them, along with a glass of water.

It is better not to offer canapés at all than to offer bad ones (the same can be said, I suppose, for everything). I would much rather have a fresh anchovy fillet on a croûton of bread than a *feuilleté* or a *vol-au-vent* that sticks to the tongue and upsets the palate before a meal. And you can use some marvellous ingredients in canapés. When I am at my house in France, I often go to one of the nearby markets, at Cogolin, Ramatuelle or Saint Tropez, and if I come across some tiny red mullet caught in the rocks, or anchovies that are still wriggling, I buy them as *amuse-bouches*.

I marinate the tiny red mullet fillets in the juice of an orange or mandarin with a drop of lemon juice, salt and pepper, for thirty minutes at the most, since the citrus marinade could burn the flesh if left longer. At the last minute I add a drop of olive oil, which has to come from the first pressing and also to have been pressed that very year. (There is a season for olive oil, just as there is a season for *Beaujolais Nouveau*.) The fillets are then served on a *croûton*.

If I had to choose one last canapé to go with my last glass of champagne, this would be a *gougère,* a little pastry *choux* bun flavoured with cheese (Emmental or Gruyère). In Burgundy, at wine tastings, they serve a piece of plain bread first to keep the tastebuds fresh, then they start to bring in the *gougères.* These are excellent with a white wine like a Bourgogne Aligoté. Another favourite in the winter, which I make when we're not too busy, is *croûte genevoise.* A piece of bread, preferably fried in clarified butter, is piled high with a creamy fondue-type mixture and baked (see p. 231).

When the *Relais et Desserts pâtissiers'* fraternity held its annual seminar at the Bell Inn in Aston Clinton near Aylesbury in 1973, the various participants put on a huge display of canapés. Around ninety of us organised a cocktail party for the last day. A central table of about eight metres in diameter held a blazing sun of canapés. All of us had worked for days, we came from different parts of Europe, and our food reflected our origins. It was a celebration of quality, quantity and colour. Even those of us who had contributed were overwhelmed by the final spectacle. I have never seen anything like it and I suppose I never shall again.

Three years later, when I entered the contest for the title of *Meilleur Ouvrier de France,* I presented eight canapés. I drew some inspiration from Aston Clinton, but I had to put forward completely new creations. The centrepiece was a crab shape made from puff pastry and filled with brown crabmeat mixed with butter and a little cognac. Around this were whites of leek on bread with mustard butter, thin slices of artichoke bottoms served with anchovy butter, *brioches* with Roquefort butter and little pieces of walnut. There were also mushrooms, filled with a mixture of hard-boiled egg and mayonnaise and coated in jelly, and a *rouleau* or *boudin* of *foie gras* with truffles and asparagus tips. At each corner of the display, I arranged crab shells containing flower-shapes carved from vegetables as decoration.

Something of a worse misfortune befell a regular French client, a know-all whose silly arrogance irritated me. In summer, we have a display of a few cold *hors d'oeuvres* on a silver tray in the bar, so that people can make a choice as they take their *apéritif.* This display, however, is false, consisting of items made from the real thing, but covered in a thick aspic, set as hard as concrete. They might also have wooden supports or foil underneath to help them keep their shape. They are made to last about three hours only, for the time of a meal service. This Frenchman always used to ask for me and one day, as someone came to seek me out in the kitchen, he decided to help himself to an *oeuf Albert* from the display. As he bit into his poached egg with smoked salmon on an artichoke heart, he suddenly found himself with a mouth full of foil, and egg, literally, all over his face. He was a little more humble after that…

Another variant is the *canapé-salle,* canapé served at table. This is a single item – perhaps a cupful of scented soup, a scallop with a sliver of truffle inside, a spoonful of melon sorbet with fresh mint in summer, or herring roe with a mustard sauce in winter. It is always offered 'with the compliments of the chef'. Yet, some people still have the audacity to send it back without touching it, saying they do not like it and imagining I am going to send them something else! I find this very strange: you send something as a gift, as a little extra, and people still think they can pick and choose.

When serving canapés, you have to work out who your guests are, avoiding anything with pork for people who might be Jews or Muslims. I follow the seasons, using red peppers from Provence, for example in August (the only time I use them). I cover these in oil and grill them until the skin chars and splits. Under cold water, I remove the skin and scoop away the white membrane and seeds. Cut into thin strips, they are cooked slowly in olive oil with garlic, thyme and a bay leaf, for about twenty minutes. I serve this on *croûtons,* and it is excellent with a *pastis.*

One of my greatest summer pleasures is preparing champagne and canapés for customers who ask if they can take the Waterside Inn's electric launch for a ride on the Thames before their meal. We put their champagne on ice and prepare a few more canapés than usual to go with them. Some of the customers are as excited as children. It is a joy to watch.

Sadly, even the best champagne can be spoilt if the rules are not observed. I had proof of this in no less a place than the Kremlin.

Boris Yeltsin and I have one thing in common: our literary agent, Andrew Nurnberg. Andrew asked me to prepare a dinner for publishers from all over the world to celebrate the publication of Yeltsin's new book of memoirs in April 1994. I had visited Moscow once before, in 1990, and been favourably surprised by some of the food available but not impressed enough to rely on what I might find locally for a Kremlin feast.

I was told I was to be the first foreign chef to prepare a meal in the Kremlin for 300 years. As a Frenchman, I felt like a culinary Napoleon. Unlike Bonaparte, though, I was not obliged to retreat, although the temptation to do so was sometimes great. In the end, the only thing I left to the Russians was the caviar. Even this was a mistake.

The menu was planned, and the wines chosen, months in advance. I warned British Airways ahead of our flight that we would be carrying substantial excess baggage, and the final tally was 450 kilograms. I took my own pans, and different types of flour for the *blinis*, for the *brioche* to go with the *foie gras* with truffles, for the bread with nuts for the cheese and for the dessert, the *tarte fine tiède aux pommes*. I took six magnums of Dom Pérignon 1985 for the *apéritif*, *terrines de foie gras* I had already prepared in Bray, the Château Coutet 1984 that was to go with it, and raw baby leeks and other ingredients for my vinaigrettes. I also took the beef for my *daube de bœuf*, the wine I was to cook it in, mushrooms, strips of bacon, celeriac and the magnum of Château Giscours 1985 to accompany. I had some early new potatoes, apples for the tart, Calvados to make the *sabayon* sauce to go with it, and the Quart de Chaume 1988 to drink with it. To go with coffee after the meal, I took the ingredients to make chocolate truffles, made of a *ganache* flavoured with fine champagne cognac, and *tuiles*. Although I was catering for up to sixty people, I took enough for sixty-five to be on the safe side, since there was absolutely no way of rustling up extra supplies on the spot.

I also took two of my cooks, Chris Sellors – a veteran of other campaigns in Australia and Hong Kong – and Marcus Ashenford as well as Diego Masciaga, my restaurant manager, and Benoît Radenne, then my head wine-waiter. Robyn, who was on the official invitation list, said she would act as liaison and help out if things became difficult. That was before any of us knew that there was a 350-metre walk – 364 steps with a long stride – between the kitchen and the hall where the dinner was to be held!

When we arrived at Moscow's Sheremetyevo airport, we were met as we got off the plane by four security men. We were kept in a VIP lounge for about an hour while our twenty pieces of luggage were gathered and examined. We were then put in cars and, with the luggage following in a van, we headed straight for the Kremlin. Arriving at Red Square, we were driven in through an entrance to the left and the van went to the right. Inside, we had to wait another forty-five minutes before being reunited with the luggage. I assume it was being passed through an x-ray machine. I was anxious to get some of the ingredients into a refrigerator and to let them rest. As we finally unpacked in the kitchen, six Russians took notes on everything, sometimes asking about individual bits and pieces, apparently worried by what we were going to serve their president. I began to get a hint of the resentment felt at the presence of a foreign chef. We were given a floor to ourselves and a *maître d'hôtel* and a waiter to look after us. Our suite was stark and simple, and furnished with ugly and uncomfortable reproduction furniture.

On the first night, we went to the Bolshoi to see *Giselle*. During the interval, we could not join the rest of the audience in drinking Russian champagne since we did not have any *roubles*. This seemed to be the only thing in Moscow that foreign currency could not buy. Afterwards we walked around Red Square for a few minutes, then in the Kremlin grounds for almost two hours. The sky was magical, pinpointed with stars, and the onion domes of so many of the buildings were outlined against it, looking like an illustration from a children's fairy story. Every few metres, armed guards, their faces suddenly illuminated by the moonlight, stepped forward to challenge us. A word from our guide made them step back into the shadows.

The next morning at quarter-past eight, armed with an interpreter, I had a meeting with Kremlin staff, all of them very unsmiling. They said they did not believe we had enough food for the President of Russia. They wanted me to add some plates of cold meat. I said I would not negotiate, and told Andrew Nurnberg that I was pulling out. I was prepared to leave all my stuff behind rather than bend to the Russians' request. Andrew, who had studied in Moscow and done a lot of business there, took this calmly and said he would handle the problem. Soon after, the Russians told me to do things in my own way.

Then I started to look over the kitchen. There were two ovens, one of which did not work at all. The temperature of the other would shoot up and down alarmingly, sometimes reaching a high of 300 degrees centigrade: it actually took five hours to get the hot plates on top heated up. There was little in the way of utensils or bowls, so I drew up a list of what I needed. About every half hour or so, a Russian would arrive with one single implement, such as a whisk, then he would go away and I would have to wait another thirty minutes for something like a rolling-pin. It was as farcical as a Jacques Tati film, but not quite so funny. It was about two in the afternoon before I had most of what I needed.

There was, however, not a single pepper-mill to be had in the Kremlin. When the time came to grind the peppercorns to go with the *terrine de foie gras*, Robyn put them in a cloth and crushed them with the Ferragamo high-heeled shoes she was wearing for the party. I was in an increasingly bad mood and I kept making her repeat the action to get the pepper evenly ground. Right in the middle of my preparation, a television cameraman came in with a note-taking assistant and began recording the scene for posterity. The interpreter said a record was needed because foreign chefs had not catered for a Kremlin boss for so long. I had to stop them when I became afraid that the heat from the television spotlight would damage my chocolate.

We had left strict instructions about the champagne, insisting that it should be opened as the guests arrived. Diego, pounding the 364 steps in a state of great distress, told us the Dom Pérignon had not just been opened but had been poured into a multitude of glasses a good forty-five minutes before the first guests were expected. I began to wonder whether this was not deliberate sabotage, provoked by jealousy.

We sent in the freshly made *blinis* (was this asking for trouble taking coals to Newcastle?) and the caviar, and I prayed there were still some bubbles left in the champagne. The *foie gras* was served next, and after that, the *daube*. Suddenly, the *daube* returned to the kitchen. A second team of waiters had set down extra cutlery and brought in a chicken *bouillon* with dumplings made in another kitchen, presumably closer to the hall. The guests were confused since this was not on the menu. Some sampled it but most waited. Eventually, it was taken away and the *daube* could be served.

Just as the cheese was despatched, there was another hitch. The Russian waiters reappeared with plates of cold meat and fish, wild boar, venison and something that looked like herring, all on the same dishes and accompanied by giant gherkins and onions. Yeltsin set down his knife and fork, refused to eat it and ordered it to be sent back. In the meantime, I was trying to cook my tart with the oven temperature rising and falling as though an unseen hand was switching the power on and off.

At the end of the meal, Yeltsin called me to the dining-room. I presented him with a gâteau in the shape of his book. He stood up and lunged towards me. I had a vision of the cake flying off into space. He grabbed it and I thought he was going to bite straight into it.

Later, Andrew Nurnberg congratulated me on the meal. He said the only problem he had noticed was that the pepper served with the *terrine de foie gras* was a little on the coarse side ...

At the end of the evening, I was furious at the behaviour of some of the Kremlin staff, which might have ruined the meal.

Back in our quarters, we were served what remained of the Dom Pérignon. We sampled the caviar that had been served at the dinner. It was salty, small-grain stuff, nothing like my first taste of caviar (at the Rothschilds', which came from the Shah of Iran) and nothing like as good as the caviar I buy for the Waterside Inn. I was shocked that the President of Russia had been served such mediocre caviar. We were also given some vodka, hot chocolate, coffee and tea.

In a private suite in the Kremlin, the first foreign chef to cook there in three centuries regaled himself with a midnight feast – a delicate gastronomic mix of caviar, coffee, hot chocolate, tea, vodka and one of the best champagnes money can buy!

Soups

I AM SURE of one thing about my childhood. My mother never had to use that well-worn phrase heard in most French households: 'Eat up your soup.' Instead, the most likely words to be heard in our family were: 'May I have some more soup, *Maman*?' And they usually came from me.

Few children really like soup, it seems to me. It's not like a chip, it's not crunchy, and it doesn't have that long, thin shape that you can nibble at and eat bit by bit. And soup has to be eaten with a spoon. I liked spoons as a child and so I never had any problem. For my mother, though, the main task was making enough soup to keep me happy.

I began to eat soup at the age of three or four. My soup-eating days therefore started around the end of the Second World War, a time when soup was often in itself the main evening meal. There was a shortage of many things then: there was not much in the markets or the shops, nor was there much money. But when things are scarce, you can always survive on soup. For this reason, soup to the French at the time was one of the basics, like a bowl of rice is still to the Chinese.

The soups my mother used to make most often were *potage parmentier,* the classic leek and potato soup, or, when we lived in the country, a *crème de cresson,* made from the strong-flavoured wild watercress she used to gather from the river.

There was only one soup I did not like very much as a child, and that was pumpkin soup (see p. 232). Pumpkin is a sweet vegetable, and I always found it hard to understand and appreciate a soup that was sweet. My mother made hers with milk, the pumpkins coming either from the garden or the market. Pumpkins in those days were enormous, cheap, a deep orange in colour, and almost sticky when you cut them open. They are rarely like that nowadays; I suppose farmers must cultivate them differently. In any case, I no longer find that sugary taste I remember from childhood. When we had pumpkin soup, I would not turn my nose up at it – I never turned my nose up at *anything* – but neither would I clamour for more.

When I was nine and considered to be in poor health, I was sent to the country, to live on a farm and build up my strength. At Escrigneul, a little village near Montargis in the Loire region, I was put into the hands of a farming couple, Monsieur and Madame Girard. They had a fairly large farm and, to make ends meet, they would take in a couple of needy children on a regular basis. They were paid to look after me by the town hall in the Paris suburb of Saint-Mandé where my family then lived. However, the Girards were anything but kind or generous. Monsieur Girard was unusually plump for a man in a physical job while his wife was as skinny as she was mean.

They would serve me and Jeannette, a thirteen-year-old also staying there, with a 'soup' made of stale crusts of bread on to which they poured boiling water. Just hot water, not even a stock. It was heated on the stove that warmed the whole house. Those farmers saved their *centimes* however they could. The only thing good about that soup was – praise be to God! – the dollop of fresh cream they put in it. Why the fresh cream? Because they kept cows which gave them milk, cream and butter and this cost them nothing. That soup would often be the only dish for dinner. On rare occasions, we would get a potato salad with herring, cut really small because the herring cost money. The potatoes were usually the ones that their pigs had refused. Very occasionally, we enjoyed a rabbit killed by the farmer, and we might get an omelette if the hens had been productive enough, but never had the right quantity of fish or meat protein that we really needed to build us up. The Girards were people without any heart or human qualities; they spent more time looking after their cows than after us children.

In September 1950, my mother came to visit me and I told her about the inadequate food and lack of comfort, let alone the absence of any affection. I told her that, although the school was about two kilometres away, they were never considerate enough to drive us there and we had to walk every day. I also told her that we had to wash under cold water that we pumped ourselves from a well, even in very cold temperatures – although on days when the water actually froze, we were allowed to bring our bowl into the kitchen! My mother reported my remarks to the social services, and I was taken away, as thin and unhealthy as I had arrived. The Girards were subsequently banned from looking after any more children.

Later, when I worked in the kitchens of the British Embassy in Paris, I discovered soups in the form of *consommé* or the thicker but smooth *velouté*, which we would prepare for banquets for up to 160 guests. I began to discover that a soup doesn't have to be a meal in itself. It can be just a precursor, it can be something to get your appetite going without really feeding you. In such cases, it is most likely to be a half cup or a ladleful.

Consommé is a soup that must be as clear as spring water and, when served, you must be able to see the bottom of the plate. A good *consommé*, when you stir it with your spoon, should sparkle like a diamond, and never have a trace of fat. It can be made from fish, game like wild duck, pheasant or wood pigeon, or meat like poultry or beef, with vegetables to add flavour.

After a first cooking, a *consommé* is sometimes a little cloudy, and needs to be 'clarified' to remove all the impurities. When the liquid is cool, this is achieved with a mixture of egg whites that have been half-whipped, plus crushed tomatoes and sometimes with some of the fish or meat used to make the original *consommé*. But this time, however, the fish or meat is minced and only the very leanest is used. This is added to the *consommé* which is slowly heated and stirred with a spatula. Finally, the solids come to the surface and form a sort of filter that traps all the impurities. In the middle, before it is skimmed off, a hole forms through which you can see right down to the bottom of the pan. The finished *consommé* is then passed through a fine conical sieve or muslin.

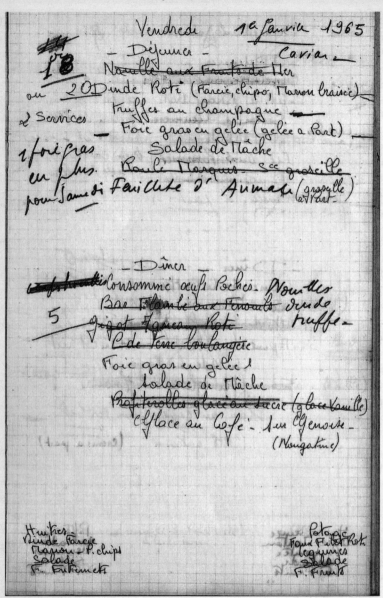

Vendredi   1ª Janvier 1965

— Déjeuner —   Caviar —

Nouilles aux Fruits de Mer

ou   2 O Dinde Roti (Farcie, chipo, Marron braisé)

2 Services   Truffes au champagne —

— Foie gras en gelée (gelée a Part) —

Salade de Mâche

1 foie gras   Roulé Marquis — Sce groseille
en plus.
pour Samedi Faillite d' Aumale (groseille
                                                        a Part —

— Dîner —

Consommé oeufs Pochés — Nouilles

Bas Flambé aux Fenouils dinde

5   Gigot Agneau Roti   truffe —

C de Terre boulangère

Foie gras en gelée

Salade de Mâche

Profiterolles glacé au sucre (glace Vanille)

Glace au Café — Sur Génoise —

                    (Nougatine)

Huitres
Viande farcie
Marron — P. chips
Salade
F. Entremets

Potage
Fond Filet Roti
legumes
salade
F. Fruits

New Year's Day. A special meal for 18–20 guests

A *velouté* soup is made from vegetables which are cooked and then sieved or passed through a liquidiser. You can use a multitude of vegetables, like mushrooms, asparagus or turnips, often with a little potato to give some consistency. It is ideally cooked in a poultry stock. Sometimes plain water is used, but this gives the soup less body and taste. When cooked, a little fresh cream can be added, and the result should be very light. Its name, drawn from the French word for 'velvet', implies something very smooth; it should have a consistency approaching that of a *beurre blanc* sauce. But it is not a sauce. It slides across your palate but does not linger there.

What I like to do is make a foaming *frottis,* an emulsion of cream and flavourings, including herbs like tarragon, or truffles, or a little Parmesan. The *frottis* combination must be in harmony with the primary flavour of the *velouté*. When the *velouté* is in the bowl, I top it with the *frottis* to enhance it for both the eyes and the palate. I want it to have a *cappuccino* effect, for some of this foam to caress the lips of the eater.

When I became chef to Cécile de Rothschild, I realised I was not the only one to appreciate soup. My boss had a knowledge of food and taste that would make a Michelin inspector green with envy. On occasion, she would head off from her house on the rue du Faubourg Saint Honoré on a half-hour window-shopping trip to food shops like Fauchon and Au Verger de La Madeleine, after which she would tick me off for not preparing some of the delicacies she had seen. Sometimes she would come back through the arched gateway to her home and phone me on my extension in the kitchen.

'Chef,' she used to say in her cavernous voice, 'go into the yard straightaway, stand under the arch and breathe. Smell the soup the concierge is making. It's ... *oh, là là!* ... How I'd love to have the same!'

Cécile de Rothschild sent me on expeditions to smell these soups literally dozens of times. One day, exasperated, I suggested: 'Mademoiselle, go and *taste* the concierge's soup.'

That made her very angry. 'No, *mon vieux,* what do you take me for?'

So she would say that the concierge's soup was better than mine, but she had never tasted it and had no intention of doing so. It was just a provocation that was somewhat typical of her. There was nevertheless something to what she said, as there were often some very tempting soup smells coming from our concierge's *loge.*

Life is a Menu

Among the domestic staff was Marcel Muet, Cécile de Rothschild's majordomo. The meek Marcel was constantly harassed on two fronts, by a domineering female boss and by a daunting dragon of a wife who also worked for the Rothschilds. During our mealtimes below stairs, Marcel would get his own back by a rare act of defiance. A country habit widespread in south-western France – known as a *faire chabrot* – consists of adding a glass of wine to the last drop of a bowl of soup. Marcel would add some red wine (often the family's own Carruades de Château Lafite) to his last couple of mouthfuls. When his wife gave him her customary withering look and began to tell him off, Marcel would say, 'Darling, I'm not drinking. It's just *chabrot*.'

The soups that I made for the Rothschilds were mostly *veloutés* for small dinners and *consommés* for larger parties. Among Cécile de Rothschild's favourites were the *consommé madrilène*, flavoured and garnished with tomatoes, and the *consommé célestine*, based on poultry, with little *crêpes* made with herbs that I rolled and cut into *julienne* as an accompaniment. She also liked Spanish *gazpacho*, which was often served at her Côte d'Azur home at Valescure near Saint Raphaël in the summer. She liked the garnish peppers and cucumbers served on a side plate so she could add what she wanted herself, never served in the soup. In her weekend house, north of Paris, when she invited other aristocrats or celebrities like the writer Françoise Sagan, she would often order a Russian *bortsch*. She always asked for horseradish from the garden to be ground into the *smetana*, soured cream. As for the *pirozhki* meat pies accompanying the *bortsch*, she would warn me: 'Careful, Chef, not just pastry, I want meat inside them!'

It was while working for the Rothschilds that I saw how the other half lived and appreciated the marvels you could achieve with money, time and taste. When I went back into her service early in 1963 after leaving the army, at the age of twenty-two Cécile de Rothschild sent me to the Banque Rothschild – later nationalised by the first Socialist government of President François Mitterrand – where I was given an advance of 100,000 francs, or around £1,000 at today's rates, and an expenses book to keep track of my purchases and justify future advances. In her service, I was to learn management skills, like running my own budget and accounts. I became accustomed to travelling and learned how to devise menus, from the most simple to the most complicated. She encouraged me to be creative in my cooking; she really wanted me to create. I discovered great wines and began to appreciate art. I learned to listen before having my own say. All of this helped me develop into the chef and businessman I am today.

The first fish soup that I made with Gilbert Picard, the chef at La Réserve at Beaulieu-sur-Mer, one of the culinary palaces of the Côte d'Azur, is one that I remember with great affection. I already thought my own fish soup was pretty good, but Gilbert's individualistic selection of Mediterranean fish, and his skill in preparing them, made his version exceptional. We had met when we were both competing for the Prix International Taittinger in 1971. That is the best spin-off of these competitions: you meet so many of your fellow chefs. Gilbert and I, both aged about thirty, hit it off from the start.

In those days, I used to rent a house on the Côte d'Azur every summer for my first wife, Françoise, and our children. They would go there for a month but I could only join them for a few days because of all the work I had at our restaurants in London. I would spend as much time as I could with Gilbert, watching, learning, laughing and – always – cooking and eating.

Gilbert and I would go to the market in Nice at seven in the morning to buy the fish for our soup. Just by the market, fishermen used to bring in their catch from the rocks near the coast, including little green crabs known locally as *favouilles*. Gilbert knew all their names by heart. We would try to find as many ingredients as possible for a good Provençal soup, fish such as wrasse, rainbow wrasse, comber, sea perch, scorpion fish or *rascasse*, blenny, sea bream, or weever fish. They were often fish that could not be found even in Paris, let alone abroad, because they did not travel well. A very good fish soup is also the essential basis for a *bouillabaisse*.

Bouillabaisse is a wonderful meal in its own right, huge Mediterranean fish poached in the original fish soup, with crayfish added on great occasions. But beware of fish bones – they can be dangerous. It is all too easy to swallow one hidden in a potato or in the thick flesh of the fish. Conversation should be stopped for a while, with total concentration given to the succulent textures and rich flavours of this great classic dish. It must be eaten hot, and is enjoyed at its best with a glass of rosé in the other hand.

After we bought our fish, Gilbert and I relaxed with a coffee in a nearby bar, then we went home. Gilbert would cook the soup and give it to me to pass through a hand mixer. Before we ate, we drank a *pastis* and then, when our families came up from the beach, we sat down to indulge ourselves. This was to become a summer ritual. Gilbert would make a *rouille* sauce, grate some Gruyère or Comté cheese, and also fry some *croûtons* flavoured with garlic. I would first eat the soup with nothing added in order to taste it unadorned, then add everything else to the second plate. I have never been able to recreate the smells and flavours of this soup in England, perhaps because, despite all the good fish available, I can't get hold of those unique little Mediterranean rock fish.

Often, as we were leaving after lunch, Gilbert would give me a jar of what remained for us to finish at home. There are some things some people do better than others, and Gilbert Picard always impressed me with his fish soup. I would have walked miles to taste it.

When Albert and I opened Le Gavroche in 1967, our menus were very short. Everything on offer was fresh, and nothing was pre-prepared. Remembering how successful my *consommés* had been in the Rothschild household, we devised a *consommé harlequin*. The crucial ingredient of this was three types of *royale,* a flavoured and moulded 'custard'. They were made with cream and eggs: the first was flavoured and coloured with tomato, the second was green with herbs, and the last was plain, seasoned only with a little salt and nutmeg. We would poach them in separate containers in a *bain-marie* placed in the oven like a *crème caramel.* After chilling, we then cut the individual custards into lozenges and put the red, green and yellow pieces in the *consommé* (thus the 'harlequin'). The *royales* were so delicate that they just melted in the mouth.

Not many people know that a good soup, with the exception of a *consommé*, can be made in hardly any time at all. So it makes me very angry that people buy instant soups. All you need are two or three vegetables. You sweat the main ingredient like tomatoes, leeks or mushrooms in some butter, you add potato, then put in some water or a little bit of chicken stock and let the whole lot cook for half an hour maximum. If you cut the vegetables into very small pieces, it can take as

POTAGES	Crème de Carotte	5/-
	Crème de Cresson	6/6
	Soupe à l'Oignon	6/-
	Consommé Arlequin	7/-

HORS D'OEUVRE -OEUFS	Rillettes de Tours (Spécialité)	8/6
	Pâté Maison Truffé	14/6
	Escargots de Bourgogne (half doz)	9/6
	Truite fumée sauce verte	15/-
	Soufflés Suissesse (Spécialité) (2 Pers)	19/-
	Oeuf Caroline	7/-
	Oeuf Poché Ecossaise	9/-
	Galantine de Gibier (Spécialité)	22/6

CRUSTACES	Homard à l'Escargot sauce Bérnaise	
	Coquille Saint Jacques à la Parisienne	11/-
	Langoustines à l'Aurore	22/-
	Mouclade d'Aunis (Spécialité en Saison)	15/6
	Nouilles aux Fruits de Mer (Spécialité)	22/-

POISSONS	Filets de Sole Cuba	21/-
	Sole Grillée Beurre Maitre d'Hôtel	19/-
	Bar Flambé au Fenouil (Spécialité) (5 Pers. sur commande)	72/-
	Turbot Poché Olga	22/6

ENTREES	Poulet Poele à l'Armagnac (Spécialité)	31/-
	Caneton Gavroche (Spécialité) (2 Pers)	76/-
	Tournedos à l'Ancienne	28/6
	Entrecote grillee au Poivre	22/6
	Pot au Feu sauce Albert	12/-
	Veau à l'Ananas (Spécialité)	28/-
	Côtes d'Agneau Maintenon	14/6
	Selle d'Agneau Orloff (Spécialité) (4 Pers. sur commande)	118/-

LEGUMES	Epinards en Branche	4/6
	Petit Pois à la Paysanne	4/6
	Carottes Vichy	4/-
	Nouilles Fraîches Maison	6/-
	Pomme de Terre Duchesse	4/6
	Pomme de Terre Noisette	4/-
	Choux-Fleur au Gratin	5/-
	Céleris braisé au porto	8/6
	Salade de Saison	3/6
	Salade Composée	4/6
	Pomme de Terre Pont Neuf	4/-

ENTREMETS	Omelette Rothschild (Spécialité) (2 Pers)	30/-
	Sablé aux Fraises (Spécialité) (2 Pers)	30/-
	Feuilleté Duc d'Aumale (Spécialité) (2 Pers)	25/-
	Roule Marquis	12/6
	Glace Amandine	9/-
	Sorbet Citron	6/6
	La Rose du Chef (Spécialité)	14/-
	Patisserie Maison	6/6
	Corbeille de Fruits	5/-

| FROMAGES | Fromages de France | 5/- |
| | Café (Petits Fours Sec) | 4/- |

The first menu at Le Gavroche

little as twenty minutes. When the potato is cooked, the soup is ready and you should take it off the heat to stop it boiling too long and losing its taste. You then put it through a mixer or liquidiser, cover the pan and put it to one side until it needs to be heated up for serving.

And you can decant it into little containers, mark the date and type of soup, and put it in the freezer to enjoy later. Even if you live alone, you can make and benefit from your own soups.

Soups can be eaten hot or cold. Hot soups are for winter, cold for summer. In neither Britain nor France are we adept at making soups with fruit. This is a pity because you can make a soup with pears, cherries or peaches that is extremely good. On Celebrity Cruises ships, for which I

Life is a Menu

ENTREES	Poulet Poêle a l' Armagnac (Spécialite)	35/-
	Caneton Gavroche (Spécialite) (2 Pers)	70/-
	Tournedos à l' Ancienne	28/6
	Entrecôte grillée au Poivre	22/6
	Pot au Feu sauce Albert	32/-
	Veau à l' Ananas (Spécialite)	28/-
	Côtes d' Agneau Maintenon	14/6
	Selle d' Agneau Orloff (Spécialite)	
	(4 Pers. sur commande)	118/-
LEGUMES	Epinards en Branche	4/6
	Petit Pois à la Paysanne	4/6
	Carottes Vichy	4/-
	Nouilles Fraîches Maison	6/-
	Pomme de Terre Duchesse	4/6
	Pomme de Terre Noisette	4/-
	Choux-Fleur au Gratin	5/-
	Céleris braisé au porto	8/6
	Salade de Saison	3/6
	Salade Composée	4/6
	Pomme de Terre Pont Neuf	4/-
ENTREMETS	Omelette Rothschild (Spécialite) (2 Pers)	30/-
	Sablé aux Fraises (Spécialite) (2 Pers)	30/-
	Feuilleté Duc d' Aumale (Spécialite)	
	(2 Pers)	25/-
	Roulé Marquis	12/6
	Glace Amandine	9/-
	Sorbet Citron	6/6
	La Rose du Chef (Spécialite)	14/-
	Patisserie Maison	6/6
	Corbeille de Fruits	5/-
FROMAGES	Fromages de France	5/-
	Café (Petits Fours Sec)	4/-

In those days a wide selection of vegetables was essential create the menus, I often offer a cherry or rhubarb soup. You must seek the right balance and it must not turn into a dessert or a *coulis*-type sauce. It must just have a taste of fruit with the right spices, like cardamom, cumin or nutmeg, or the freshness of a herb like mint. I have developed a number of cold soups for the ships to be served in hot destinations like Bermuda and the Caribbean.

Many people think the only cold soups are *vichyssoise* or *gazpacho*. At the Rothschilds, I also used to serve a *crème Caroline,* made with maize. It was slightly sweet and included maize, milk and a little onion; it was served very chilled, dusted with paprika or cayenne pepper.

At the Waterside Inn, there is not a day without a soup on the *table d'hôte* menu at lunch time. This is because I like soups, and I only offer my customers what I like. I do not make food for a market or for a niche. Now, as many as twenty customers take soup, whereas there might only have been ten in the early days. The lunch-time soup might be a little *velouté* made with sorrel from the garden, or a pea soup – if there are good fresh peas available – with diced bacon and *croûtons* served on a side plate. Otherwise, it could be a *consommé* of lobster or crayfish, with some crayfish tails as a garnish or, even more delicate, *a consommé* with a little *ravioli* floating in it, stuffed with crab, crayfish tails or wild mushrooms. It goes without saying that we make our *raviolis* ourselves; I do not buy in my pasta. It is true that I employ twenty cooks and have the staff to do this. It is also true that sometimes the garnish can take longer to make than the soup itself!

Another soup we serve is a *velouté de coquillages aux huîtres.* This is made with several shellfish, cockles, mussels and clams among them. We keep all the juices after cooking the shellfish, then mix them, after sweating some finely chopped onion, with a little fish stock, some cream, and a carefully chosen quantity of herbs. This produces a soup that has a unique whiff of iodine, of the sea itself. An oyster is then placed raw in the soup. Since the liquor is very hot, the oyster is poached on the outside, but still temptingly raw in the middle.

We also have a *consommé double de volaille,* called 'double' because it is cooked twice. I make a stock base first with a whole chicken, then cook it again, adding minced raw chicken breasts and aromatic vegetables, and then I clarify it with yet more raw chicken and vegetables. The result is almost an elixir. I infuse some lemongrass in it, and serve the soup in little ramekins in the middle of five-course meals in winter. This replaces the more common sorbet, which I think should never be served in cold weather.

Alain Chapel, a French three-star chef who sadly died suddenly in 1990 at the age of fifty-two, developed a *consommé en gelée, crème Dubarry et caviar Sevruga,* at the restaurant which still bears his name at Mionnay near Lyons. This dish is so refined that it is impossible to describe the nuances of taste it contains. The chilled *consommé* is of chicken with tarragon, just beginning to gel as it is put in the plate, covered with a Dubarry cauliflower purée topped with a generous helping of Sevruga caviar.

In 1980, the British branch of L'Académie Culinaire de France – since then known as the Academy of Culinary Arts – held a fund-raising dinner at the Bell Inn at Aston Clinton near Aylesbury, with the title 'Entente Cordiale Culinaire'. Several chefs, including Paul Bocuse, Joël Robuchon and Pierre Troisgros from France, were called upon to make the dinner. We worked in pairs – one British-based chef with one from France – on each course. Alain Chapel and I were assigned the first. During a series of phone calls, we agreed to adapt his *consommé* recipe to a winter one, using game instead of chicken, a beetroot cream and Oscietra caviar. On the day itself, Alain Chapel could not come, and I had to make the dish alone. The whole meal was excellent, but I honestly think this Chapel-inspired *consommé* was a revelation. I still make it today, but for private dinners, not for regular menus, because of the time, cost and difficult preparation involved.

Soups from the East fall into a category of their own. The Chinese birds' or swallows' nest soup, which I tasted in a wonderful restaurant in Hong Kong, is one of the most delicate I have ever eaten. Men climb up cliffs to collect the nests, which is highly dangerous. The soup may be very expensive because of those dangers, but it is so delicious, it is worth it.

One of the favourite soups of my wife Robyn is the Thai *tom yum goong*, which she always orders when we arrive at the Oriental Hotel in Bangkok. Even before our luggage has been brought to the room, and at one or two o'clock in the morning, she will persuade me to order her a bowl. This is a hot, sweet and sour prawn soup flavoured with lemongrass, chillies, lime leaves and lemon juice. It's particularly good eaten in Thailand because you can find fresh straw mushrooms there. They go off too quickly to be exported, meaning that the soup cannot be properly re-created abroad. The smell when *tom yum goong* arrives in the room is fantastic, it's the start of the holiday. One mouthful, and you know you're in Thailand. When Robyn is nostalgic for that wonderful country, she makes this soup for dinner in Bray (but without straw mushrooms, sadly).

Another soup inspired by the East, and which really took me by surprise, was one made by a highly gifted Scottish amateur, Gerry Goldwyre, winner of the BBC's 1994 *Masterchef* competition. I judged him along with some other winners for *Masterchef 2000* in the first February of the new millennium, a programme celebrating the tenth anniversary of what is, to my mind, one the best food programmes on British television. Gerry's soup was billed as Sweet Potato and Sesame Soup with Coconut Pesto. These are ingredients not usually to my taste, but his treatment of them was spectacular. The sweet potato was, like potatoes in my own *veloutés*, used as the bland, thickening element. The other ingredients, all fairly strong in flavour, were blended in such a masterly fashion, with none overpowering, that I could only compare the end result to the subtleties and complexities of a *grand cru* wine.

I was a judge on the programme with Julia Sawalha, Saffy in *Absolutely Fabulous*. In an earlier season, I had been a judge with her sister Nadia from *Eastenders*. The normally relaxed and expansive Julia was nervous at the start, and whispered to me that she was not much of a meat-eater. She asked me to taste all the meat dishes and said we would average out the marks afterwards. (She liked the soup, though!)

The British are a bit funny when it comes to soup. They discovered gastronomy a little late (better late than never), but they know soup should be served hot. There is a generation of Britons (my generation in fact) that wants soup not only hot, but *piping* hot. The younger generation has a little more gastronomic education, and knows that a *velouté* and other soups would be spoiled by being over-heated. When we first opened Le Gavroche, people would complain that the soup was not hot enough and would sometimes send it back to the kitchen to have it heated up. However, this is slowly becoming a thing of the past. Even so, there are still some who will still say, very politely, at the end of their meal: 'The soup was excellent but not hot enough.' You don't find that on the Continent, it's very English!

Hors d'Oeuvres

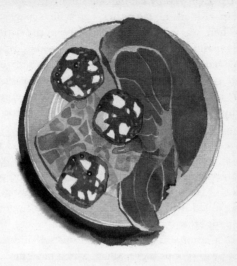

T HE *hors d'oeuvres* in any meal should be the precursor of the pleasures to come, never just a filler or afterthought. All too often, *hors d'oeuvres* are ill-considered items served in portions that are too large, so small that they are silly, or whose quality has been neglected. In reality, they should be light, tease the palate and be visually attractive. The starter should never be considered secondary because it is not the main dish.

Caviar is, of course, the most luxurious of all starters. Here I would go for both quantity and quality. I believe such a delicacy should be treated with reverence and consumed rarely, even for those rich enough to buy it all the time, otherwise it becomes ordinary or everyday. When available, however, it should be eaten with unashamed greed and in large portions!

Once I took a press party to see how a Roux Brothers' Scholar – a promising British chef whom we sent to work in one of the great French restaurants – was making out with Roger Vergé near Cannes. Nick Rowe, a Diners Club executive accompanying us, asked Robyn – whose knowledge is encyclopaedic and dates back to long before we met – to teach him about caviar. We were all in a *brasserie*, and Robyn told Nick that the only way to learn was by eating. She summoned up both Oscietra and Sevruga caviar with all the garnishes, egg whites, egg yolks, parsley, onions and toast. There was a hush from the others in the party – who had just begun eating pasta – as Nick and Robyn ostentatiously gorged themselves on caviar, pretending not to notice their companions' astonishment and envy. Later we organised a second caviar induction course in Bray. We also invited Roy Ackerman, one of the great figures of British gastronomy, who arrived with a very theatrical 'prop', a pedestal, gold-painted wooden dolphin from Maxim's in London. We perched the silver tray of caviar in a moulded ice base – which was inset with flowers and leaves – on top of the wooden fish, which had pride of place next to the table. We began with pressed caviar and salmon eggs, and progressed to Sevruga, Oscietra and Beluga, eaten with *blinis* or new potatoes from the garden, and accompanied by different kinds of vodka, including the classic Moskovskaya, a pepper and bison's grass herbal vodka. Without the slightest *soupçon* of a complex, we revelled in our self-indulgence, using horn or mother of pearl spoons (never silver, which tarnishes).

I buy my caviar from W.G. White Ltd, of Feltham in Middlesex, and they have been a rich source of delight and information over the years. There are over thirty different types of sturgeon, but primarily three that produce caviar, the three mentioned above. Beluga is the most expensive, and tastes very walnutty and creamy. Oscietra, whose eggs are about the same size as Beluga, tastes a little like a mature Brie. Apparently a lot of restaurants pass off the cheaper Oscietra as Beluga, but there is a handy way to tell the difference: if you press the eggs of Beluga, a grey oil will appear; the eggs of Osciestra when pressed exude a yellow oil. It's not foolproof, but a fair guideline! Then there is the Sevruga, whose eggs are the smallest. This means they take on more of the salt used in processing, and thus have more a 'taste of the sea'. The caviar market is in turmoil at the time of writing because of hefty price increases in Iran and Russia, rather similar to the July 2000 oil crisis.

I love caviar with *blinis,* and just thinking about *blinis* conjures up the taste of caviar. I like them totally covered in caviar and this is our special treat for New Year, which we celebrate at our house in the south of France. We always have at least two kinds of caviar, but Oscietra is our favourite. For the past ten years, Kate Gignoux, a friend who lives just over the hill from our house, makes *blinis* at home. She and her husband Peter carry them to us, plump and still warm, in a wicker basket, wrapped in a napkin with aluminium foil on the outside.

She also brings a pot of thick, non-pasteurised soured cream, what the Russians call *smetana*. As Kate and Peter come in, our fire is blazing and the Dom Pérignon or Krug is out of the cellar. Recently, Kate has started spreading her wings and now she is making *blinis* based on a recipe of Georges Blanc, a Michelin three-star chef whose *crêpes de la mère Blanc,* made of potatoes, are world-famous.

Another luxury starter is *foie gras.* As some people smuggle drugs, I used to smuggle uncooked *foie gras* into Britain. For the first five years after Albert and I opened Le Gavroche, Britain was not a member of the European Community, meaning that there were still strict customs controls on goods, especially raw and fresh food, coming from France. Albert, although he agreed it was necessary, used to worry about me getting caught. As many of our clients in those days were from the establishment, often aristocrats or politicians, I had little fear that we would run into lasting trouble. I explained my illicit substances away as a 'pâté' to a customs officer at Heathrow. As he let me through, he said 'It doesn't look very nice'. . .

At first we marinated duck *foie gras* in a little port and Armagnac, then cooked it wrapped in a cloth and served this as a *ballotine* cut into slices that melted in the mouth. The British entry into Europe in 1973 came just in time since we needed increasing supplies of *foie gras,* not only for Le Gavroche but for the Waterside Inn which had just opened. Restraints were also lifted and we were able to start serving our *foie gras* hot, a new departure for Britain and a clear indication that we had imported it raw. At the time, hot *foie gras* was still rare even in France. We cut *foie gras* into escalopes – four from the small lobe of the liver and six to eight from the large lobe. We pan-fried these escalopes fiercely and served them with a sweet and sour sauce, segments of orange and grapefruit and some *julienne,* little strips, of lightly candied lemon rind.

In general, I like *foie gras* hot in winter and cold, in a terrine, in summer. To make a *foie gras* terrine, I place duck *foie gras* in a terrine mould after cooking, one lobe at a time, with a layer of lightly poached figs or rhubarb spread on top before other lobes are added. It could take around six lobes to fill up a terrine mould. Once the mould is filled, it should be covered in clingfilm and a light weight placed on top. After cooling in the refrigerator, the terrine is turned out of the mould, sliced, and served with toasted *brioche.*

For Cécile de Rothschild, I prepared only goose *foie gras.* Goose *foie gras* is larger and whiter than duck. It usually weighs between 600 and 800 grams, whereas duck livers are just 300–500 grams each. She did not eat the *foie gras* as an *hors d'oeuvre* but with salad – possibly of lamb's lettuce and walnuts – after the main course. It could be served as a terrine stuffed with large pieces of truffle and covered in a rich jelly.

To prepare the liver, I left it to soften at room temperature, then, with the point of a knife, I took out the nerves and veins from the lobes. I put the liver in a flat dish with salt and pepper, some cayenne and a little drop of port and cognac, and left it for up to half an hour in the refrigerator. I then wrapped it tightly in a napkin like a large white *boudin,* and poached it in a strong poultry stock at a maximum of seventy degrees centigrade. (The centre of *foie gras* should never be heated to more than sixty degrees or the fat escapes, leaving behind a poor, dry lump of liver.) I always left it to cool in the stock. Not until the next day did I remove it from the stock, and take off the napkin. I would then place the cold and firm-textured *foie gras* in a terrine mould and pour over some of the half-set, clarified poultry stock used for the cooking.

Cécile de Rothschild would decide just as I was about to start preparing the *foie gras* whether she wanted truffles or not. When her cousin, Lord Rothschild, was coming from Britain, she would tell me just the day before to prepare him some *foie gras* to take back, giving me scarcely the time to buy and prepare it. On one occasion, I complained that this would be difficult because her English cousin had taken away three of my best terrine dishes the previous year and had never returned them.

For me, one of the first things that jumps to mind when I think of *hors d'oeuvres* is *charcuterie*, with its multitude of variations on hams, *saucissons*, pâtés and terrines, recalling those comforting odours of my childhood. And *charcuterie*, of course, remains more affordable than other *hors d'oeuvres.* It's more homely and simple in its approach more a family *hors d'oeuvre* than one for grand receptions.

For me, *boudin noir*, black pudding or blood sausage, is the epitome of the peasant nature and simplicity of *charcuterie*. The concept exists in many cuisines, and is always different: I have eaten it in Lancashire and Scotland, where it is more powerful than many French varieties, and in Italy. Every region of France has its own recipe. Cooked too quickly, the skin burns and bursts and the inside stays cold and goes dry. Over too gentle a flame, the inside will also go dry, as the constant heat 'steams' the *boudin,* forcing out the moisture. My mother used to cook *boudin* in foaming butter, just a little at first and then adding more as time went on. This produced what I called *'le chant du boudin',* its slightly whistling song. A little of the filling, or rather blood, would begin to protrude at each end when it was cooked after about five minutes. My mother served it with apples from the garden. Cut roughly, not regularly as I would do now, she cooked them on all sides in a little frying pan. She would throw in a pinch of sugar to compensate for the apples' acidity and caramelise them. When she made *boudin* as a main dish, she would accompany this with some mashed potatoes.

The *boudin blanc* is more elegant than its black cousin, and is made from poultry, sometimes with some pork and occasionally with some truffles. It is a great favourite at Christmas and New Year in France. When we finally opened our own *charcuterie* shop, we were inundated with orders for white *boudin*, which Albert made and served with a Périgord truffle sauce at Le Gavroche. I have never tasted such a delicate, tasty *boudin blanc,* and this is something that Albert must have in his genes, passed down from his father and grandfather. Whenever Albert makes them now, I always ask him not to forget his brother and to put some aside for me.

Pork is the mainstay of *charcuterie*, either used by itself in *saucissons,* etc., or to give texture and moistness to dishes made principally from poultry or game, from elegant *galantines* to the more mundane terrines.

Rillettes are easy to make, from pork (the original), duck, goose or rabbit flesh, and pork fat. The flesh is cut into pieces and cooked very slowly together with the fat, some white wine and spices, until it breaks down into fibres. It is then taken off the heat and left to cool. Then it has to be worked with the fingertips to make long strings of flesh that combine and 'melt' into the pork fat. This holds the meat together and gives it its unctuous rich quality. This again is something that Albert does particularly well. I often serve *rillettes*, sometimes with grilled hazelnuts inside, accompanied by toast and segments of grapefruit to offset the dish's fattiness (see p. 234).

When I saw the high quality of British salmon, I began to make salmon *rillettes*. I poach a large salmon steak in a vegetable *court bouillon*. When cold, the flesh is broken into shreds (without being crushed), then mixed with a little softened unsalted butter, whipped cream, salt and pepper, a few green peppercorns, and snipped chives. I store this at salad level in the refrigerator – it must not be too cold to spread – and serve it with Melba toast. During Ascot Week, when the Waterside Inn sometimes makes up picnic hampers, this is a favourite.

At the same time as we could start importing raw *foie gras* into Britain, we were also allowed to bring in live snails. I used to salt them, then wash, drain and blanch them. I arranged them in little pastry flan cases with a strong-flavoured but delicate parsley purée – *en habits verts* (green coats). I made up a light herb soufflé mixture, piled this on top of the snails, and baked the flans for three to five minutes. This was to remain one of my signature dishes for about fifteen years, and was also a dish I took to the Mandarin Hotel in Hong Kong when I cooked in the Le Pierrot restaurant there. One evening, I noticed that the first flans to be served looked fine, but the later ones were tired and flat. I found that the Chinese cooks helping my team were taking a short cut by whipping huge quantities of egg white in advance and freezing it; this deflated, collapsed egg white was thereafter used on each individual order. When cooked, the soufflé collapsed, turning into a sort of pancake. I was so angry that I threw one of these pancakes at a wall. The freezing ceased immediately.

In the early days at Le Gavroche we served snails in their shells. One evening when Albert was absent, Tony Battistella called me from the kitchen. The dining-room, although full, was strangely quiet. You could have heard a pin drop. But instead there was a crunching, cracking sound. Tony motioned discreetly with his chin towards one of the tables of four. I quickly moved round the room, talking to customers briefly on several other tables so as not to look too curious. Then I homed in on that last table. Three of the diners were eating their starter in silence; the fourth was noisily crunching his *escargots de Bourgogne,* shells and all! Snail tongs were untouched, and a thin line of blood trickled from the corner of his mouth. At that time, Le Gavroche offered six, nine or a dozen snails. Luckily, he had only ordered nine, and he was on his last. The next day, Albert and I discussed banning snails in their shells from our menu but, since the customer in question was not from the British Isles, we decided against it.

Our love of *charcuterie* was to lead to one of our London ventures, the establishment of a French-style shop selling all that comes from the pig. We wanted to set this up near Harrods but, after failing to find anywhere suitable, I noticed a shop for rent in Lower Sloane Street about fifty yards from Le Gavroche. Two days later, negotiations were under way. We finally took over the shop, to be named 'Le Cochon Rose', the pink pig, in February of 1969. Its proximity to Le Gavroche was a plus, meaning that it was easy for us to keep an eye on it.

Work on Le Cochon Rose was carried out at the same time as on our new restaurant, Le Poulbot, in the City. Work at the shop, however, was comparatively simple and was completed in four weeks. The façade and the insides of the shop were in blue and white with the sign outside in a vivid and contrasting pink. I had asked the interior designer, David Mlinaric, who had made such a good job of Le Gavroche and who was also in charge of Le Poulbot, to leave a good deal of room for the *laboratoire* where all the serious preparation was to take place. In the end, this took up 60 per cent of the total space, and was largely based on the layout of the *Pâtisserie des Marches* where I had served my apprenticeship. To equip the *charcuterie*, I turned to the French company La Bovida, and got so excited by the diversity in the catalogue that at first I drew up a list long enough to equip two shops!

At the end of March 1969, we opened to the public. This was the first authentic *charcuterie* to open in London. Everything was prepared on the spot – we did not want to import from abroad and lose freshness and quality in the process. Sylvette, a young French, slightly plump brunette, took care of the shop itself. Two *charcutiers*, both excellent professionals, arrived from France. My task was to draw up recipes and to assume the privileged role of chief taster. The refrigerated displays were soon overflowing with dozens of different pâtés, sausages with herbs, knuckles of ham in breadcrumbs, goose and pork *rillettes, galantines* of chicken, guinea fowl or veal, a pâté made from pork *museau* (snout) with a shallot vinaigrette and piles of snails that were constantly pillaged by customers. My grandfather would have been very proud of his grandsons, setting up a shop in the family tradition, so like the one he had in Charolles. How he would turn in his grave now if he knew that the French government has been considering replacing the traditional skin made from beef intestines on sausages with plastic substitutes because some scientists say there may be an outside risk of mad cow disease.

The actual job of *charcutier* had few secrets for me, but Le Cochon Rose gave me first-hand confirmation of how hard this branch of butchery was. The hands of a *charcutier*, swollen from contact with salt and brine and marked by the many cuts caused by the slip of a knife, are ample testimony. The temperature in the *laboratoire* was kept at a wintry level all year long and we frequently had to throw sawdust to stop the damp floors from becoming dangerously slippery. Albert and I knew these hardships from childhood, and this awareness had made us choose *pâtisserie* as our first speciality rather than follow family tradition.

Every week, several whole pigs were cut up on the wooden bench by our two *charcutiers*. The back legs were made into ham, the loin was cut up into chops, and the shoulders were used to make Toulouse sausages. The bones were kept to make jelly, used to surround soft-boiled eggs in *oeufs en gelée* or to glaze pâtés and *galantines*. The blood went into our *boudins* or to clarify the jellies, and the head was used to make pâtés. The trotters, after being cooked for hours in a *bouillon*, were sold breadcrumbed, leaving it to the customer to grill and serve them with a *béarnaise* sauce. (It was then that I learned that a pig's trotter contains no fewer than 32 bones, a fact that I would often verify by counting them as I ate.) The curly, corkscrew tails ended up in *choucroûte*. The entrails went into *andouilles* or *andouillette* sausages. Nothing was wasted.

Albert and I were delighted with this project. We had become determined not just to shine at the summits of gastronomy but to play an educative role in developing British taste. A few weeks after the opening, we were given a boost by a highly complimentary article in the *Illustrated London News* by the food writer Margaret Costa. It was accompanied by a series of photographs, and explained the important place that *charcuterie* plays in the diet of a French family. As Albert and I had decided not to advertise our new shop, but let the business grow by word of mouth, that article was extremely important. The French community in London was immediately at our door and British customers soon followed. On Friday and Saturday afternoons, the queue stretched out along the pavement, even when it rained. On Saturdays, wearing my chef's jacket, I used to help out and nothing would please me more than the frequent sight of customers, who had come with the intention of buying just one or two items, leaving with their arms full.

In the very first weeks, our turnover was above expectations. Albert and I were eager to expand, suggesting we could open similar shops elsewhere. Naïvely, we suggested that Golder's Green would be ideal. Michael von Clemm, our chairman, said it might work, 'But you'll have to change the name.' We had no idea that Golder's Green was known for its large Jewish community!

Even with just the original shop, we realised we needed more qualified staff to keep standards up. In June of that year, we took on our sister Liliane as the main shop assistant with her husband Paul in charge of production. Both were excellent in a trade that they had been practising for twenty years. Liliane was smiling, friendly, cheeky and a born saleswoman. Paul was hard-working and produced extremely tasty goods. Unfortunately, he became interested in matters that were no business of his. Several years later, this led to a breakdown in our relationship, giving me early proof that it is not always easy or desirable to work with close relatives. They went back to France.

I began the new millennium by attending the slaughter of a pig, known as '*tuer le cochon*', on a farm near Lyons. It was something I'd always wanted to do, both because it represented a return to nature and to truth, as well as a tradition, part of a civilisation, that I fear may be disappearing. This winter ceremonial has been commonplace for centuries on all farms. Individual farmers would slaughter their pigs in rotation and invite their neighbours to share in the meat. This ensured an even supply and avoided an excess. This practice is only tolerated now provided that the farmers do not *sell* anything. A local official, like a *gendarme* or a village mayor, is usually invited – taking his share of the pig with him at the end – to bear witness to the proper conduct of events. I went there with Daniel Giraud, a *pâtissier* from the town of Valence who is a close friend, a fellow *Meilleur Ouvrier de France* and a lover of rural life, on the eve of the Epiphany on 6 January 2000. A pig is slaughtered on this farm on the Monts du Lyonnais three or four times a year in a ritual that turns into a true celebration with a professional *charcutier* officiating. The farm was at an altitude of 600 metres, with fresh, clean air ideal both for raising pigs and for drying their meat.

The animal, weighing some 250 kilograms, was pulled into the yard on a rope attached to the ring through its nose. It had been fed on a traditional diet, a ground-up mixture of Jerusalem artichokes, nettles and potatoes, never with any industrial feed. It was killed with a revolver shot to the head so it did not suffer. The carcass was laid on wooden planks on the ground, then was pulled up on pulleys by four of us. The blood, extracted by cutting the pig's throat, poured into a bucket. This was whipped by hands and forearms with a little vinegar to stop it coagulating. The carcass was then lowered on to straw scattered over the planks. This straw was set alight to singe off the hairs on the pig's skin. The skin and the hooves were then scraped and the pig cut into pieces. The odours were powerful. If this account may distress some animal rights defenders, then I can only reply that we cannot turn our back on the world that created us.

Daniel and I put on aprons to butcher the meat which was still warm. We put the fat to one side, the lean to another on a bare white table, quite unlike the fancy boards I use in my kitchen. We drank some light white wine from the Rhône valley as we worked. About two hours after the slaughter, the blood was mixed with lightly cooked chopped leeks, onions, apples and parsley, then milk and cream from the farm were mixed in. We tasted this for seasoning with spoons and our fingers before putting it in *boudin* skins.

That was how I began the new century. The dinner that night was 'our' *boudins* with a couple of bottles of Châteauneuf du Pape. To start we had a vegetable soup, made by the farmer's wife, just as good as the soup that Paris *concierges* used to make.

The next morning, we were up before dawn to make *saucissons* from the lean shoulder meat, seasoning them with salt and pepper and putting them in skins. With no colouring agents and smelling strongly of the original pig, it is not the sort of product that townspeople normally like. The *saucissons* were destined to dry for at least six months in the lofts where maize was lying on the floor and apples were stacked by size and type. There were mixed smells of corn, apples and *saucissons*. We all took away a little basket with *boudins* and *grattons,* pieces of crackling. Outside in the yard, dogs and hens picked at bits of the pig that had been discarded. . .

Eggs

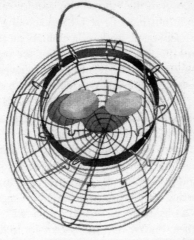

HAD I BEEN asked as a child about which came first, the chicken or the egg, I would have had no doubt. It was the chicken. In my birthplace of Charolles, my family had a hen called Julie who was more of a pet than a farm animal. She followed my mother around everywhere like a dog or cat, competing with me for my mother's attention.

It was war-time and, with food rationing, the rare times when Julie gave vent to her voice were greatly exciting for me because I knew we had an egg and that this would please my mother. Food was so short that my mother would practically cut the egg in four. When Julie stopped laying, a time when any normal hen would have been retired to the soup-pan, we left her alone. She was too much of a pet, and she went on to die of old age.

More than ten years after the war ended, I was to begin to discover the multiple uses of eggs, and to realise that they did not exist to make omelettes alone. In June 1956, I left school and was eager to get started as an apprentice in *pâtisserie* like my older brother. My mother took me in my

Life is a Menu

Sunday best to the Saint Michel employment office of the *Société des pâtissiers français* which was just by the Palais Royal in Paris. There, a young woman ruffled through some papers until she came across a letter from Monsieur Camille Loyal of the *Pâtisserie des Marches* in the working-class district of Belleville in northern Paris. He was looking for an apprentice. The young woman telephoned, made an appointment, and my mother and I were soon back on the *métro*. Within an hour, we were at the shop, an imposing place with a marble facade and gold engraved letters promising the customer that everything inside was made with real butter. Monsieur Loyal looked the part. He was a large man dressed in white, with a magnificent starched chef's *toque*. After he gave us a speech on the unsocial hours and life of a pastry-cook, I was taken on.

That was to give me a painstaking and laborious introduction to eggs which, I quickly found out, were one of the four basics of *pâtisserie*, together with butter, flour and sugar. Our egg deliveries used to arrive in what we called *canadiennes,* crates carrying an impressive 360 eggs. It was my job as the latest recruit to 'clarify' the eggs, to separate the yolks from the whites. I would go through them one by one, taking care not to let the slightest hint of yolk taint the whites. This would have ruined them, introducing the fatal grease that would make it impossible to beat the whites into a *neige*, or 'snow', for meringues or biscuits. Monsieur Loyal watched over me like a hawk, making sure that I cleaned out the shells with my thumb – a technique that would be totally forbidden today because of hygiene regulations – to extract every last drop of white. Now, apprentices are saved this ordeal because there are machines that break the eggs and separate the yolks to perfection, provided the eggs have been well chilled beforehand.

Despite this tough start and a conviction that eggs and I were not to become good friends, they were destined never to leave my life. Eggs, after all, are a crucial element in *pâtisserie* and the emulsifier in sauces of the mayonnaise and *hollandaise* families. And, just as a cabinet-maker varnishes his furniture, *pâtissiers* use eggs to put the finishing touch to their work. They use the yellow yolk with a little bit of white or some milk, and brush it on the pastry. A layer of egg must be applied very carefully, not just splashed on, and too much egg will peel off in the oven and ruin the final effect.

Having followed my brother into *pâtisserie*, I now followed him into my first job in a kitchen. Two and a half years later I joined Albert in the

Macaron Noisette : 250 gr de pâte d'amande, 125 gr de poudre de noisette, 375 gr de sucre glace, 50 gr de fecule, détendre au blancs

Macaron Nancy : 250 gr de pâte d'amande, 250 gr de tant pour tant, 250 gr de sucre glace, Vanille, 50 gr de fecule, détendre au blancs.

Macaron Sherbet : 600 gr de tant pour tant, 200 gr de sucre glace, melanger avec 8 blancs montés avec 50 gr de sucre.

Miroir ou Progrès : 500 gr de tant pour tant, 50 gr de farine 8 blancs montés avec 50 gr de sucre, miroirs garni avec crème d'amande à pithivier.

Tirliton : 3 œufs de poudre d'amande, 3 œufs de sucre glace, 3 œufs de beurre fondu, 6 œufs en tout, 1 noisette d'abricot dans chaque fond.

Madeleines : 200 gr de beurre, 200 gr de sucre glace 4 œufs, 250 gr de farine, 1 pointe de licot, citron ou Vanille

Mousse chocolat : (moule à charlotte papier beurré) 250 gr de chocolat a cuire fondu a l'eau, incorporez deux blancs montés, 3 cuillère de crème fouettéez, mouler avec couche de nougatine ecrasée, demouler (frais) Sauce café crème et bien avec grains de café liqueur a part.

Macaron chocolat : 108 gr de chocolat rapée très fin, 50 gr sucre glace - 100 gr Amande Poudre - 5 blanc monté - 50 gr beurre fondu - Laissez reposer 1 Heure avant de mettre au Four - doubler pour la cuisson - Four à 150°.

Meringue Suisse : 1 Blanc - 50 gr sucre semoule, blanc monté au 3/4 mettre alors le sucre et laisser monter (mettre le sucre doucement - chetter poudrer de sucre glace

My well-used page of petits fours from my apprenticeship

British Embassy in Paris. This was my first contact with Britain, even if I had no inkling then what Britain was going to mean in my life. Under Gladwyn Jebb, who was then ambassador, breakfast at the British Embassy was a true egg festival. They were fried, poached and scrambled, jostling with big black country mushrooms – uninviting to the eye but full of taste – tomatoes, sausages, black pudding and bacon. It was there, too, that I first sampled salmon kedgeree where chopped hard-boiled eggs, carefully cooked so they were not too hard, added taste, colour and a soft texture to the fishy rice. I loved making kedgeree and, when the guests had gone, I would always treat myself to a bowl.

This contrasted with another view of eggs *en masse*. On my first trip to Moscow in 1990 where I went to seek out Russian art for my private dining-room at the Waterside Inn, I was staying in the Hotel Moskva near the Kremlin. I came down to breakfast on my first morning to find that the breakfast eggs had already been fried and laid out on the tables in a huge banqueting hall. There were two congealing eggs on each plate, on tables for ten or twenty, multiplied by fifty. Row after row after row of eggs just staring at me. Needless to say, I decided to pass on breakfast. . .

A few doors from the British Embassy, when I moved along the rue du Faubourg Saint Honoré to the home of Cécile de Rothschild, I was treated to lectures on the omelette. My employer told me just how she thought an omelette should be. She was a sentimental, emotional woman and her eyes would shine. At times, when she got really carried away, there might even be a small tear.

'Chef,' she said, 'I want to see this omelette very rounded, pale with a little golden sheen, a film of tenderness. When you touch it, it must bounce back a little but it must not be firm. When you touch it, you must want to bite into it. It must be like a baby's bottom. Why am I telling you this, Chef, you've just had a baby!'

Cécile de Rothschild and her eggs would put me through another culinary endurance test. A favourite *hors d'oeuvre* was what she called *oeuf en brioche* 'with a little truffle'. A *brioche* was hollowed out, and partly filled with a fine purée of chicken. A lightly poached egg then went in, to be covered with a Périgueux truffle sauce. The result was sublime. It is the sort of dish you simply could not justify nowadays. In terms of man-hours and ingredients, it would be too expensive. First, you have to make a

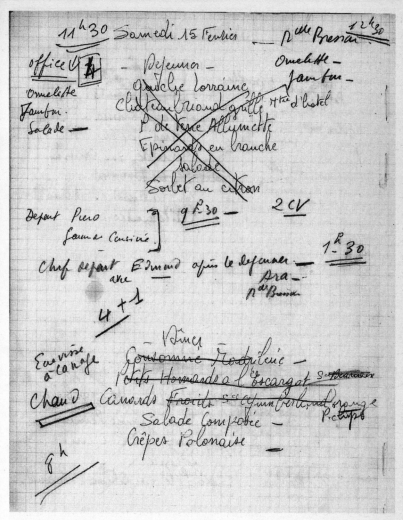

Lunch in Paris, then a rather sophisticated dinner for five in the country

suprême de volaille, a dish in itself. You have to be a bit mad to go and turn that into a purée. You must also make the *brioches* and then you have to poach the eggs. The truffle sauce alone takes about two hours to make, as one of its ingredients is veal stock. You can make this ahead, but it still takes half an hour of preparation and an hour's simmering! The sauce also needs thirty grams of finely chopped truffles...

On Thursday evenings, she would call me after dinner at around ten-thirty or eleven, and I would go up to the salon. She would say, 'Chef, I'm going to the country tomorrow after lunch. I'll write the menu for lunch in your order book.' She would not give me that menu straightaway, which would have made things too easy. For the Friday dinner in the country, at Noisy-sur-Oise in Picardy, where her guests included the rich and famous, she would, however, give me a few guidelines.

'We'll be six in Noisy and we'll have a little egg dish. You know how I like them, Chef, in a *brioche* with a little chicken purée, something not too complicated. After that, we'll have a country dish, perhaps a *navarin d'agneau*. Ask Charles the gardener for vegetables from the garden.'

I would have to make the dough for my *brioches* in the morning. Then I would poach the eggs. I would put them in jars of chilled water. If they broke, they were ruined, but preparing them in Paris saved me a precious half-hour. Once lunch was finished, I would put the jars in my Citroën 2CV and head north to Noisy. On those Friday afternoons, there was always a rush to leave Paris. There were no motorways and, on days when I was unlucky, I could take about two hours to reach my destination, even though it was only around thirty miles away. All the time, as I bounced along the road, stopping and starting in traffic jams, I was watching over my eggs, the most fragile part of my load. Once in Noisy, I would put them straight in the refrigerator.

When the time came to prepare the dish, I drained the eggs through a strainer, put them in a bowl and poured boiling water on them to heat them up. Then I dried them carefully on a cloth and put them into the *brioche* which I had previously lined with the purée. The finishing touch was the sauce.

'*Un petit plat facile,*' Cécile de Rothschild liked to call it. 'An easy little dish ... '

On one of the weekend trips to Noisy, I was pushing my 2CV, loaded with food, to the limits. Coming into the village at about forty-five miles per hour, I hit a hump in the road which sent the car, with its bouncy suspension, right into the air. My usual thrill at this experience turned to horror when I saw my employer at the wheel of her Bentley, coming the other way, heading straight for me in the middle of the road. We missed each other, but she looked visibly shaken and angry. When she returned home shortly after, she called me in immediately. Without letting me speak, she told me I was a road-hog and a public menace. When I could get a word in, I replied that her Bentley, even when driven very fast, would not take off when it hit a hump. I suggested that her inability to keep to her own lane would make potential accidents more likely. I also pointed out that, after making a lunch in Paris, I had been hurrying to prepare her dinner and that she would not have been pleased if I made her wait.

She said nothing for several seconds then, to regain the upper hand, remarked as she left the room: 'Since you like speed so much, I'll buy you a Jaguar. But don't expect it immediately, it'll be for your retirement!'

Truffles became intimately associated with eggs to my mind when I visited Mont Ventoux in Provence at the end of the 1980s. I go there every year to buy my truffles, of which I need about thirty to forty kilograms each season. In the nearby town of Carpentras, my contact is a fellow *pâtissier*, Frédéric Jouvaud. His wife, Nicole, said one day she would make some eggs. 'I hope you don't mind,' she said, 'it's very simple.' She was trembling a little at the idea of making something for a three-star Michelin chef. The result was so good that the dish is now one of the favourites of both myself and of Robyn, my wife. We make it for ourselves when the Waterside Inn is closed and we are at our house near Saint Tropez.

Egg shells are porous, which means they can pick up the taste of other ingredients close to them. An egg that has been left too long on the straw where it was laid will taste of straw. An egg next to onions in a refrigerator will absorb the flavour of onions. Preparing for her dish, Nicole had left eggs in a closed jar with truffles for a day or two to ensure that they were permeated with the flavour of truffles. First, Nicole warmed up some cream. As it boiled, she threw in some fine slivers of truffle. Then she let this divine truffle cream cool under the lid of the saucepan. Next she grated a little Emmental cheese. She greased individual cups with a little butter, added a little grated cheese, then some cooled truffle cream and broke her eggs on top. She finished by adding a little more cream before she put the eggs in the oven. It gave eggs a completely new dimension, and this dish remains one of the best things I have ever eaten in my life.

As with most food, an egg's beauty lies in the pleasure it can give both when eaten simply and when used in complex recipes. When Françoise, my first wife, and I were visiting her parents at their farm at Ognon in Picardy, I would take eggs just laid and still warm. I would make a hole in both ends and swallow the warm egg raw. Professional singers are encouraged to eat raw eggs to help their voices. I used to feel that I was getting the best part of being a singer: eating fresh eggs raw, but not having to go through the ordeal of the concert platform!

The only egg that I have never been able to accept is the Chinese 100-year-old egg. I have adapted to everything else in the Chinese repertoire, including snake served in different shapes and forms. The only thing that is worse than the sight of that translucent green white of the 100-year-old egg around the squelchy greenish yolk is the actual taste. At first, when served this at Chinese banquets, I would ask for some tea to help me wash it down. Soon, I gave up altogether and simply declined.

I tried an ostrich egg once, to discover that it was not much different from a hen's egg. Out of curiosity, I made an ostrich egg omelette and an ordinary omelette to compare them. We found little to choose between them. The main advantage is that you need fewer ostrich eggs to make an omelette!

The speckled quail's egg is both pretty and tasty. The size of the tiny chocolate eggs wrapped in foil for Easter, it requires a lot of skill and patience to peel and to get it out of its shell without spoiling. Quails may be adorable little birds, but they come with unspeakably difficult eggs.

As for gulls' eggs, we serve them with *apéritifs* at the Waterside Inn during Ascot Week in early June when it is the tradition to eat gulls' eggs. They are pretty to look at but I find they have little taste. They are served with celery salt and paprika and lightly buttered wholewheat bread. We bring them in napkins folded into artichoke shapes. They must not be cooked too long because they are best served soft.

Spain is a country famous for its egg-yolk desserts. At the Waterside Inn, we have a *consommé* in which we put *cheveux d'ange*, or 'angel hairs', made in the Spanish way. We make a syrup of equal quantities of sugar and water, then we add just a little of this syrup to egg yolks mixed in a bowl. The rest of the syrup is then heated up. We take a spoonful of the mixture of yolks and syrup, put this in a cornet-shaped paper piping bag, and pass this over the rest of the syrup which has since been brought to the boil. Tiny strands of yolk then slip into this hot mixture and are instantly

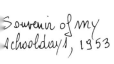

Family

Newly arrived in
St Mandé. Liliane
was 12, Albert 11,
and J was 5.

Souvenir of my
schooldays, 1953

Françoise in
Paris in 1959,
the first year
we met.

Alain aged 10

Francine aged
18 Months

christine aged 4

Mother with her Two sons on a Happy outing
in Gassin, 1991

A sea food feast with
Mother in dordogne 1997

Albert in his element
at rungis market

Early days with
Robyn in our house
in the south of France

on holiday with my
Three pretty grand-
daughTers, Aurore,
Marine and Claire,
and Francis my
son-in-law

Four happy chefs in the family; Albert
and my self with Alain /on the left/
and Michel

Apprenticeship

Monsieur and Madame Loyal
in front of their shop

Returning from a delivery
of Croquembouche on a
Sunday in May, the month
for first communions

The market at Saint-Eustache as it was when I shopped there as an apprentice.

At the British Embassy

My Chef Emile Rouault (left)
My first pièce montée for Stella
Jebb's wedding

Army

The five o'clock desert ritual — galettes bretonnes with Yvon Castel and fanfan hoping for crumbs

A desert feast. The young gazelle is stuffed with potatoes and onions and seasoned with harissa.

poached. After that, they are plunged into iced water before being served in our *consommé*. They keep a slight sugary taste that surprises the customers. It is just a traditional Spanish method of preparing eggs, often used by Spanish cooks to decorate cakes.

When he was president of France in the 1970s, Valéry Giscard d'Estaing said in a famous interview that his favourite dish was scrambled eggs. At the Waterside Inn, I include scrambled eggs with crab and asparagus on my spring menus. A layer of liquidised brown crab meat is spread over the centre of a plate and heated in the oven for a minute. We pour scrambled eggs over this and add the flesh from a crab claw and asparagus tips before garnishing the dish with chives. This dish has become so popular that regular customers often call to ask when the spring menu will be in force so they can be sure of finding it (see p. 236).

In 1982, Albert and I took on a most unusual challenge. Edward Booth-Clibborn, then chairman of *Design and Art Direction*, was organising a media awards ceremony, with people from advertising, public relations and the media, at the Royal Albert Hall. He said people at big conferences were sick of eating badly and asked if we could cater for up to 3,500 people. We agreed and decided to serve a cold meal, one that would contain only fresh food and nothing frozen, tinned or packed. The starter was an *oeuf poché Albert,* a poached egg on artichoke hearts with a salmon mousse topped with a slice of smoked salmon. To follow was *aiguillette de boeuf en gelée,* with a *tarte au citron* and *délice cassis* as desserts.

All the logistics were monumental. Sylvano Giraldin, our restaurant manager, had to recruit 400 waiters. They had to be experienced and competent, and he made multitudes of telephone calls to find them. The result was a mixture of waiters of different nationalities since many of them came from Chinese and Italian restaurants. I honestly think Sylvano's hair started to go grey during this exercise. And I have no idea how London restaurants coped that day without waiters because Sylvano seemed to have hired them all for the Albert Hall!

It is impossible to carry 3,500 eggs in containers, such as I used to for the Rothschilds, so we decided to do the poaching on the spot. The day before the ceremony, we were allowed into the basement of the Royal Albert Hall.

Technicians installed compressors to turn some of the rooms into giant refrigerators. We had three or four refrigerated trucks parked outside as back-up. We installed giant burners in adjacent rooms to do the cooking. Michel Roux Junior, my nephew, was in charge of the team of cooks doing the poaching. One of their tasks was to count the eggs, which is not the same as counting six or a dozen! It would have been awful if even a single guest had not had his or her egg. We had 3,500 eggs and 3,000 guests; the remainder ended up hard-boiled to keep them from being wasted.

We had ice-makers to manufacture ice on the spot. We used this to cool water into which we plunged the eggs to stop the cooking and chill the egg right down for reasons of hygiene. We wanted 3,000 happy, not sick, guests. The cooking took a day and a half. The artichokes were cooked at Le Gavroche and the assembly was done on trestle-tables in the Albert Hall.

We have always liked taking risks and accepting challenges, but that Albert Hall job was nearly the limit! Our restaurants outside were still working, so it was difficult to detach people for this operation. They were difficult and tense days, and everyone had to weigh in, driving trucks and helping wherever they could. Organisation counts on occasions like that: you cannot succeed if things have not been well thought out. In the end, though, the Design and Art dinner was a great success, and was a steep learning curve for us in the intricacies of mass catering!

Eggs were the subject of the first television programme that Albert and I made together for the BBC in 1988. When the first programme went on the air, containing much banter between us on our different approaches to cooking scrambled eggs and whether an omelette should be pale or well browned, it was heralded as a triumph by many, including the food critic, Egon Ronay, who also said we were doing marvels for cooking in Britain.

Just after that came the statement by the then Conservative Health Secretary, Edwina Currie, that eggs could carry salmonella. The consumption of eggs in Britain dropped by more than half, doing enormous damage to producers, of whom only a few were really guilty of bad practices likely to engender illness.

A few years later, during a literary lunch in Sheffield, I sat at the same table as Edwina Currie. I took advantage of the situation to let her know how strongly I felt on the eggs issue. I told her jokingly that she had not only nearly ruined my programme but, more seriously, that she had also done enormous damage to the egg industry. 'It had to be done,' was her reply.

I suggested she could have found some other way and pointed out that the problem had not arisen overnight. 'You should have handled the problem as though you were walking on eggs,' I told her. Her reply was along the lines of most politicians' replies, having little bearing on the question. Whatever her reasons, not only did Edwina Currie endanger my programme, she almost killed the British breakfast!

Health matters, or rather an obsession with them, achieved huge significance at the Waterside Inn in later years. In the early 1990s, we regularly won the top 'merit' award for food hygiene. This was based on visits by inspectors from the Royal Borough of Windsor and Maidenhead who would arrive without warning to see our kitchens. We would then hang the merit certificate of what the council called its 'Clean Food Campaign' on the kitchen wall.

In 1995, in a letter carrying the stern heading 'FOOD SAFETY ACT 1990', the council told me we were only being honoured with a lesser 'Highly Commended Award' that year. The reason given was our use of fresh, and not pasteurised, eggs in mayonnaise and dishes 'which are only lightly cooked'. As a three-star Michelin chef, I cannot risk losing taste, and nothing pasteurised ever tastes the same as fresh produce. Pasteurised eggs, milk and cheese lose some of their essential flavour, and for that reason, I refused to consider the use of pasteurised eggs. I was also very angry at being downgraded. For me, the most important point at issue was that the staff would see the difference in the certificate, and wonder why we were only second best in the council's eyes.

In subsequent correspondence and after a number of conversations, the council suggested that I explain on the menus that 'Central Government advice' was to use pasteurised eggs and to warn that the Waterside Inn used fresh eggs. I wrote back that I did not believe customers 'need to see the words 'Central Government' in the text. This is a restaurant and not an office.' In the end, the council accepted our wording explaining that fresh eggs were used, and we started getting the top award again.

There have been so many food and health scares since then that it seems they are no longer worried about eggs.

Life is a Menu

When Albert and I opened Le Gavroche in 1967, Albert created a twice-cooked *soufflé suissesse* that quickly became a very popular starter. The individual *soufflés* were baked briefly to set them, then unmoulded into a small dish in a sea of cream, sprinkled with Cheddar and Gruyère or Emmental cheeses, then baked again until airy and golden. But it was the half dozen eggs that went into that *soufflé* that nearly involved me in a diplomatic incident.

Albert and I had planned to alternate in the evenings, one cooking back in the kitchen, one front of house in the dining-room. At the beginning, my English was so bad that I could not take the orders, so I stayed in the kitchen. Towards the end of that year, though, on one of the first occasions when I was in my dinner jacket and welcoming customers, an elegant and determined young woman came thrusting into Le Gavroche although the restaurant was already full. I pursued her and even took her by the arm. I told her she could not come in, but she replied 'I'll have my usual table', and pointed to one that was already occupied. Tony Battistella, my *maître d'hôtel*, was horrified and tried to stop me arguing. Finally, he hissed at me, 'It's Princess Margaret.' It was too late. I told her I was sorry, but that I could not let her in because she had not reserved.

Her passion was Le Gavroche's *soufflé suissesse*. Usually she did not even bother to order it, but would sit down and wait for it to come. There was a chill between us for a while, but Princess Margaret continued to be a regular customer. And she always sat at the same table. . .

Shellfish

S HELLFISH play a unique role in gastronomy, bringing the distinctive iodine flavours of the sea to the table. Nowadays, oysters, lobsters, crabs and even jumbo shrimps are usually exorbitant in price because they are considered luxury foods for special occasions. Yet it was not always so. In the 1950s, most shellfish, including lobster, were very reasonably priced.

My first introduction to shellfish was the grey shrimp. Like many a little boy on a seaside holiday, I boasted a shrimp-net and bucket. On the beach at Saint-Gilles-Croix-de-Vie on the French Atlantic coast, I used to scoop up these twinkling, wriggling little creatures and put them in my pail. In those days there were plenty of shrimps in the sand at the water's edge, and there was no talk of pollution. (The very word was far from entering everyday usage as it has today.) Back home, my mother would heat a little of the seawater in which we had kept the shrimps, and drop in some onion peel, which deepened the shrimps' grey colour. When the water boiled she would throw in the shrimps, which cooked immediately. We would then drain them and they were ready for eating. I was usually so anxious to get started that, to my mother's dismay, I would eat the shrimps without bothering to peel them, leaving only the heads. It was a modest but tasty foray into the mainly grown-up world of seafood.

Crustaceans, such as lobster and crab, fascinate me because they are so full of life. For the average consumer, however, the complete opposite is true. Many will buy crustaceans that are not just dead but already cooked and have no idea of the life and flavour that was there shortly before. Much of the shellfish sold ready for eating has soft flesh with little taste.

Although shellfish may have been considerably cheaper when I was a child, we still could not afford to eat them much at home. So it was when I worked for Cécile de Rothschild that I gained my first real experience. My boss liked me to serve *demoiselles de Cherbourg,* tiny Breton lobsters, for the buffets she would organise after an evening at the theatre. These little parties were exclusive affairs. Guests could include Régine, the famous Paris nightclub-owner, or Georges Pompidou, then a senior executive at the Banque Rothschild and later Prime Minister of France before he succeeded Charles de Gaulle as President in 1969.

Cécile de Rothschild's buffets, although employing the most excellent ingredients, were nonetheless quite uncomplicated. I would set the lobsters up in a *buisson*, literally a 'bush', or a pyramid, decorated with tufts of parsley, and serve with them a simple green sauce, a concoction of finely puréed fresh herbs.

She never wanted the lobsters out of their shells or otherwise prepared for gracious eating. All she would allow was a scissor-cut through the membrane on the underside to make them easier to break. She loved fighting with them, breaking the shells herself. She loved doing the things with food that most people don't like. She used to say cooking should be savoured with the fingers as well as the palate. She was a gourmet through and through; she should have been a cook. As with all of us who enthusiastically eat with our fingers, she would end up speckled with the juices; there would even be bits of flesh caught on her rings. (In fact one of her habits at any meal was to remove her rings and roll them in bits of bread, causing a permanent nightmare for the kitchen staff and her chambermaid who would spend their time ensuring that precious heirlooms did not disappear into the rubbish bins with the leftovers!)

CHATEAU LAFITE ROTHSCHILD
Le 9 Octobre 1964

DINER

Crême de Cresson

Homard grillé

Pintadeau poêlé

Haricots verts au Beurre

Salade

Ananas au rafraîchi

Petits Gâteaux

HIRCHBERG 1955

Château LAFITE ROTHSCHILD 1957

Château LAFITE ROTHSCHILD 1945

:-:-:-:

My first time cooking for the Rothschild family at Château Lafite

In summer, when she moved the household to Saint Raphaël, Cécile de Rothschild would send the chauffeur, Edmond Oger, through the Côte d'Azur traffic jams to buy a *langouste,* a crawfish or rock lobster, from a well-known fishmonger who sold crustaceans on the road into Saint Tropez. Three or four hours later, Edmond would drive back with a solitary and angry crayfish in the boot of the Rolls-Royce. It was always very much alive and remonstrating, straight from the fishmonger's tank. I would grill this crayfish and serve it with a little *anchoïade,* anchovy butter. I had to make the *anchoïade* from fillets of fresh anchovies, never from a jar, with olive oil, a little wine vinegar and a clove of garlic. I would then serve this in a side dish so she could put it on herself. 'I like *anchoïade*, Chef, but you would put on too much,' she would say. 'I still want to taste my *langouste.*'

One of my greatest surprises when I arrived in England in 1967 was to discover the wonders of the seafood and fish at Billingsgate market in London. What struck me most at first sight was the size of the huge common or edible crabs from Scotland (known as *dormeur* in France), which were much bigger than any I had known at home. It was a real shock. In later years, three-star chefs visiting me from France, like Paul Bocuse and Roger Vergé, were also open-mouthed when they saw the size of my crabs. However large, they still taste every bit as good as the smaller, Continental variety. But what was most satisfying of all about Billingsgate was that the quality was as good as in France and prices were often half those I had known.

As a result, I had no hesitation in putting crustaceans on my menus. One of my favourite recipes was a *gratin de crabe*. This consisted of crab flesh that I flaked into small pieces while it was still warm after cooking. I then covered it with a sauce made of an Alsace Riesling, a little finely chopped shallot and some sliced mushroom. At the last minute, I would put in a small spoonful of a *sauce hollandaise*, place into a serving dish and glaze it for thirty seconds under the salamander grill. The result melted in the mouth. On top of the dish I would place a little crab-shaped piece of puff pastry. I cut this out using a cutter I had commissioned from a craftsman who worked near Le Gavroche. It was one of our most popular dishes in the 1970s.

In the mid-1970s, when my work was split between Le Gavroche and the Waterside Inn, I began to travel in the quieter months of the year, in January and February when the Waterside was closed and trade was slow at Le Gavroche.

It was a trip to China that marked me as much as any. I went there with Bill Vine, a gourmet friend who is a writer on gastronomy. He and I had met in 1973 when we were both made *Hospitaliers du Pomerol*, members of the fraternity of Pomerol in Bordeaux. As a young journalist working for the trade magazine, the *Caterer and Hotelkeeper*, Bill had spent a lot of his time watching in the kitchens of restaurants like Le Coq d'Or or La Mirabelle to improve his knowledge of what was going on backstage. In this, he differed from many food critics who have never taken the trouble to set foot inside a professional kitchen. In the 1960s, he started taking the leading lights of the British catering trade to the United States on study tours to see the enormous strides their American colleagues were making.

Bill is also an expert on ethnic cuisines, so I decided to go with him to China and Hong Kong on a six-week trip. Through his contacts in the trade, he helped me discover real Chinese cuisine. As I watched Chinese cooks work, I developed a new recipe for the Waterside Inn, *tronçonnettes de homard au porto blanc,* medallions of lobster in a white port sauce. This has since become one of my 'signature' recipes, and it has been singled out by Michelin for mention in its guide.

The lobsters must be alive – this is vital. They should always be heavy, firm, combative and tense, their eyes must move, and they must be ready to snap your fingers with their claws or to try and make a break for freedom. Those with bubbles around their heads, that do not react and that appear light for their size are already at death's door and should be discarded.

Available are European, Maine and Canadian lobsters, among others. The European, or native, lobster is now almost twice as expensive as the North American varieties. As a result, thousands of tons of lobsters are flown by Boeing 747 from North America to Europe. These American lobsters are often from lobster farms, and have a soft shell. They have a pleasant enough taste, but are neither as firm nor as succulent as the European species which might be fished off Cornwall, Scotland, Brittany or the Channel Islands. However, the lobster used for my medallions is American or Canadian because its flesh is more supple. When cooked very quickly, it gives a better result than the European lobster, the flesh of which contracts and becomes hard in a hot pan. I use Europeans for the slower, poached dishes such as *homard à la nage,* poaching being a technique which brings out their full finesse.

To make my *tronçonnettes,* I kill the lobster with a needle or a sharp knife between the eyes, a technique that goes straight to its nervous system, killing it immediately and ensuring that it does not suffer. The lobster is immediately cut into medallions, slicing along the natural rings on the lobster's shell. These medallions are seasoned with salt and cayenne pepper and then sealed with just a drop of olive oil in a very hot pan to keep in all the juices. They are finished in the oven while the frying pan is deglazed with white port and a little fish stock. Sometimes I add a drop of veal stock to enrich the sauce and make it glisten. The medallions are then laid on a *julienne* of thinly shredded, crunchy carrots, leeks and fresh ginger. The cooking of the lobster takes a maximum of five minutes (see p. 238). And this is the secret of much Chinese cooking: shellfish, especially crustaceans, should be alive right up to the moment of cooking; then it should be cooked quickly and served immediately.

Another of my lobster dishes was the *homard à l'escargot,* or 'snail' lobster, so called because the final result is curled like a snail, cooked in a garlic butter normally used with snails, and served with *béarnaise.* I devised this when working for the Rothschilds. If imitation is the sincerest form of flattery, then I was hugely flattered at the end of 1997 when Jonathan Meades, *The Times'* food critic, included a description of this very dish, in his review of the year's innovations, but attributing it to another chef in Britain (who spends at least as much time working on his image as in his kitchen). In Meades' words, this 'marvellous' lobster, seemingly identical to the one I first made more than thirty years previously and which has been on the Gavroche menu since 1967, was 'grilled, excised from the shell, cut up, replaced in the shell with a bath of garlic butter, and lightly glazed with *béarnaise*'. I could not put it better myself.

On holiday on the Thai island of Phuket in the early 1980s, I came across mangoes that were fleshy and tasty, most unlike the fruit that then reached Europe. Lazing in the sun, my mind wandered into the mango grove, side by side with a lobster, and I had the idea of making a mango purée into which I would mix a little sherry vinegar, some lemon and green peppercorns. Not long after, this became part of a recipe, in which I poured mango sauce over a salad containing cold lobster medallions, mango and avocado slices, two types of lettuce and a *julienne* of truffle. This dish was such a success that I kept it on my menus for about ten years. When British Airways gave me a contract to devise its first-class and Concorde menus in 1983, this was one of the first recipes I proposed.

Working for British Airways was an unusual task for me since it meant planning and preparing food for hundreds of passengers flying Concorde and first class. This involved devising dishes to be cooked in a central kitchen in small batches, plated then chilled, taken to the aircraft to be reheated and served in difficult and cramped conditions. I was issued a security badge that allowed me to go right into planes on the tarmac to make spot checks. On only two occasions in sixteen years have I found things not quite up to standard and ordered dishes to be changed just before take-off.

In another excursion into high-volume cooking, working for Celebrity Cruises – when I added cuisine at sea to my existing cuisine on land and in the air – I began to use Alaskan king crabs. They look more like spiders than crabs! They have long legs or claws that are full of flesh, and which turn pink when cooked.

I served broiled king crab for sittings of between 1,500 and 2,000 passengers. The crabs' claws are put in the freezer for a few minutes to harden them up, then they are cut down the middle with a ribbon saw. They are brushed with butter and cooked immediately on a flat hot-plate, seasoned with lemon juice and coarse pepper. As accompaniment, I served a butter sauce with some dry sherry, lemon juice and a little paprika, and small oven-cooked potatoes.

On several visits to Australia, I was to discover three new sorts of crustacean. One was the marron, a very large freshwater crayfish to which some wine-growers from the Margaret River region treated me. The second was the Balmain bug, a prehistoric-looking creature with a head and tail like a crayfish but with a strangely flat body and no claws. The third was the yabbie, a crayfish commonly living in creeks and behind the dams in man-made irrigation lakes.

The marron, accompanied by a light Australian Cabernet Sauvignon, impressed me so much that I briefly tried to include it in my menus. Coming from rather muddy lakes, the animal looked like a lobster but had smaller claws. Its white, succulent and slightly sweet flesh went right up into its head. Tasting better than any lobster I have ever eaten, I asked whether it was exported and was told that a few were sent to Sydney but no further. So I decided to take a gamble and order them for the Waterside Inn. First, there was a mass of red tape: I needed sanitary certificates for the British customs. Once these were obtained, the marrons were packed in ice in refrigerated polystyrene containers to keep them fresh and alive, and flown to London. I sent a courier to pick them up as soon as they cleared customs. However, I had to stop after two or three weeks because between a third and a half of the marrons would die en route. Those that survived were cooked in a vegetable *court-bouillon* and served with a little melted butter or a champagne sauce. The flesh was so perfect, it needed nothing else. For the others, the combination of a good day's journey and the prospect of ending up in the hands of a Frenchman whose intention was to feed them to customers on the banks of the Thames, was clearly too much. Much later, I learned that the first marron farm had opened off Kangaroo Island in South Australia, but I was not tempted to repeat the experiment.

In Sydney in 1985, I used the Balmain bug, which lives in the sand on the sea edge, for a dish I made during a promotion of the Waterside Inn at the Intercontinental. I was introduced to the Balmain bug by my brother-in-law Christopher on a tour of Sydney fish market, the best fish market in Australia. When I drew up my menu, I decided to use it for a *cassolette,* a medley of ingredients and flavourings, with a dressing served in a small dish. I made a vinaigrette with Meaux mustard, sherry vinegar and olive oil flavoured with crushed lobster heads. I used this to dress some fresh linguini pasta and the Balmain medallions, and topped it all off with some snipped tarragon. This was served warm as an *hors d'oeuvre*. It was one of the most successful dishes on my Australian menu.

That particular working trip to Australia was for me perfect: I learned as much as I gave. I had brought my knowledge, my philosophy and my skills to the southern continent, and shared them with the cooks who worked alongside me, but at the same time I was discovering new concepts and ingredients that made me reflect and galvanised my creativity. I encountered many a marriage of ingredients that I would not have thought of otherwise, which helped me invent new dishes when I returned home.

My first long-clawed yabbie – which is reddish-brown in colour, not green like its European equivalent – was served to me by Sally and Neil Rob at Redbank Winery. We spent more time on a pre-lunch wine-tasting than we should have and when we went back into the kitchen, the yabbies, caught especially by the Robs' children, had escaped from the bowls in which they had been placed. We had to run here and there to recapture our lunch, after which they were plunged into a fragrant *court-bouillon* that Sally had made, using dam water. Moments later they were brought straight to the table and the bowl placed in the middle of a table-cloth of newspapers. That's what I call a direct producer–consumer chain. Those yabbies were so tasty, juicy and delicate that my fingers became sore from plunging into the bowl and from peeling off the shells in the two hours we spent gathered round that table. That is the only way to eat them, for pure culinary pleasure in their simplest state and without complicated sauces. But you have to be willing to roll up your sleeves. . .

As for oysters, I started my travels knowing only the varieties that are common in Europe such as Marennes, *belons* or *fines de claire*. On my first trip to the United States, on a Bill Vine study tour for British catering trade executives in 1978, I came across huge 'steak' oysters, so big that I could hardly believe they were really oysters. Bud Grice, the senior vice president for Marriott Hotels, presided over a meal served for us in Boston. On the buffet were oysters that were bigger than a man's hand. I watched in astonishment and admiration as Bud, a gentle giant, took one and ate it in one gulp. As for me, a little smaller, I had to ask for a knife to cut mine into four. Although its flesh was firm, it lacked some finesse, but it otherwise had a good taste.

We went also to Pier 4 in Boston, the restaurant which then served the greatest number of meals in the United States, some 2,000 a day. People have to queue to get in; they are given a number, then summoned by loudspeaker. There were probably about 400 customers in the restaurant when we arrived, and as we walked in, I saw a lobster tank that was easily thirty yards long. It was full of lobsters and even they were elephantine, weighing between four and eight pounds. They were nothing like the tender little *demoiselles de Cherbourg* lobsters that Cécile de Rothschild used to send me out to buy, which weighed under a pound.

I remember being surprised at how young the waiters seemed, all aged between eighteen and twenty and handling twenty customers each. Only older waiters, rarely under thirty, would usually have direct contact with the client in European restaurants. In Boston, the youngsters serving us were in the American entrepreneurial tradition; they were untrained and unsalaried, working only for tips. Smiling and cheerful, they were plainly more interested in the dollars they would earn at the end of the meal than in proper professional service as we Europeans knew it. Our party of catering executives represented two-thirds to three-quarters of the restaurant trade in Britain. We were all amazed at the size of the restaurant, and I was praying that we would never see such a thing in Europe. However, nearly two decades later, a few in the British trade have put into practice things learned about mass catering on that trip (most notably, although he was not there, by Sir Terence Conran).

When our Pier 4 lobster arrived, it was a monster served with lemon butter. In the biggest restaurant I had ever seen, people ate lobster as though it were herring.

I adore oysters. I can eat two or three dozen in a sitting, but I like them raw or just lightly poached – if cooked too much they lose their taste. In the 1970s, soya-bean sprouts started to become available in London and this helped me refine an oyster recipe that became another of my 'signature' dishes. Paradoxically, it was the sprouts' watery, neutral taste that attracted me. Together with this, they are crunchy, have a cleansing quality and their presentation adds a touch of exoticism.

I made a *vol-au-vent* in the shape of an oyster shell. I cooked it in the oven, when cooked, sliced off the top and put it to one side. I took some chopped shallots, sweated them lightly, added a little reduced raspberry vinegar, a little raspberry purée, a small spoonful of cream and the oyster juice. I would cook this together for a few minutes, add a tiny piece of butter and then pass it through a *chinois* sieve. The sauce was tangy and fresh. Its slight acidity compensated for the oyster's rich and fatty quality. I would then roll an oyster in this nearly boiling sauce for a minute. I would put slightly sweated soya sprouts with some *al dente* French beans – sliced lengthwise exactly the same size as the soya sprouts – in the pastry and place two oysters on top, with four around the *vol-au-vent*. I then put a few winkles and fresh raspberries on the plate. The sprouts brought a fresh touch and crunch, exactly as I intended.

A favourite shellfish of mine is the king prawn. I have particularly fond memories of eating them in Barcelona, a city that I adore because you can find an enormous variety of seafood there. I like to eat my Barcelona king prawns on the port near the Olympic Village. Everything is still alive, just like in Hong Kong; all the seafood is wriggling on the display shelves or in tanks.

When at my house in the south of France, at Gassin near Saint Tropez, I enjoy myself most when the fishmonger has fresh king prawns. As I've said, I never go to buy seafood with a shopping list or a fixed idea in my head. I always see what the fishermen have brought in and then make up my mind, depending on the freshness of the products. When I find really fresh prawns, my wife Robyn and I like to eat them cooked in a slightly Chinese style. We pan-fry them for less than a minute on each side in a little olive oil with finely sliced hot chilli peppers.

We are always very careful not to eat all the heads or carcasses even though the heads of king prawns, when absolutely fresh, are delicious. Not eating the heads requires iron discipline. So why do we hold ourselves back? Because we're thinking of the next meal ... We're already planning Robyn's seafood risotto for that evening. We put the head and other remains to one side and in the afternoon, I use them to make a little stock. Then we cook some mussels and slice in some squid, always at the last minute to stop it becoming rubbery, add the juice from the mussels and, of course, a small glass of white wine. This is what we call our 'double-it', getting double the pleasure out of our lunch-time king prawns!

If Robyn and I really want to indulge ourselves on seafood, and fill ourselves to bursting, we head for the Château de Montreuil on the French Channel coast. This is run by Christian Germain, who was my head chef after Pierre Koffmann at the Waterside Inn. His wife Lindsay, whose gentle smile never seems to leave her face, also worked for me in the dining-room. Christian was one of the chefs whom Albert and I helped to set up in their own business and Christian's restaurant is particularly well appointed and enchanting, being in a property that once belonged to the Rothschilds. The Rothschilds donated it to the town of Montreuil, and the local council sold it for conversion to a restaurant and hotel.

When Robyn and I go there, the Germains always join us for a late lunch that lasts a full three hours once they have finished their regular lunch service. We first open Loire whites and then move on to white Burgundies because these are Robyn's favourite. (I am not, incidentally, opposed to red wines with seafood. Reds, though, must be young and light, without too much tannin, what the French call *vins de soif*, wines more to assuage your thirst than to delight the palate, such as those from the Loire, the Beaujolais or even a light Bordeaux.)

The quality of the seafood at Montreuil reminds Robyn of Australia because it arrives straight from the sea, supremely fresh. The table groans under the weight of the seafood platter: there will be winkles, mussels, razor and other clams, such as *praires* or 'Warty Venus', crab, Dublin Bay prawns or *langoustines*, lobster, and at least four types of oyster. Christian, like many of my former chefs, has earned a Michelin star, and seafood platters, more a *brasserie* dish than one for a restaurant specialising in fine cuisine, are not on his menu. He prepares them for us out of friendship as a special treat. One year, Robyn went there with some friends for her birthday when I was away. They drank their wine, ate their shellfish and spent the afternoon in the pool. I was so jealous that I have never since let Robyn celebrate her birthday without me.

Mussels are not expensive, they are easy to prepare and the result is a very sociable dish, something to share with several people. My mother always said we should eat them more often. When I was a child, mussel shells were covered with their own little barnacles, not scrubbed as they are now, and my task was to scratch them clean with the back of a knife.

A cuisine exists for all occasions: there is everyday cooking, weekend cooking and cooking for special occasions, and a category I call *cuisine ménagère*, housewife's cooking. This is not in any way pejorative, but a term I use to designate a dish that is easy to make and does not take too much time. In the *cuisine ménagère* class, I make a dish of mussels in a Roquefort sauce. The sauce consists of the juice of the mussels and a small spoonful of fresh cream to which I add just a little Roquefort – never so much as to spoil the taste of the mussels. I reduce this a little, then put some young spinach leaves, tossed in butter, at the bottom of the serving plate, shell the mussels and lay them on the spinach. I spread the sauce lightly over the mussels and glaze it under the grill. The whole dish takes around 20 minutes to make while the cooking of the mussels takes between two to three minutes. It is a dish that I like to make in Gassin, and it is a way of making a good meal without spending the whole day in the kitchen.

Not all my memories of seafood have been joyful.

In 1984, I was in Sydney, and Damien Pignolet, then one of the best chefs in Australia and a gastronomic celebrity, invited us to a very good Chinese restaurant, the Imperial Peking in the Rocks. The restaurant had a few Japanese-style dishes and he ordered a crayfish *sashimi,* the flesh served raw in the Japanese style. There were about ten of us and all the others let out cries of joy when the crayfish, that had been cut down the body rather than in the more usual thin medallions, arrived. I took a piece and put it in my mouth. It was still twitching, it was chunky, cold, and I just could not swallow or chew it. It remained stuck between my tongue and palate. Damien took one look at me – I must have been turning green – and called out, 'Waiter, could you take all of this away and bring it back as soup.' That was the closest I shall ever come to eating a crayfish *sashimi.*

Another time, in the early years after we opened Le Gavroche, my brother and I were frequently invited to lunch by wine merchants. We could rarely go together because we could not afford to be away from the restaurant at the same time. In 1975, we made an exception for Hedges & Butler who invited us to lunch at their headquarters in Regent Street. They had a beautiful cellar and a stunning dining-room where the directors served nothing but the best. They had a team of *Cordon Bleu* women chefs who could turn out some exceptional meals.

Albert and I both like simmered dishes, dishes that have been cooked slowly for a long time, what the French call *plats bourgeois.* This is a taste that we inherited from our mother's side of the family. The main course that day was steak and kidney pie with oysters, a great British classic. The sauce, the meat and the kidneys were all succulent. The puff pastry was both crisp and tender at the same time. The oysters had been added right at the end of cooking and were just lightly poached. Albert and I both jumped at the chance of a second helping when it was offered. It was accompanied by a 1964 Mouton Rothschild.

Albert and I took a taxi back and we were both very contented, pleased with the food, the wine and the company. We went back to work in the kitchen in the afternoon but at the end of service, Albert was not feeling well and he went home slightly earlier than usual. The next morning, early, he was due to do the market. However, my sister-in-law Monique woke me with a telephone call to say Albert had been taken to hospital. He had eaten an oyster that had poisoned him. It just takes one. That is the problem with shellfish, and it is something that the public rarely understands. There is no way to establish that an oyster is safe. You need just one mussel or oyster that is dead or polluted, or that is just simply rejected by your body, to suffer.

The blood vessels in Albert's eyes had burst and he spent a whole day in hospital. Two days later he came back to the Gavroche but he was very pale, and his eyes were hollows. To this day, Albert cannot go near an oyster. If he touches one, he wants to vomit and it gives him a skin allergy. The oyster he had eaten that day was indeed fateful.

Every winter, we have one or two clients who call to say they fell ill after a meal at the Waterside Inn. They will say they have not slept all night and have been violently sick. Almost always, they have eaten shellfish. Sometimes, I tell them what happened to my brother but this is little comfort for people who are really ill and suffering. The customer often imagines there is a hygiene problem or that things were badly prepared or not fresh enough. In fact, it is nature, which is not answerable to anyone. That is the mystique of shellfish. They are, after all, living things.

Fish

THE PART that fish plays in the British diet has changed radically over the last few decades. In France, habits have changed too, but not in the same way. In the 1950s when I was growing up, French fishmongers' displays used to groan with a huge variety and quantity of fish. The average French household would not hesitate to plan fish for dinner and do all its own preparation. Since then, there has been a fall in the consumption of whole fish in France. Housewives there now tend to buy fillets, steaks or escalopes (even the vocabulary is borrowed from meat). Today's French housewives seem to want their fishmonger to start the cooking for them. I suppose this has a lot to do with people wanting to buy a more 'sterile' product – and fillets leave you with less debris and odour. It seems strange to seek out something that is odourless, bland even, when the smell should be a large part of the pleasure. A rich and plentiful display of fish is pleasing and evocative, and its smell, whether raw or cooked, is a precursor of the joys to come.

When you buy a fish, it must have bright, bulging eyes. It should give you a challenging stare. When you pick it up, it should be firm and stiff, especially big fish like sea bass or salmon. If the tail bends downwards when you hold the fish up, that is a sign of fatigue, an indication that it was caught a few days before. The gills, when you open them, should be a bright, deep red colour, never dull; the gills should give off a clear iodine smell.

On my arrival in Britain in 1967, the fish-eating habits of the two peoples on each side of the Channel could not have been more different. When we had John Dory on the menu, Gavroche customers would often ask us to spell it and to explain what it was. The British had only ever heard of cod, sole (which always had to be on the bone), turbot or salmon. Most of the other varieties caught by British fishing boats were exported straight to Europe.

It was not until the 1980s that the British seemed to become truly aware of monkfish, John Dory, bass or bream. Since then, prices have soared and fish has become a luxury product. On some days now, a full half of the customers at the Waterside Inn will choose fish for their main course. This compares with around a fifth when we first opened Le Gavroche. This modern trend gives me great pleasure since I love working with fish. It is a noble product and I find I am more original and more innovative in thinking up sauces for fish than I am for meat. Fish sauces are lighter, more delicate and more tasty.

Nowadays the British customer is more blasé about fish, but when I close my eyes, I can still remember what it was like in 1967. The portion had to be enormous, extremely thoroughly cooked and burning hot. The flesh near the bone had to be well cooked, never a little pink as we liked to serve it. I remember one of my first experiences of a cooked fish in a British restaurant. When I cut into it, it was so hot the bones were actually steaming. For twenty years, we were insulted and our fish was sent back because the portion was not big enough, hot enough, cooked enough or because 'I cannot pull the fish off the bones.' We refused to compromise, and continued along the same purist path – and obviously to good effect. Now many of those same erstwhile complainers think they have invented a new way of eating fish.

Fish has many nutritional qualities. It contains protein, vitamins and minerals, and is low in fat, so is therefore considered a very healthy food. This, together with a growing awareness of the varieties of fish available, goes a long way towards explaining the rise in fish consumption in Britain over recent decades.

Some people think fish is good for them just because it comes from the sea. They may be a bit misguided when you think of all the oil-tankers illegally cleaning out their tanks at sea, and of all the sewage, industrial and other waste that is poured into the sea. Sadly, the sea is not always the paradise that some people imagine, and there have been some disasters involving the eating of polluted fish – the mercury in tuna in Japan some years ago, for instance.

Modern fish-farming methods may in time add other uncomfortable details to this picture. Many farmed fish – up to now, usually salmon – are kept in extremely cramped conditions, in water that is still, not moving, where they are prone to disease and lice. They are fed artificial, man-made products instead of a natural diet. Because of this second-rate life, their flesh is softer, fattier, less bright in colour, and they lack the substance, taste and texture of their more muscular, wild counterparts.

Now there are also turbot, John Dory and bass farms, while sole-farming is starting. I was once a bit shaken when I was buying fish from my usual Saint Tropez fishmonger. He was gutting a small sea bass for the woman in front of me. As he did so, he not only pulled out all he should have but also some little strips of fat that should not have been there. When the customer had left, I asked the fishmonger, who knows I have a professional interest in food, for an explanation. He acknowledged that it was a farmed fish, and said that, in his opinion, fish-farmers were pushing things too far. Some fish farms appear to be extremely well organised, though, like that of Northern Salmon in the village of Glenarm in Country Antrim, Northern Ireland. The Glenarm fish swim against the waves in near natural conditions in large pens in the open seas, battling against real tides and swimming distances like those of their wild cousins. The quality of the product – the company uses no chemicals, antibiotics or artificial colouring agents – is excellent. It is one that I buy on the occasions when there is no wild salmon on the market.

Those methods contrast strongly with new plans to produce genetically modified salmon that will grow five to six times faster than natural fish. The real point, of course, is that these fish will make money five to six times faster for the producers. The principal question is: 'Do we really need this?' The answer is 'no'. Apart from questions of taste, something must go wrong in the end. What will happen if some of these modified fish escape from their farms – as fish do – and start breeding with fish in the wild? The real species could be permanently damaged, with immeasurable consequences.

My fear is that, with both fish-farming and genetic modification we may be heading for battery fish with problems like those that afflicted battery chickens in the 1970s and 1980s. After chicken that tasted of fish, are we now going to eat fish that tastes as bland as chicken? You only have to look at sea bass that, caught by line, costs up to 300 francs a kilogram in France, while farmed bass is a quarter that price and has nothing like the same quality. It may be wonderful for people to have food that they did not know existed before but, for myself, I would rather eat a potato that tastes of potato than a fish that no longer tastes of fish. I hope that a really beautiful food is not about to be killed off or damaged, and that we are not heading for another food scare.

I was around eight or nine years old, on our seaside holidays on France's Atlantic coast, when I first took an interest in fish. Saint-Gilles-Croix-de-Vie was a place known for its newly caught sardines, sardines with a good, strong taste. Cooked on a barbecue of vine twigs, which gives a far better flavour to fish than charcoal, they grill easily and very quickly.

I used to watch the fishing boats returning and the fishermen land their writhing and glistening catch. One day, a fisherman asked me why I was constantly hanging around the port. On another, he gave me some sardines to take home. Later, he invited me to go to sea on his boat and watch him and his crew at work. My mother agreed and I got up at dawn to go with them. At first, I really enjoyed the experience, then the seas became choppy and I went below decks to avoid the waves washing over the deck. I was down in a sort of a hold, breathing the thick, pungent smells of the boat's fuel, and this made me very sick. Nevertheless, the beauty of watching the fishermen pull in their nets filled with sardines made up for this.

At home, my mother used to cook whiting, with its white and light flesh, because it was inexpensive. She could not afford sole or turbot. Our fish diet in those days amounted virtually to whiting in Paris and sardines on holiday. So it was much later at the Rothschilds that I became properly acquainted with fish. It was a real festival of discovery.

One of my early memories is of cooking turbot. If I had to prepare three turbots for a dinner for eighteen people, Cécile de Rothschild would make sure I kept the heads in the kitchen for a dish of turbot cheeks for the following day's lunch. I served these cold with a lemon mayonnaise or slightly warmed with a *sauce mousseline*. The three pairs of cheeks would only be enough for a couple of people. Occasionally my boss would invite extra guests, and then she would authorise me to buy another turbot, extract the cheeks, which were a mother-of-pearl white and slightly gelatinous, and serve the rest of the fish to the staff.

In my time, there were no diplomas in cooking. You left school at fourteen, with a school-leaving certificate at most. There was no need to take the *baccalauréat*, still less a degree, to be a chef. So one of the few ways to stand out professionally was to enter competitions or take part in exhibitions. I was anxious to test my performance against my contemporaries so I entered a number of competitions in the 1960s.

In 1963, I entered a competition held in Arpajon, just south of Paris. I cooked a turbot which the Rothschilds' chauffeur, Edmond Oger, very kindly transported in the boot of the car. I poached the turbot whole, let it go cold in its stock and removed the skin delicately with the point of a knife. I made a creamy sauce to which I had added a little gelatine and I covered the fish with this just before it set, essential to make an even layer. The turbot became snow-white in colour. I then decorated it with thin crescents of truffle to resemble scales and sealed it all with a fish aspic. This was a *chaud-froid,* literally 'hot and cold', cooked fish covered with a cold sauce and glazed in aspic.

To set the dish off to its best advantage, I borrowed a silver platter from the Rothschilds. The only problem with this was that I omitted to ask Cécile de Rothschild for her permission ...

In a contest involving fifty people, I was placed in a very good silver category. Cécile de Rothschild was delighted, proud that her chef had done so well and asked to see the photographs. 'A *chaud-froid*, Chef, and of a turbot, such a noble fish,' she said. 'It's mean of you! You never make it for me.'

The tone suddenly changed when I produced the photographs.

'What's that?' she murmured, then her voice started to rise. 'It's a family heirloom, my inheritance!' The time for congratulations was over and I was in for a good scolding. It was the only time I ever heard Cécile de Rothschild's language approach that of a fishwife, yet I understood her anger. It was another lesson that I learned from her: to ask before taking.

My success, however, inspired me to enter other competitions. I thought this might help me build up a reputation which would be an asset for the restaurant Albert and I were planning to open. Just as our London

Dîner

Consommé à la Royale

Filets de soles soufflés Favorite

Gigue de chamois

Sauces poivrade et groseille

Jardinière de légumes

Canards froids Bigarrade

Salade

Gâteau Africain

A typical formal dinner at Cécile de Rothschild's

plans were coming to a head in 1967, I entered the Prosper Montagné chefs' competition. In the last round, the six finalists had to choose their own dish and I decided to make *filets de sole soufflés au Parmesan*. This was especially ambitious since I was making the soufflés without flour which made the exercise rather hazardous. But I have always liked taking risks. I filleted the sole and poached it, keeping back the bones for the sauce. I cooked some mussels, scallops and shrimps, and cut them into large dice so that each ingredient would remain identifiable. My presentation was on *un socle,* a base made of two loaves of bread which I joined together with wooden cocktail sticks, sculpted into an interesting shape, then brushed with melted butter. Once this emerged from the oven, it looked like lacquered wood.

My fillets were poached, the base was ready and my seafood was cooked and diced. One of the judges told me I had fifteen minutes in which to complete the preparation. This was just right. I beat the egg whites and mixed them into my soufflé base. I put a first layer of soufflé on the sole fillets, then another until they were well rounded. I had seven minutes left and I slipped the dish into the oven and closed the door. I was already imagining myself on the winner's podium.

Then I looked round and what did I see? My seafood which I had forgotten to add to the sole! The judges all had my recipe and knew there should be seafood in the dish. Instead, I had to serve it separately. I would have liked the earth to swallow me up. . .

People often ask me what disasters I have known professionally. I reply that, to keep three Michelin stars, you cannot afford much in the way of catastrophe. That competition, however, was a disaster, and a moment of inattention cost me a prize. The episode taught me of the need to concentrate, and also that you can never be really sure of a dish until you have put it on a plate and served it to a customer.

I left for Britain shortly after that. From London in 1971, I entered yet another competition for the Prix International Taittinger, a Europe-wide contest for hot dishes. More than 100 chefs entered each year. When the finals were held in Paris, the other five remaining contestants and I were each given exactly the same recipe to follow, for a *turban* of sole and salmon. On arrival, we were handed the recipe, the ingredients and the utensils.

I really enjoyed myself. I had to make a *beurre blanc,* white butter sauce, and a mousse. I was given a cake mould to make the *turban*. The dish, contrasting the white of the sole with the pink of the salmon, was a treat for the eyes. The cooking was delicate since the *turban* had to be poached in a *bain-marie*. When I took it out of the oven, I tested it with a poultry needle. The needle came out clean and shining, meaning that the centre was properly cooked. A judge told me I had five more minutes. This gave me just the time I needed to turn the mould out and place my *turban* on a serving dish, a delicate manoeuvre. I let it drain a little, slipped it on a pan cover and then to the plate. Not a fibre of the fish was damaged or out of place. It looked like a piece of ceramic. I varnished the *turban* with some clarified butter and sent the dish with its accompanying sauce to the judges.

A young chef next to me, Michel Nicoleau, from the Connaught in London, was due to follow me. He had problems getting his *turban* out of the mould. He began to shake it, a manoeuvre that could have ruined the *turban*. I went over with a flat knife to help him. This calmed him down and he extracted his *turban* with just a tiny blemish.

That evening at the Crillon Hotel, the results were announced. Gilbert Picard of Beaulieu was third, I was second and Michel Nicoleau was first .... Nicoleau told me very kindly that the prize should have been mine. This taught me another lesson, that in competition I should never help a rival! My second prize, however, enabled me to take back a handsome cup to display in Le Gavroche and earned me some useful mentions in a British press that was trumpeting the success of London's new generation of French chefs.

A few years after that, I decided to retire as a contestant from competitions. I changed hats and became a judge and it was at one of the Mouton Rothschild competitions, which I judged for some fifteen years, that I ate one of the best fish I have ever eaten. This was a braised turbot cooked to perfection and served with a *sauce hollandaise,* by Charles Somerville of the Black Bull in Yorkshire, a pub and restaurant. The only problem was marrying a Mouton Rothschild with the turbot as, obviously, it had to be a light, young vintage. Somerville's victory proved that you do not have to come from one of the top stables to win a top prize.

Somerville's boss was George Pagenham, a large man who contrasted somewhat with his thin chef. One of the rules of the competition was that the winner had to repeat his menu for a guest list of around fifty, including food critics, that year at the Mouton Rothschild château in Pauillac. Pagenham drove Somerville there in his own Rolls-Royce with, in the boot, all the food needed for the party, including the turbot and tanks to hold lobsters. Arriving at the château, Pagenham spotted a shabbily dressed elderly man. In his best French, he asked him to help unload the car. It was only the next day that he realised that the man who had helped was in fact his host. After that, Baron Philippe de Rothschild liked to tell friends that whenever he saw a Rolls-Royce approaching his château, he would hesitate before venturing outside for fear it might be a mad Englishman trying to press him into service.

Personally, I knew I was on the right track with my own fish when Roger Vergé, a long-time three-star chef from the Moulin de Mougins, dropped in at the Waterside Inn in the late 1970s when he was changing planes between Nice and the United States at Heathrow. He called ahead and asked for fish because, as he said, Britain was known for the quality of its fish. I made him *goujonnettes de sole au Sauternes* (see p. 240). The Sauternes I chose was a very good one, a Rieussec. (I must emphasise that wines are not just made to be drunk; they are also there to make sauces.) My sole, poached in the Sauternes and fish stock, was accompanied by mushrooms, carrots and courgettes. I reduced the sauce to a light syrup, and added some cream and a little pistachio butter. Passed through a *chinois* sieve, this sauce was poured over the sole, with the vegetables served *al dente*. At the end of the meal, Vergé told me this was a truly creative dish, something worthy of three stars. At the time, I had two Michelin stars and these words from an established three-star chef of Vergé's renown were almost as good as if they came from Michelin itself. This was another recipe that was to become one of my classics.

My brother Albert has always adored fishing. It is more than a hobby, more like a passion. As for myself, apart from a period as a child when I caught tiddlers and tadpoles, I have never been an enthusiast.

I did go after frogs once or twice with my father. Even though frogs are not fish, the methods used to catch them – using a three-pronged hook – are similar. As perch and pike are tempted by brightly coloured red and yellow spinners, the frogs are attracted by a piece of red rag tied to the hooks. Frogs would respond to my father's imitation of their croaking and fall victim to the lure. At home, he would deal with them straightaway. It was a scene that I always fled. He would slice off their heads, eliciting heart-rending squeaks from the frogs, and skin them. The smell was unpleasant but, after the legs had been thrown into a pan with some cream and tarragon or chives, they were delicious.

In the 1960s, before I moved to London, I used to visit Albert and we would go on early-morning fishing trips in Kent. Albert would dig up worms and buy maggots – pink, white, large and small. All I really enjoyed about the trip was organising the picnic. This usually consisted of a cold chicken, served with mayonnaise, a tomato salad with fresh herbs, pickles and a bottle of wine.

After about ten minutes of waiting for the fish to bite, I would get restless. I wanted to walk, talk and do all the things anglers must not do, and that annoyed my brother. I also had the bad habit of snagging my line every time I tried to cast. It would catch in the bushes behind me or in branches overhead. Irritated by my incompetence, Albert would finally tell me to give up any thought of catching anything. You need too much patience to be an angler and patience is not one of my virtues.

My son Alain was about ten at the end of the 1970s. One day I was in the Waterside kitchen when I heard an unusual commotion coming from the restaurant. I realised it was applause. I knew it was unlikely to be a spontaneous and collective outburst of enthusiasm for my cooking since only half the dishes had left the kitchen. I went to see what was going on. A number of customers were standing. Then I saw Alain with a pike of around ten to twelve pounds. He had been fishing and caught his first big fish. Some of the customers sent him a drink to celebrate, and in a few minutes, he had a trayful of orange juices and Coca-Colas.

The episode gave some of the staff ideas. Pierre Dufossé, who looked after the garden and parked customers' cars, said that, if the Thames had such good fish, he would catch them too. He turned this into a small trade, rushing into the kitchen with his catch, taking first a bottle of wine in payment and later champagne.

My more regular fish suppliers are people who are willing to bring their produce to the Waterside Inn. In the mid-1980s, a young man called Tony Allan asked for an appointment. He said he planned to supply fish from a new wholesale business based in Billingsgate. This was a tough undertaking since it was not easy to break into the market, the work is hard, and the hours are long and unsocial. He turned out to be a former cook from the Dorchester, and looked me straight in the eye as he explained his plans. I agreed that he should become a supplier for a trial period of a few weeks. He is still doing so twelve years on!

The quality of his fish and the efficiency of his delivery system were spot on and at the same prices as the others. He had the knack anyway, allied with the heart of a chef and an unquenchable desire to get on. It was and is heartening to see young people succeed like that. The venture provoked envy at the beginning, and I started getting anonymous calls hinting that the business was dodgy, a sure sign that Tony was doing well and upsetting some of his competitors. Now running some restaurants called simply *fish!,* he has done extraordinarily well, and recently floated his company on the stock market. Before he did so, he asked me to become a non-executive director. Knowing the man and knowing his standards, I readily agreed.

I really enjoy discovering new species of fish when I travel abroad. I saw the greatest variety in Australia. At the Sydney fish market, I met Peter Doyle, a great character whose name was synonymous with fish throughout Australia. He first had a fish restaurant at Rose Bay, to which my Australian wife, Robyn, was introduced as a young child, then, as his empire grew, Peter Doyle turned into a supplier too. Peter led me on a tour of the market and his knowledge and passion for all fish, from the tiniest mollusc up to a tuna, that he exported on a regular basis to Japan, were phenomenal. The assorted fish were amazing, literally all the colours of the rainbow, and included many hitherto unknown to me: there were southern hemisphere garfish (long, shiny and dark), flathead (flat, with a fairly strong, dark skin, loved by the Chinese as much as by the Australians), and jewfish, which Peter told me had delicate, moist white flesh. Peter had inherited this passion from his own father and he passed it on to the rest of his family and to those who came into contact with him. I remember being surprised to discover that he was a fifth-generation Australian. Being from Europe, I had always assumed that every Australian had grandparents who came from elsewhere.

In Hong Kong, too, I was to come across a huge variety of fish. In 1980, I was on holiday and staying at the Mandarin Hotel with Bill Vine, a travelling companion. Learning that I was a guest there, the hotel's general manager, Andreas Hofer, asked if I could prepare a couple of dinners for ten to twelve in the hotel – one for the media, another for favourite clients. Before I put together my first menu, I had to see what the Hong Kong market had to offer, so I met up with the Mandarin's buyer at four o'clock in the morning. My sights settled on a garoupa or grouper, a huge fish resembling a sea bass in both size and appearance (and a member of the same family). I had about fifty different fish to choose from, and the buyer told me this was only the tip of the iceberg. He said there were 1,500 types of fish in the seas around China, and 700 freshwater fish, of which carp is the most often consumed.

When the time came to prepare that first meal, the executive chef, Josef Kunzli, a German, was nowhere to be found. Although he had been present at the meeting setting up the meals, Kunzli was never in his office when I looked for him, nor was he in the kitchen. However, this was the first time that a guest chef had ever cooked at the Mandarin, and although most chefs are pleased to accommodate a visiting colleague, a few take umbrage. Because he was not there, I had problems finding even the simplest ingredients and it was Bill Vine who had to become my *commis,* or assistant chef. I would give him a list of what I needed for the hour ahead, and he would scurry to and fro around the kitchen, from section to section.

I carried on preparing my *garoupa aux écailles dorées,* garoupa with golden scales. I opened the fish along its back, and removed the bones, ready to receive its vegetable stuffing. For this I sweated mushrooms, onions and fennel in butter separately so that all three would have the same consistency when I mixed them together. Mushrooms, for example, cook quickly, fennel takes a bit longer and onions longer still. Once seasoned, I added a little cream to make the mixture smooth and left it to cool. I cleaned the inside of the garoupa with a damp cloth and inserted the stuffing. I wrapped the fish in savoury pancakes to insulate it from the puff pastry that was to encase it. The pancakes stopped the water from the vegetables and fish reaching the pastry and softening it. I cut scales and eyes into the pastry with the point of a knife. It cooked for an hour and a half and came out of the oven lacquered like a piece of wood.

To follow, I made a *granité de poires au Brouilly*: pears were poached in red wine, liquidised to a purée and then placed in the freezer but frequently stirred to give a sorbet-like *granité*. This served as a refreshment before the *daube de boeuf* still to come. When this *granité* had been served,

Andreas Hofer came to see me. To judge by the surprise of the Chinese cooks and of Kunzli, who had finally condescended to make an appearance, the Mandarin's general manager was not in the habit of venturing into the kitchen. Much to my pleasure, Hofer told me he was eating one of the best meals of his life and that, from that moment on, I was his guest in the hotel. I was very touched. Hong Kong, after all, is one of the world's greatest gastronomic centres, and people are not easily impressed by a good meal. In fact, he insisted that I served exactly the same meal the following night – he said he didn't want anyone to miss out on such an experience!

That same year, I encountered another fish dish that was remarkable for its simplicity and fun. The annual congress of the *Relais & Châteaux*, the association that groups together most of the world's finest hotels and restaurants, was being held in London, and the main dinner reception for 600 people was at the Dorchester. Anton Mosimann, the Dorchester's well-known Swiss chef, had brought in barrows from Billingsgate to serve as tables for the buffet. These were filled with oysters and a variety of other seafood. The surprise, however, came when Billingsgate porters, in their flat hats, waterproofs, boots and aprons, advanced into the room carrying Billingsgate cases filled with newspaper cornets of fish and chips. Here we were, owners and chefs of the world's most reputed and refined restaurants, eating fish and chips from newsprint. They were exceptionally good, though, and I take my hat off to Mosimann for showing us that good cooking is not always a matter of expensive ingredients like caviar or *foie gras.* I must have eaten three or four of those cornets myself. . .

Cécile de Rothschild

A formal portrait a few
years before her death.

A most remarkable woman
who knew exactly what she
wanted and from whom
I learned things one could
never learn from books

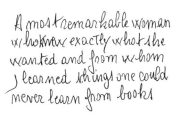

Le Gavroche

1967 and our dream comes true.

'Spring'
My entry in the
'Pièce Artistique'
category for the
Meilleur Ouvrier de France
1976
All in sugar, it took
2 weeks to make.

Le Cochon Rose

A first for London,
our charcuterie only
a stone's throw from
Le Gavroche.

25th Anniversary of the
Waterside Inn

Celebrating with my head Chefs
Pierre Koffmann 1972 - 1976
Christian Germain 1976 - 1981
Michel Perraud 1981 - 1987
Mark Dodson 1987 -

Pride of my summer cold starters. Parfait!

Success - it is the team that counts
Mark Dodson and Diego Masciaga

Le Gavroche

1981

A turning point. Le Gavroche moves to
Upper Brook Street

The Waterside

From our electric launch, a romantic view of our new venture The Waterside Inn

The original kitchen in 1982, just before its transformation

My brigade in 1989
now working all over the world

  2 in Adelaide
  1 in Singapore
  3 in France
  1 in Washington D.C
  1 on a Ship
and the others in the UK

Red Meat

O NE BEEF dish of mine that used to be a great favourite of my regular customers was the *joue et queue de boeuf à la beaujolaise,* using the two ends of the animal: its head, from which I drew the cheeks, and its tail. Both these pieces of beef are very tasty. The tail is full of bones that lend flavour while the cheek is tender, even gelatinous. The two complement each other and I liked to cook them in a *daube*-style stew. I would marinate them in red wine for a full twenty-four hours, drain the meat, pat it dry then quickly brown it on all sides. After that, I would braise it in the marinade to which I had added a little *fond de veau,* a veal stock base. Before serving, I would take the meat out, then reduce the sauce, taking care to arrive at a smooth end result that was neither too thin nor too thick. I would serve this with root vegetables, large mushrooms, little *grelot* or button onions, big, healthy chunks of diced bacon, and heart-shaped *croûtons* cooked in butter topped with chopped parsley.

BSE, or mad cow disease, killed all that.

In all the cacophony of claims and counter-claims since the scandal erupted around bovine spongiform encephalopathy, we have been treated to what the French would call *'tout et son contraire'*, anything and everything. First, we saw politicians from prime ministers down telling us not to panic. We saw them gorging themselves on beef on television. A week later, they told us not to eat beef at all or not to eat too much of it; then they banned beef in schools. At the end of 1997, we were told we could eat beef but not on the bone, and it became illegal to sell beef on the bone in Britain. This meant that I could keep the cheek in my recipe but not the tail.

As it happened, the day the ban came into force, I had prepared the annual Wedgwood Hospitality Industry Dinner. I had already planned to include my beef dish, and the menu had even been immortalised on special Wedgwood plates produced for the occasion. In a short speech I made as the dinner began, I excused myself by noting that the beef had begun to marinate before the ban had been announced and that there was no way of changing the menu, given that it had been glazed on porcelain. I offered to replace the dish for anyone who did not want it, but there were shouts of 'We'll have the beef!' and not one diner took up my offer.

It is consumers and honest producers, those who have always been careful about how they raise their animals, who suffer in a situation like the BSE crisis. Nervous politicians put the fear of God into whole populations, just as they once did with eggs, after earlier allowing greedy multinationals to go after quick profits by producing industrial feed. These firms hoodwinked many farmers into thinking they could produce cheaper meat, leading to a scandal that was to ruin many good and scrupulous farmers, not just those with doubtful rearing methods.

I have eaten both good beef and bad beef in my life. Even though Europeans object to the American practice of raising beef herds with hormones, a speciality beef restaurant that I particularly like is Peter Luger's in Brooklyn. I go to New York at least twice a year and I always head to his huge restaurant that serves 600 a day with excellent, mild-tasting meat. The restaurant has its own herd and it serves gargantuan portions, of almost a kilogram per person, on chopping-boards. The first time I ordered a T-bone there, I thought I would never get through it. I rose to the challenge with ease when I discovered how good the meat tasted. It melted in my mouth, the restaurant atmosphere was good, and I had a delicious American Cabernet Sauvignon to go with it. I may come from the Charolais, where the best French beef is produced, but Peter Luger's beef is also one of the tastiest you can find.

Like many Frenchmen, I eat not only to survive but also for pleasure. This means not just choosing careful and ingenious ways of preparing food, but taking an active interest in its quality and origins. Of the meat I choose to serve at the Waterside Inn, 100 per cent of the beef is British, Aberdeen Angus. Ninety per cent of my lamb, too, comes from Britain, from Wales and the West Country. I buy most of my meat on the carcass and we do our own butchery, meaning that we have the closest possible controls over the treatment our meat receives. I do, however, have to buy some extra beef fillets and saddles of lamb. Even then, we do all our own preparation of the meat, excising the nerves and trimming the fat ourselves just when it is needed for cooking, never before.

When purchased, beef should be a bright red colour. A firm, white or slightly cream-coloured fat shows that the animal is young. When beef arrives at the Waterside Inn, guaranteed free from additives, hormones or recycled protein, it has been matured for three weeks in conditions of controlled temperature and humidity. It comes only from steers; cow meat is quite different. We leave it in our cold storage facilities for another three to seven days before preparing it. Lamb is similar. It needs to have firm, white fat. The paler the colour of the meat, the younger the animal. Dark red meat is more likely to be mutton than lamb, although mutton is now rarely available, unfortunately. It made for a tasty winter dish.

Another advantage of buying meat on the bone means that we can cook it on the bone, giving it more taste. But even when small, boned portions are required, nothing is lost. We keep all the bones and cook them with aromatic vegetables and herbs to make the veal and lamb *fonds* we need as the base for sauces. This takes me back to my days with Cécile de Rothschild, who hated waste. She used to tell me, 'Chef, don't lose anything, especially with lamb. If there is some cold leg of lamb left over, in summer you serve it to me in a *moussaka*. In winter, make me a shepherd's pie with a little fresh tomato sauce in a side dish. Not ketchup, Chef, but a sauce you have made yourself. Even if I am not here, do the same thing, then the staff can eat it. How lucky you all are!'

Our policy of doing all the work from carcass to plate means that we never have meat that has lost all its blood, leaving it with the taste and consistency of cardboard. This also means we have to train our staff extremely well. We always have cooks cutting and preparing meat, and others scaling, gutting and filleting fish. When we employ a new cook, he or she must always start in the cold kitchen, preparing meat alongside someone who is already experienced. This helps young cooks gain the knowledge they will need to buy their own products from suppliers in their later careers. Butchery is the start of everything. If the preparation is not up to scratch, how can anyone produce a dish of top quality?

In the late 1970s my brother Albert and I took part in what might in Britain be called a culinary revolution. Clinton Silver, the director in charge of Marks & Spencer's Food Division, wrote to us and asked us to help them train their butchers in French meat-preparation methods. At the time, there was little butchery tradition or skill in Britain. We took Marks & Spencer buyers to France and helped them set up training. They went to the Rungis food market south of Paris and to the Boucherie Lamartine on the avenue Victor Hugo in the city's 16th *arrondissement,* at that time one of the leading Paris butchers. Where Marks & Spencer led, others followed, so this quickly resulted in the first meat appearing on British supermarket shelves marked 'French cut'. This more punctilious preparation of meat, trimming nerves and fat along the fibres until only the good, edible meat is left, became the fashion and now the cuts of meat in British shops are closer to those you would find on the Continent.

My first memories of red meat as a child were not just of beef or lamb but also of horsemeat. Despite the British aversion to eating meat that comes from a loyal servant and friend of man, it is a product that I like. In the 1950s, horsemeat in France was cheap, but then it became popular and now it is as expensive as beef. My mother would often buy horsemeat and she asked for either a piece from the *bavette,* skirt steak, or from *l'araignée,* the 'spider'. This was so named because, originally a round piece of meat, would end up looking like a spider once the butcher had cut out the nerves, leaving several strings of meat sticking out from the centre. Horsemeat can have a rather strong taste, but it is good accompanied by separately simmered shallots, with parsley added at the last moment. Some like it with garlic but I find this inappropriate.

When I was a child, lamb was expensive and rare. My mother would send me to do the shopping – there was no compulsion in this, I adored doing the shopping – and she always asked me to buy *côtes découvertes*. These are the chops near the neck, as high as you can get. They are streaked with fat, unlike the more lean *côtes premières* which are little kernels of meat attached to long, thin bones (and which were Cécile de Rothschild's preference). My mother liked lamb chops because you could suck the bones. She also used to heat up the accompanying vegetables – French beans, spinach or other greens – with some of the lamb fat to give them more taste.

I adored the so-called secondary pieces of lamb, like the collar or the shoulder which are delicious in a *navarin* stew. My mother used to make what she called a *navarin d'agneau,* but it was more a mutton stew, as the meat came from an animal that was too old to be considered lamb. She made it with white kidney beans and big chunks of carrot rather than with new vegetables as in a real *navarin*. It was delicious nonetheless but nothing like as fine as the *navarin* I was to make twenty years later for Cécile de Rothschild with spring vegetables from the garden at her country house outside Paris. I was lucky to know such contrasts. If you only eat caviar or the best fillet of beef every day, how can you appreciate simple pleasures and the value of a mutton stew?

As for my early consumption of beef, my mother liked to buy minced steak. This came from fat-free meat that was too tough to be sold as ordinary steak but was more suited to cooking in a sauce. When my mother brought the steak home, I would often lift a little of it with a spoon from around the edge and eat it raw. I hoped I wouldn't be noticed but my mother always did, and told me off. On other occasions, she would sprinkle a little of the raw meat in my soup. Since I was a sickly child, this was considered a way of building up my health and strength.

I have always adored raw meat. In my kitchen, we cut meat only when a client has ordered a portion. Sometimes I cannot resist, and cut a sliver of beef on my chopping-board, about as fine as a piece of Parma ham, season it with a little salt and pepper and pop it in my mouth. One of the most widely accepted ways of serving raw beef is as a *steak tartare*. This dish is hard to find with just the right amount of seasoning. It is better eaten in a restaurant with a large turnover to ensure that the meat is constantly freshly chopped. My favourite version is that offered at Le Vesuvio in Cannes, a restaurant just by the Hotel Martinez on La Croisette, where the specialities also include pizzas cooked in a wood oven. The clientele is varied, from students eating pizzas to elderly *bourgeois* coming for the *tartare*. Whenever I am flying into Nice in the evening my main concern is whether I will land in time to get to the Vesuvio before they take the last order, for the quality of the meat and seasonings are just right. The chips served with it are piping hot and crisp on the outside, soft inside. To go with all this, they toast slices of country bread alongside the pizzas in the wood oven. I like this nearly burnt. This mixture of the *tartare,* chips and bread is sheer delight.

At the Rothschilds, I would sometimes prepare a *boeuf Stroganoff* with fresh pasta. Cécile de Rothschild adored this, especially when there were just a few guests. Many people have errant notions of how to cook this, even using meat that has been already boiled. In fact, it needs good raw fillet of beef, cooked quickly at the last minute, with fresh paprika (not one that has been sitting in the larder in an opened jar for six months or more), freshly chopped herbs, lemon juice and soured cream (see p. 242).

A beef dish that I really like, which is equally delicious hot or cold, is *aiguillette de boeuf,* the silverside from the leg. The *grosse aiguillette* will serve six to eight people, and the smaller and more delicate and juicy *aiguillette baronne* is very good for just two to three. With a layer of fat on the outside, both pieces of meat first have to have the nerves removed and then they are pierced with a long larding needle to insert long strips of back fat before being marinated in a good Bordeaux. At Cécile de Rothschild's, this was always a wine from the family vineyard, often a Carruades de Château Lafite. I would add aromatic vegetables and a *bouquet garni.* After marinating it for a day, I would seal it and brown it all over in a hot pan and then braise the *grosse aiguillette* in the oven for four to five hours, just over two for the *aiguillette baronne*. I would then serve it with root vegetables, like carrots and celeriac, small glazed onions and boiled potatoes. This was a rich, heady winter dish, real *cuisine bourgeoise.*

The summer variant, served cold, is equally delicious and visually spectacular. I take the same sauce, and clarify it like a consommé to obtain a jelly with a powerful taste and a deep amber colour. The beef, covered in this shimmering jelly, is a dish that should never see the inside of a refrigerator.

It was a cold beef dish that won me an award in 1966, just a few months before I left for London. I had entered the Arpajon competition's Cold

Dîner

—

Turbot soufflé
Pommes de terre à l'anglaise
Poularde Mercédès
Riz créole
Petits pois au beurre
Aiguillette de bœuf à la gelée
Salade
Glace Jubilé
Petits gâteaux

A Château Lafite was served with my slowly braised aiguillette de boeuf

Dishes category with a sirloin of Charolais that I ordered from Monsieur Daumain, a butcher at the covered market of La Madeleine. Monsieur Daumain himself looked a little like a bull, with a thick neck. He was always deep red in the face, as though he was about to lose his temper. I ordered the meat ten days in advance and he kept it in his cold-storage room to let it mature. I removed the nerves, trimmed all the fat and, with a small larding needle, inserted strips of back fat and truffles, one arranged neatly behind the other, a job that took the best part of three hours. Then I roasted it, turning it every ten minutes and sprinkling the cooking juices over the meat. As well as stopping the meat from getting too dry, the aim was to achieve a perfect symmetry, giving a uniform colour on the outside. When it was sliced, this cooking would also ensure that the well-cooked exterior would change to a medium-cooked pink halo around the rare red centre.

For a base, I cooked some rice in milk, then, when it was still hot, I added a few leaves of gelatine to make it firm. I put this in an oval dish, and as it cooled and set, I laid it on a silver platter (this time borrowed with Cécile de Rothschild's permission!). I added some *al dente* macaroni cut into short pieces and pushed into the rice base to give a pattern of little circular holes round the edge. This all took yet another two hours. Then I put the beef on top. The result, with the white ermine-like macaroni surrounding the purple-red meat, resembled a prince's crown. As decoration, I carved the heads of little mushrooms, poached them in lemon water, placed a little dot of truffle on the top and put a row of them on the meat. Garnished with artichoke bottoms and roundels of carrot and turnip, I covered the beef and the garnish with aspic jelly. I had to apply this just as it began to set, when it was no longer thin but before it thickened, to be able to spread an even layer. I surrounded it with little green beans tied with a tiny 'string' of hard-boiled egg white and white palm hearts similarly tied with minuscule threads of red pepper. The decoration, the lustre of the jelly and the use of a base gave the dish relief and helped it stand out visually among the entries.

This effort required about forty hours' work in all, and won me the solid silver medal of the City of Paris, the second prize out of fifty competitors, at the age of twenty-five. Cécile de Rothschild's pride was almost palpable.

In 1970, I wrote to Paul Bocuse, the famous three-star French chef, who was to me a national hero. I asked if I could visit him at his restaurant at Collonges-au-Mont-d'Or near Lyons. He agreed that I should come and stay for two days. Paul has hospitality in his blood.

On the first morning at about six, Paul took me to his local market at Les Brotteaux in Lyons. It was then that I understood how much more there was to Paul than just the ability to cook. He seemed to have an aura. Everywhere he went, it was a bit like an emperor passing through, with other cooks as his court. La Mère Richard, whose business is still one of Lyons' best known cheese shops, was devoted to Paul. She was later to work with her daughter with whom she shared the same Christian name, Renée, (which earned the business another nickname, *Les Deux* Renées). The elder Renée would choose cheeses – goat's cheese, Saint Marcellin and Vacherin – for Paul Bocuse and set them aside. Only once he had been to the market would she release what remained to the rest of the trade or to the general public.

When we had finished at the market, Paul turned to me and said, 'I don't know how you live in England, but here every effort earns a reward and you need something of substance.' He took me to a *mâchon,* or *bouchon,* one of those little Lyons bistros where food is served at any hour. It was about eight-thirty in the morning. Paul ordered some *tripes à la lyonnaise* 'to get your appetite going' and a carafe of Beaujolais while we waited for our braised *boeuf à la beaujolaise.*

The next day, Paul took me off to see the Troisgros brothers at their three-star restaurant in Roanne. Paul drove his van at high speed through a network of back roads with the same dexterity that he ran his kitchen. Jean and Pierre Troisgros, with their labradors, were waiting for us when we arrived at around nine in the morning. Jean said it was time for a bite – the Lyonnais seem incapable of welcoming people with anything but a meal. He took a fillet of Charolais beef, from my home region, cut thin slices straight from the middle (giving us the best, like the considerate host he was), and then diced a shallot into a frying pan. In his kitchen where fifteen cooks were already bustling around, he held the pan of shallots over heat in one hand and the pan with the beef in the other. A few minutes later, he ground some pepper over the meat, and it all arrived on the bistro table. (At that time, the Troisgros restaurant still had a bistro side for the locals as well as its more elegant dining-room.) It was all so simple, but an ingredient of that quality should always stand by itself. Again we had Beaujolais, this time in a bottle, with the Troisgros pressing me to try different *crus*. I began to understand why the Lyonnais call Beaujolais 'the third river of Lyons' alongside the Rhône and the Saône! We followed this with a tour of their cellar and their precious selection of cigars.

That was how I discovered how unique Paul Bocuse was, something that subsequent meetings have confirmed. He and the Troisgros taught me what it is to be Lyonnais, and thus why the Lyons region has so many starred restaurants...

The Rib Room of the Carlton Tower was one of my favourite places when I was living in London. I would go there for lunch at weekends when our restaurants in the city were closed. Bernard Gaume, the chef, used to prepare some succulent ribs of beef from animals that were a cross between Hereford and French Charolais. The beef was always left to rest between cooking and carving, as it should be, ensuring that the meat would be tasty and juicy. The rib joint was carved in front of us, dark outside and pink within, and was accompanied by generous and crisp Yorkshire pudding and potatoes baked in the oven. The presentation might have been simple, but the result was a delight for the palate.

One of the most popular French beef dishes is the *pot-au-feu,* served with a marrow bone that should be eaten with a sprinkling of coarse sea salt. The marrow has to be eaten first because it must be hot. Different types of beef, from oxtail to blade, knuckle and tongue, are simmered with carrots, leeks, turnips, cabbage and potatoes, to make a dish that is as nourishing as it is tasty. The *bouillon* in which these vegetables cook is often served on its own as a soup, either before eating the *pot-au-feu* or at another meal. This is a dish at which my brother Albert excels, and his *Pot-au-feu sauce Albert* was one of the favourites on the Gavroche menu. Rather than serving it with the traditional Dijon mustard, Albert devised a horseradish sauce that was a perfect accompaniment.

A particular *pot-au-feu* enthusiast was a retired American colonel, Colonel De Muth, who had been on Eisenhower's staff during the Second World War. One day in the 1970s, the colonel had booked at Le Gavroche during a spate of IRA bombings in London. A few days before, a bomb had exploded at a restaurant in Knightsbridge. The noise of that explosion, followed by the police and fire brigade sirens, brought me out of the kitchen to see what was going on. Fearing the same might happen to us, we had put up grills outside the restaurant and plastic film over all our windows to limit any damage that might be caused. Just as Colonel De Muth was about to tuck into his *pot-au-feu*, a police car drew up outside and two officers told us to clear the restaurant immediately. The colonel adamantly refused, protesting, rightly, that 'the marrow must be eaten hot.' He insisted that he had heard an explosion and that the alert was over. We realised that the colonel, who was hard of hearing, had taken the loud clatter caused by clumsy handling of the nearby serving lift to be a bomb. After failing to move him, we left the colonel alone to finish his meal. Fortunately, events justified his determination and, after a short evacuation, staff and customers filed back into Le Gavroche.

Albert and I once tried to take British beef to Paris when we thought of opening a British restaurant there. In the early 1980s, we were offered the Pavillon Laurent restaurant on the Champs-Elysées, in one of the elegant pavilions towards the Concorde end of the avenue. We already had a twenty-ton refrigerated lorry travelling twice weekly to and from Paris's Rungis market, and thought we could put it to good use on the outward journey by sending Aberdeen Angus, smoked salmon and game like grouse to the new restaurant. Our plan was extremely ambitious: we had also decided to turn the building into a British showcase, with shops selling British clothes and a whisky boutique among others. Always ready to run before we could walk, we even drew up menus for the restaurant. We offered £200,000. In the end, however, another buyer appeared on the scene from nowhere – Sir James Goldsmith – and he snatched the deal away by outbidding us by £20,000.

In 1985, I received a call from Hong Kong to tell me that Li Ka Shing, one of the territory's most powerful *taipans*, whom I had met on a visit there, wanted me to introduce him to France, a country he had never visited, and to French *savoir-vivre*. Li and I had been at a dinner party together at the Red Pepper restaurant in Hong Kong. He came on foot, I seem to remember, while his chauffeur-driven Rolls-Royce followed behind. This was his usual behaviour, and the local joke was that he walked his Rolls-Royce like a dog.

Li had already made plans to come to London and we left in a private jet for southern France. I had booked one of the most elegant hotels in the region, L'Oustau de Baumanière at Les Baux-de-Provence. It was the beginning of June and the setting was idyllic. On the first evening, we ate the hotel's best-known signature dish, a *gigot d'agneau de lait en croûte,* a milk-fed lamb born four to six weeks before. Li, who shyly spoke only a few words of English, was delighted by his initiation into France and French cooking. The following evening, he insisted on having the same dish again. When I tried to tempt him into trying something else, he replied that the dish was unique and he might never have it again. I have to admit that eating that same dish two days running was not a punishment, given the succulence of the meat and the delicacy of the preparation. But I had to explain to Li that not all of France lived like the residents of this magnificent Provençal palace.

In France, lamb is often served with an excess of garlic. In Britain, to me the excess is the mint sauce. It's strange how southerners seem to overdo garlic in cooking, while northerners add too much that is sweet. I find mint jelly with cold lamb, alongside other pickles, quite acceptable, but have never taken to mint sauce served with hot lamb.

Agneau de lait, milk-fed lamb, is rarely found in British restaurants, but goes on my menu in February. The first come from the Pyrenees, where the ewes give birth before those in Britain, then we take English and Welsh lamb. We use a lot for things like stuffed saddles of lamb, completely boned and filled with a stuffing that contains shallots, parsley and morel mushrooms. Roasted, this is carved in the dining-room by Diego Masciaga, my restaurant manager, whose skill and delicacy make him one of the best carvers in Europe.

In 1981, Hedges & Butler asked Albert and myself to cook a dinner for sixteen people at which the guest of honour would be the Queen Mother. They said she had specifically asked for us to prepare the meal. The Queen Mother had always had a lot of affection for Albert since the days he cooked for Major Peter Cazalet, her race-horse trainer in Kent. It was almost unknown for us to leave Le Gavroche together to cook for anyone outside. As was normal on any unusual assignment, Albert left the practical side to me. 'You draw up the menu,' he said, 'bring what's needed and tell me what I should do when I get there.' I arrived at about five o'clock with one of our cooks. Half an hour later, Albert arrived with the comment, 'I hope you haven't forgotten anything.'

For the main course, I prepared a *gigolette d'agneau*. This was a boned leg of lamb cut into cubes and lightly pan-fried a few minutes before serving with a very light juice made from the bones of the lamb. It was served with a Mouton Baron Philippe 1961, an appetiser for the grander Château Mouton Rothschild 1953 that was to accompany the cheese.

The Queen Mother has been to the Waterside Inn several times over the years. Last time, like many of my other guests, she stepped outside to throw bread to the ducks and swans on the river.

Lamb also featured in the most important royal occasion with which I have ever been involved. In March 1996, I received a telephone call from Prince Edward. An important family birthday was approaching and he and his brothers wondered if the birthday dinner could be held at the Waterside Inn. I told him that the ideal would be to take the private dining-room which could accommodate up to fourteen people in comfort. As it was so close to April, I had an inkling of what the occasion might be. Two weeks later, Edward called back to make more definite arrangements, saying that they wanted to treat their mother, confirming, as I had suspected, that it was the dinner for the Queen's seventieth birthday. We finally settled on *selle et carré d'agneau de lait* from Wales for the main course with spring vegetables from the Loire Valley, tiny blue turnips, peas and baby carrots. The latter are so tender that they needed hardly any cooking and certainly no addition of herbs.

Edward and I were in touch over the next few weeks on the organisation of this dinner. No one on my staff knew what was going on. I kept the plans completely secret. I did not note the details in the reservations book so no one knew who the guests were or who had booked the private dining-room that night. It was only two or three days before the event that I confided in my chef and restaurant manager, Mark Dodson and Diego Masciaga.

Perhaps it is because I worked in aristocratic houses as a young man that I have a special affection for the monarchy. After all, I served people like Henri d'Orléans, the Count of Paris and the pretender to the French throne, and I cooked for the Duke of Windsor quite often when I worked for Cécile de Rothschild. As a rule, the French like other people's monarchies, but not their own. So I started shining my pans, very excited at the idea of having the Queen at the Waterside Inn for such a personal occasion. I inspected all the nooks and crannies of the private dining-room to make sure everything was spick and span.

Two days before, on my own birthday, I received a phone call during a family dinner. It was the *Daily Mail*. A journalist said the newspaper had been reliably informed that the Queen was going to celebrate her birthday at the Waterside Inn. Of course, I denied it all. I tried to make a joke of it and to get them off my back as politely as possible because, had I been harsh, they were capable of printing my words. The caller told me that, in any case, the article would be printed on the Saturday morning, and he kept his promise.

I had dozens of calls from customers and colleagues wanting to know if it was true. Scotland Yard turned up, so did the Maidenhead police with dogs. Even our local Bray constable was there, offering his help. It was a bit like a Fernandel film. The only person not getting a good laugh out of it all was me, although I made sure I was always smiling to try and defuse the situation. I tried to look relaxed but I was really very tense because I was sure the whole event would be called off. I thought the security problems – the Waterside Inn is after all in a *cul-de-sac* – would be too great.

Photographers began arriving to take up position with their telephoto lenses. Television crews followed. By the Saturday evening, the day before, security men were in place. There were some twenty-five to thirty people dealing with security a full day ahead to ensure that the dinner could proceed without any problems. They insisted on taking the rooms above the dining-room so they could watch the road outside. I was beginning to wonder if the poor Queen could enjoy herself on an evening out like that.

On the Sunday morning, I had the phone call I had been dreading. It was Edward to say that good sense had dictated against holding the dinner at the Waterside Inn, since it had become impossible to hold the private family party he and his brothers had wanted for their mother. Would it be possible for us to cook and serve the dinner at Frogmore in the grounds of Windsor Castle? He asked me to come and meet the butler which I agreed to immediately. I jumped into the car, it was only a twenty-minute drive, and set off for Windsor Castle. I was given a guided tour of Frogmore from top to bottom, at least of the kitchen, salon and dining-room. These great houses may be very fine but they were not always built with happy cooking and serving in mind. The kitchen and the dining-room were on different floors and there was a distance of about seventy-five yards between them. Already I was worried for the lamb, but what bothered me even more was the preparation of the raspberry soufflés the Queen adored. So I decided then and there to change the menu a bit and make *sablés aux poires*, a dessert that would not suffer so much from the long walk between kitchen and dining-room.

Another factor involved the gas cooker at Frogmore, which was adequate, but it was more of an ordinary domestic cooker than the professional ovens I was used to. The refrigerator was similar. It was a kitchen that could be used for small and simple meals but not for a great gastronomic occasion, so I was not going to be in the best of my elements. I knew that it was going to be a difficult evening, and that I would have to make up for some things that were missing. I came out of Frogmore and called Edward, to tell him that we could not serve the soufflé, but that this would be the only change. Six people were coming with me, three kitchen staff and three to serve.

Back in Bray, there were lines of police and barriers outside the Waterside Inn as if the original royal dinner was going ahead as planned. For us, it became an under-cover operation (my main pleasure, though, lay in the prospect of giving the Press, which by now had invaded Bray, the slip). I put my Renault Espace by the private dining-room in the middle of the afternoon and we loaded it gradually, crouching down SAS-style to hide from the photographers' zooms. That night Bill Wyman of the Rolling Stones came to dinner at the Waterside Inn and was flabbergasted to see old ladies and children waiting with flowers while photographers and television crews jostled behind lines of police.

At Frogmore, we started organising things with the Windsor staff. Before dinner, Edward came to see me in the kitchen with Sophie, now his wife, and cracked some jokes about the quality of the equipment. I explained I had finally decided to make an exception for the Queen and the Queen Mother and would prepare them each a soufflé because this was really their favourite. I said I hoped this would not offend the others. I carried the soufflés to the dining-room myself, then I was invited to join them all for coffee and port. I talked to Charles about the training of young chefs and changing standards of cuisine in Britain. Just before I left, Edward told me that he believed the leak about his mother's birthday plans had come from someone close to the Royal Family. However, on subsequent occasions, members of the Royal Family, including the Queen, invited by others, have been to our private dining-room, and we have managed to serve them without anyone finding out.

This event gave me a burst of publicity such as I had never known before. There were newspaper articles everywhere, in Britain and abroad, as well as radio and television reports. For me, another immediate consequence was that I lost my voice, a result of nervous tension, and I was unable to speak properly for close to a month, much to the joy of my staff. . .

White Meat

A S THE SON and grandson of *charcutiers,* French pork butchers, I was conscious of the importance of at least one white meat from my earliest childhood. Others are veal and veal offal, and kid.

Pork is the basic meat in *charcuterie* and, as such, is a very important element in the diets of both the French and Germans. The quality varies with the breed of pig and with the way the animal is fed and raised: if happy in its environment, its growth will be healthier and the final product will be good. In my childhood, I ate pork frequently, as it was and is a fairly cheap meat. It was usually a grilled pork loin chop, served with a potato purée, the ideal accompaniment.

Veal, on the other hand, is an expensive meat because the animal does not live long and has to be reared carefully. The best veal comes from calves that, as the French say, were 'raised under their mother' and have not been weaned. We ate this less frequently at home.

When I worked for Cécile de Rothschild, my boss would boast to her guests about my skill at making *blanquette de veau,* something she ordered quite often. This was a classic French veal dish that my mother would make for special occasions when I was a child. 'It's a concierge's dish,' my boss would say, underlining her respect for traditional, rather than *haute* cuisine, 'a dish of mothers and grandmothers. I'm lucky because my chef was so well brought up by his mother.' *Blanquette* is a dish I now make mainly at home, especially in winter. It is not really appropriate for a three-star Michelin restaurant, although I sometimes put it on my *table d'hôte* lunch-time menus.

As spring vegetables began to come on the market, like baby onions and field mushrooms, my mother would make us a celebratory *blanquette*. She bought cuts of shoulder, breast and *tendron,* or flank. The *tendron* contains cartilage but no bones, and contributes much flavour to the dish (I liked chewing it). My mother watched her *blanquette* like a hawk, making sure it never boiled. The meat was cut into similarly sized pieces so it would all cook evenly, to guard against the pieces being overcooked and disintegrating. Covered with a little water, she simmered it at no more than ninety degrees centigrade. She hated seeing meat boil, since this toughens it. After about ten minutes, she let me lift off the greyish-white foam of impurities that formed on the surface, which I would throw away. Then my mother put in an onion that I had studded with cloves, some carrots and a big *bouquet garni* of herbs. This she would tie to the pan-handle so that she could remove it easily, because 'I don't want to go on a fishing trip.' The herbs always included curly parsley which, she said, had more taste than the flat-leaved variety.

After letting the meat cook for up to an hour and a half, she transferred it to a bowl and covered it with a damp cloth. She took out the herbs, carrots and onions and set about reducing the cooking juices. Next came my moment of glory. She put cream and egg yolks into a large bowl for me to mix. Then she slowly poured on the cooking juice which I stirred with a fork, turning it into a sauce that began to look like a *crème anglaise* or custard. She then put all the sauce, the meat, baby onions and mushrooms back in the stewing pan with a little lemon juice to sharpen the taste, and placed it on the edge of our coal range where it would be warm but would not boil. She served it with some *croûtons* fried in a little butter, or, in winter, with boiled rice (pilaf rice was something she simply did not know). My mother's preparation of this dish was so good that Albert and I decided not to change anything, and we entitled our own recipe for the dish, 'Our Mother's Blanquette of Veal'.

Another dish that my mother used to make for special days was *paupiette de veau,* or veal olive, which brings together both veal and pork, a combination that reduces the price, making it more accessible to a modest budget. It is a thin veal escalope enclosing a pork stuffing which is encased in barding fat and tied in a small parcel with strong string. Mother used to brown this in a cast-iron stewing pan for about twenty-five minutes until the outside had caramelised and the centre was soft and inviting. One of my greatest pleasures was to take off the string which had become soaked in the sauce, fat and juices. I kept this until the end and sucked it until only the taste of string remained... (see p. 244).

It was at the British Embassy and with Cécile de Rothschild that I came across nobler cuts of veal, such as the *longe*, or loin, and the saddle, and encountered some of the great veal dishes of classical French Cuisine. It was only in the great private houses such as those, where time and money were irrelevant, that many dishes of the past would be cooked. Many would be wonderful to recreate today if we had the time, but very few have the skill. Indeed I have only cooked the following dish once or twice during the last thirty years, for private parties. Perhaps I'll cook it at New Year, instead of my normal capon. . . .At the Rothschilds', I cooked half-racks of veal, until the meat was 80 per cent cooked. I removed the centre of the loin from the bones, taking care to leave a good two to three centimetre slice still attached at either end. I carved the meat I had removed and then sandwiched it back together on the bone with a *duxelles* of mushrooms and slices of cooked *foie gras* between each slice. The end slices on the bones acted like two book-ends, holding the loin in its original shape. I poured a Mornay sauce, mixed with one-third *hollandaise* to lighten it, over the meat. It went under the salamander grill for thirty seconds before serving. This was veal in all its splendour.

At the beginning of 1963, my sister-in-law Monique called me in Paris with the alarming news that my brother had been seriously injured in a car accident. Fortunately, neither Monique nor their son, Michel, who was then nearly three, had been in his Mini that was crushed like a sardine can. Albert was in hospital at Pembury in Kent with fractures to the pelvis and the hip. Doctors told him it would take three months of treatment and physiotherapy to get him back on his feet. They even feared for a while that he might be permanently disabled. A combination of the surgeons' skill and Albert's own ferocious determination ensured that he recovered.

Albert, with Monique beside him in the kitchen, was working for Peter

Cazalet, a boss whose severe demeanour concealed huge kindness and generosity. When Albert left to set up Le Gavroche, he gave him a parting gift of £500 to help the restaurant on its way.

A few days after her first call, Monique telephoned again to say Albert had suggested I should come to Fairlawne in Kent for an important weekend that his boss was planning. The Queen Mother was to be the guest of honour. Albert had drawn up the menus with the Cazalets before his accident and he wanted me to run the kitchen because, although my sister-in-law was an excellent assistant cook, she did not have the training to cope with a busy weekend. I told Monique that Peter Cazalet's wife Zara would have to ask Cécile de Rothschild directly.

Cécile de Rothschild summoned me shortly afterwards and announced with a theatrical flourish: 'The English want to borrow you.' She behaved as though she were sending me on a crusade and took to telling her guests, 'I'm lending him to the English for a royal weekend.' *Un weekend royal* ...

The main dish was to be a saddle of veal Prince Orloff. Monique asked what she could do to prepare the way and I asked her to make the *soubise* sauce, a three-hour task. She did this beautifully, blanching the onions to remove their pungency but not their taste, then she cooked them in butter without browning them for half an hour, mixed them with a classic *béchamel* sauce and cooked all of this in the oven before sieving it.

As I embarked on my journey, Cécile de Rothschild, who wanted to know every detail of the menu, was happy to give advice. 'Careful, Chef, don't overcook the veal or it'll go dry,' she said, and 'Don't be nervous just because you're cooking for the Queen Mother, be just as you are with me.'

I removed the meat from the oven while it was still quite pink, and carved it into one centimetre thick slices. Monique laid a spoonful of the *soubise* sauce and a thick slice of truffle between the slices fifteen minutes before serving. We re-formed the meat and put it back in a low oven. Just before it left the kitchen, we coated the veal with Mornay sauce flavoured with a little of the *soubise*, sprinkled a tiny quantity of freshly grated Parmesan over the top and put it under the salamander grill. It was served with vegetables from the Cazalets' garden – carrots, runner beans, new potatoes and green English asparagus.

The next day, the Queen Mother came to see us in the kitchen. She enquired after Albert's health – she had often tasted his cooking on her visits to Fairlawne – and asked me both to transmit her best wishes to Cécile de Rothschild and to thank her for lending me for the weekend. But, as I might have expected, the most gruelling part of the whole exercise was still to come. When I got back to Paris, I had to tell my boss everything from A to Z and then repeat it, again and again and in every detail. It was like an interrogation. For months, Cécile de Rothschild told guests, 'My chef was the Queen Mother's cook. Just look at him. At twenty-two, he prepared a dinner for the Royal Family!'

At the Rothschilds' I created a *veau à l'ananas,* veal with pineapple. I cut some very thin escalopes from veal fillet, and beat them until so transparent you could almost read through them (rather like a *strüdel* dough). I cut them into small squares and cooked them very quickly and lightly in butter for a few seconds. Then I added a little mild curry sauce to which I always add a little apple so that it is not too strong. I mixed in a little *hollandaise* to give it a smooth texture, taking care not to boil it, and put in the veal on a very low heat. I added diced pineapple, sprinkled on a few flakes of grilled almonds, and served it with pilaf rice. For years, this dish was a Gavroche speciality.

At one point, Cécile de Rothschild decided she needed to lose weight and constantly asked for veal *piccata.* For about six months, she wanted her escalopes so thin that they were almost transparent. I would cook six to eight at a time in the hope that two or three would not stick or tear on the very hot grill. Demonstrating the stupidity of which only really intelligent people are sometimes capable, she would then order fresh pasta to go with it – and plenty of it!

Most of the veal I serve now comes from the Limousin region of central France or the Dordogne. There is nothing to compare with this in Britain. Cooked, the flesh is white and both its texture and taste are delicate. Two million calves are raised each year and France is Europe's main producer. To be classified as 'raised under its mother', a young calf needs to drink the milk from two cows, one its mother of course, each day in order to be properly fed. A couple of weeks before slaughter, whole eggs are added to its milk feed. Only 7 per cent of the total production are fed this way and come with a certificate of origin.

From the calves I buy, we sometimes make *tête de veau,* using all parts of the calf's head. This is a well-known French dish but not one that can be served in a gastronomic restaurant, more in a *brasserie*, as the Brasserie Lipp in Paris does so well, with a *ravigote* sauce of sunflower or peanut oil, wine vinegar, capers, small gherkins, snipped herbs and onions. This dish underwent a revival in the late twentieth century. Jacques Chirac, during his campaign for the French presidency in 1995, made a point of eating it repeatedly, setting himself apart from his less earthy rivals, the Socialist intellectual Lionel Jospin and his fellow Gaullist, the more patrician and technocratic Edouard Balladur. Charles de Gaulle, who was Chirac's and Balladur's political mentor, liked to dismiss the French as *veaux,* people who follow anything and any trend. In French, the word means both calves and their meat, veal. An English-language equivalent is to liken people to sheep. De Gaulle would surely not have missed the irony of the spectacle of a spiritual successor elected to the Elysée Palace after eating so many heads of veal!

As Chirac campaigned, I cooked *tendron* or flank of veal on the barbecue, and served it very unusually, with a caramelised lemon. I have always liked lemon and its combination with sugar, the sweetness of one making up for the acidity of the other. I wash and prick the lemons with a skewer then poach them for a few minutes in a syrup made of equal quantities of sugar and water. Then I leave them to cool in the syrup before poaching them again for fifteen minutes. The end result is a lemon that is still whole but with a soft skin and an inside half sweet, half acid. I marinate the *tendrons* themselves in honey, lemon juice, paprika and crushed black or white peppercorns, and leave them overnight in the refrigerator. I cook the veal on the hottest, middle part of the barbecue, with the lemons on the outside of the grill. When the meat looks as if it is almost caramelised, with all the sugar and honey coming out of the meat, I serve it with the lightly grilled whole lemon, a great combination.

Of all animals, the calf offers the most noble offal – liver, kidneys, sweetbreads, tongue and brains. When I used to go to the old Les Halles in the centre of Paris as an apprentice, to buy mushrooms and scallops, I always had a look at the offal market. As the son of a *charcutier*, I was fascinated by the lungs hanging there, slimy with blood, and by the vats containing hundreds of tongues, that looked like squirming fish. There were dozens of stallholders and long queues of customers.

In London in 1967, Albert and I had to move heaven and earth to get veal kidneys or sweetbreads. We repeatedly heard that there was no demand so no one had any, but from the first day, we managed to put kidneys on the menu. Veal kidneys are encased in a hard white fat. When you slice into this fat with a knife and pull it back with your fingers, there is a cracking sound before the pale pink flesh of the kidney is revealed. Ideally, this process, which is almost sensual, should also remove the membrane on the kidneys. If not, this has to be taken off separately.

I love preparing kidneys for my own recipe, *le sauté de rognons de veau à la moutarde*. I cut them into big cubes after taking off the fat and the nerves from the middle, sauté them very quickly until about half cooked and put them aside. I deglaze the pan with a glass of dry white wine, put in some chopped shallots and reduce this before adding a mixture of strong Dijon mustard and Meaux mustard grains, a spoonful of veal stock and a little cream, just enough to make the sauce smooth. I return the kidney cubes to the pan, roll them in the sauce and leave them for a few minutes to soak up some of the sauce. I add some parsley and serve this with a pilaf rice or spinach.

Albert had another excellent recipe, *l'émincé de rognons de veau au porto*. He removed the fat, cut the kidneys very fine, and sautéed them quickly. He then made a port sauce with some veal stock, and added cranberries. He cooked the kidneys for just thirty seconds in this somewhat sweet and sour sauce, and served the dish with fresh pasta. The regulars used to delight in these two recipes because they could tell from the menu which of the brothers was working in the kitchen that evening.

It was more difficult to sell *ris de veau*, or sweetbreads. Sweetbreads come from the calf's throat and, for some reason, this put many people off. There are two parts: the kernel, which should be very white in colour and firm; and a longer, more fibrous part which I discard. I wash the sweetbread, then blanch it and cool it again. After removing the nerves, I then press the sweetbread between two cloths with a weighted plate on top to make it keep its shape. My favourite way of cooking it is whole with a few slivers of fresh truffle inserted with a sharp knife. I sauté it in clarified butter to form a crunchy golden exterior, like a thin caramel layer. Inside, the flesh should be unctuous, like fresh cream.

In the early 1980s when I went to water my herb garden one day, I noticed that the tarragon had gone and very little of the chives and flat parsley remained. I stormed off to the kitchen, demanding to know who had ravaged my herbs. Michel Perraud, then my chef, owned up, saying he was preparing a new dish. He had taken a whole calf's liver, a big one, covered it in herbs and wrapped it in pork caul, a lace-like veil of fat (used to make faggots in England). He then roasted it. We first served this in thin slices one Sunday. The ends were well cooked and it was rarer towards the middle, providing something for all tastes. We served it with a potato purée and a sauce containing a little Madeira. We have made the dish since, many times; my only regret is the depletion of my herb garden.

Another white meat that Albert and I promoted in Britain is *chevreau,* kid, which is usually found on the market for a few weeks around Easter. There is only enough for six portions in a kid, which is about the size of a big rabbit. It is very similar to the *agneau de lait,* or milk-fed lamb. At Le Gavroche, we served kid from very early on, cooked at the very last minute. I sautéed some whole garlic cloves in their skins in foaming butter in a frying pan, and then put in the pieces of kid. I sprinkled thyme leaves over this and cooked the meat on all sides, leaving it pinkish near the bone. I melted more butter until foaming in another pan, then added a hint of chopped garlic with some breadcrumbs that I tossed until lightly toasted. I added chopped parsley and snipped tarragon and then poured this mixture over the plated kid. I liked to serve it with mangetout and carrots. When the slightly pink meat was cut and the juices mingled with the sauce, the effect on the palate was sublime. We were the first to serve kid in Britain, just after Britain joined the Economic Community in 1973. By then, we had enough regular customers who trusted us enough 'to give it a try'.

I tasted one of the best kid dishes I have ever had one Easter in Portugal. I was buying port from the Symingtons, a British family of port and Madeira shippers and growers whose port brands include Graham's and Dow's. The kid was roasted with roughly chopped lemons fresh from their garden and whole cloves of garlic. It was served with green cabbage, carrots and tossed potatoes, a simple garnish that was ideal with such delicate meat. The lemons brought out the flavour of the kid, and I thought it so delicious that I ate several helpings, even sucking the bones. (They had to call for a finger bowl for me, because I was behaving so badly!) The dish was prepared by a local woman cook, not a chef, but I could not have done better myself.

White Meat

On my first visit to China in 1980, I suffered several culture shocks. The first was seeing the disgraceful state of the animals in Beijing Zoo: they were hungry, skinny, dirty and unhappy. Another was attending a classical music concert to which Chinese peasants with no interest in the proceedings had been bussed in. They chatted, spat on the floor, walked around on the creaking wooden floor of the concert hall and even farted loud and strong while the conductor and the Beijing Symphony Orchestra soldiered on. Then, when I was walking through the city in freezing temperatures, I saw skinny pig carcasses, frozen by the weather rather than by any refrigeration process, thrown from a truck on to the roadway, pavement and even into the gutter, for delivery to a hotel restaurant. How different from Europe where Brussels now requires us to note the temperature inside the refrigerated trucks which deliver meat to restaurants! However, the fat from those same pigs was used to flavour some of the best rice dishes I have ever eaten.

The pork I buy comes from a farmer on the border between Essex and Suffolk. I know the breeder and I know his pigs are happy pigs. He delivers them whole which, as with red meat, means we can keep it on the bone until served. We make *pâté de tête* from its head, especially for serving in canapés. We only ever say it is a little pâté, omitting to mention that we have used the tongue, cheek and ears, because many customers might send it back. Sometimes we tell them the contents of the pâté later, and hear remarks like, 'Oh dear, what have I done?'

From the rest of the carcass, we make stew and *goulash* for the staff and keep some for making game or poultry terrines, which always need some pork meat and fat. We sometimes serve roast loin or legs with all the trimmings for Sunday lunch in the restaurant. We used to make hams in the good old days, putting the legs in salt, but we stopped, however, as it is a long process, and very tedious.

As a young man, I also used to visit Les Halles to go to the twenty-four-hour Pied de Cochon restaurant in the early hours. There I would eat a grilled pig's trotter in breadcrumbs with *béarnaise* sauce and *pont-neuf* potatoes. I would walk this off by touring the market to watch the trucks disgorging their produce. The restaurant and the dish exist to this day.

A pig's trotter is something that Pierre Koffmann, one of my former chefs and a cooks' cook, has developed into a signature dish at La Tante Claire. His is boned, filled with a stuffing that includes veal sweetbread and truffles, and then braised in a rich stock. Pierre's cooking is real, back-to-the-roots cuisine. He brought to the restaurants of both the Roux brothers much pleasure and a lot of professionalism, and was responsible for training a multitude of youngsters over the years.

For training is vital, and only a few places now have butchery as part of the professional kitchen. When someone new joins my kitchen, he or she has to cut his or her teeth on preparation, cutting meat, learning how to use boning knives, cleavers and saws. But the practical side is not all they learn. I like to watch new recruits at work to gauge their attitude and see how they work under pressure. My preference is for people with basic experience but not much more than that so that I can hone their skills along my own lines. They must all be tidy and organised and clean their work table after each preparation. I consider these methods have proven themselves because I have never had spoilt brats or a primadonna in my kitchen. I insist on team work and we all have to help each other. If ever I see one of my staff pushing another around, I grab him and make him apologise in front of everyone. If it happens again, he goes.

In our early days at Le Gavroche, Albert and I worked together in the kitchen during the day and took turns in the dining-room. One week, I would take the orders in my dinner jacket, with Albert staying in the kitchen. The next week, Albert would serve and I would cook. One of the major differences between our cooking was the size of the portions. Albert used to chew me out for being mean, while I considered his portions too big to the point of being ungainly for real gastronomy.

People rarely came to the restaurant more than once a week. Fortunately, when one of our more famous visitors came, for three evenings in a row, and ordered exactly the same dishes each time, it was the same configuration.

Sir Charles Chaplin was in England in the early 1970s and came once to Le Gavroche, then booked again for the next two nights. Each time, he ate a *soufflé suissesse* followed by *veau à l'ananas*. He signed the visitors' book with a little drawing of his famous cane. The portions, incidentally, were mine. I was in the kitchen that week.

Poultry

O NE OF THE first things I learned in history lessons at school was that King Henri IV, who led France into the seventeenth century, wanted all his subjects to be opulent enough to cook a *poule au pot* on Sundays. This chicken stewed with vegetables is not only a nourishing meal in itself, but it also provides the chicken stock that can be an ingredient for so many other things. By underlining the importance of this dish, Henri IV could perhaps be described as one of the most important culinary figures of France!

For me, this was something of a revelation since I had no idea as a small child that chickens were there to be eaten. My only knowledge of poultry had been Julie the hen who was our pet when I was a toddler, and her sole connection to our meal table was as an infrequent egg supplier. In fact, the variety of poultry available is enormous, and includes all birds reared for the table, among them pigeons, guinea fowl, goose, quail, turkey and duck. Until a few years ago, capon – a young cockerel castrated in order to become fatter – could be included in this listing, but it is now illegal in Britain, although capons can be enjoyed elsewhere in Europe. A few years ago on our way to Shaun Hill's Restaurant, we saw a sign for the Wernlas Collection in Ludlow, 'a living museum of rare poultry'. We took the turning, imagining a fleeting visit of ten minutes. Three hours later we were still there, completely mesmerised. There were forty different breeds of chicken, of such astonishing variety and beauty they quite took our breath away. Though in truth their bodies were all much the same, their feathers gave them an amazing variety of shapes, colours and sizes; and their eggs were similarly varied.

I had my first taste of chicken when I was ten or eleven, on the day of my first communion. I remember vividly the smell of that roast chicken when we went home to our flat, my nostrils registering something new. There were eight of us, and I ate a drumstick. I took care not to stain my clothes, especially my new grey tie. I remember the sensation when I bit into the skin, and found this to be the best piece of the bird. After that, I enjoyed sucking the bones. I liked the meat, but the skin and bones gave me the most pleasure. My favourite piece of the actual flesh is the soft, dark meat of a chicken's back, the underneath of a roasted chicken, which is known in English as the 'oyster' or *'sot-l'y-laisse'* in French. This means literally 'the silly one leaves it'.

Later, as an apprentice in Monsieur Loyal's *pâtisserie*, I was to see masses of poultry when our customers brought their Sunday roasts to be cooked in our pastry ovens. The chickens they brought were plump and healthy, their skin smooth and not in the least uneven. Their beaks – chickens in those days often still had their heads on – could be easily bent, proving that they were young. The wings, too, were flexible and the legs, especially the 'knees', were plump, a sure sign of quality. The customers attached a note to their birds with the time they wanted to collect them. Some of them put potatoes, onions or carrots in their roasting tins to cook alongside the chicken. It was my job as the newest apprentice to prepare the chickens and then to take my big wooden spade and push them into the coolest of our ovens, to allow them to cook slowly, forty-five minutes for a small bird, seventy-five minutes for a big one. I turned and basted them several times during roasting. It was a chore that I enjoyed even if I was a little frustrated since I could not, as I would have liked, pluck off a bit of skin and share in the meal. I did on occasion dip my finger furtively in the sauce to get a taste. When the customers came to reclaim their lunch, the boss's wife would call me on the intercom to bring the relevant roast to the shop, and I felt a wrench as my work was taken away. Some customers gave me a tip; I would have preferred a piece of their chicken.

When I was serving in the army in Algeria, I was posted to the B2-Namous base near Colom-Béchar in the Sahara desert which, I later discovered through press articles, was an experimental chemical warfare station. Fortunately for me, no active exercises were carried out in my time.

One day, outside with my Lebel service rifle, I killed a little bustard with one shot. The bird was like an oversized farm hen or capon and was technically out of range. My tastebuds must have been guiding my trigger finger that day for me to be so lucky. Cooking was my job, so I brought it back to the camp and plucked it while still warm, then covered my fingers in peanut oil and pushed some snipped parsley in between the breasts and skin. Other more powerful herbs like rosemary or thyme would have been too strong for such fine meat.

I had a choice between keeping the bird hanging in the cold room for two or three days until the meat matured or cooking it immediately. Out of sheer greed, because I was in a hurry to see this rare example of poultry on a plate, I decided to prepare it for that day's dinner. I cooked it for over two hours with some chunks of carrot and onion. As I basted it, I revelled in the meat's change in colour from off-white to hazel. I pan-fried some potatoes to a light golden colour then put them around the bird for the last 20 minutes or so. The result was incomparable. The flesh was plump, meaty, moist and juicy, slightly unexpected for a bird living in the desert. I would have thought it to be slightly gamey in flavour, but the taste and texture were more like capon, dense and rich. There were six of us round the table but there was enough meat for eight to ten people; nonetheless, in under ten minutes, it had all been stripped off the carcass. For us desert dwellers, this was a true feast.

After I left the army, I used to prepare a turkey every New Year's Eve for Cécile de Rothschild. This would always be a gift from a friend and come from the Dombes region near Lyons. One important detail I learned then was that, in every large piece of poultry, it is important to remove the nerves from the legs which, in a turkey (or capon), are very thick. To do this, you must make an incision in the leg just above the claws, twist a needle under the nerves that go the full length of the leg and pull them out one by one. This guarantees a bird that is completely tender. Another good tip that few people know about is removing the wishbone before cooking for easier carving. The skin of the neck needs to be pulled back and the wishbone eased out with the point of a knife. The skin is then folded back into the opening.

When I cooked the Rothschilds' New Year turkey, I would buy a second bird to make the sauce. The meat from this would be used for a staff meal. I filled this staff turkey with a pork stuffing containing eggs, herbs, shallots and chopped mushrooms. I put this in the neck after taking out the wishbone. I sewed up the neck and roasted the bird, saving the carcass and bones afterwards for my sauce. (Cooked poultry bones should always be kept to make and flavour soups.) I would cook the main turkey slowly in a very low oven to keep it soft, adding a little water from time to time.

A turkey recipe that Albert and I tried *en masse* in 1980 at the Krug Awards of Excellence ceremony provided a new test of logistics. The champagne house had asked us to cater for about 150 in the Banqueting House in Whitehall. The setting was magnificent, and the guests – the men in tails and the women in evening dress – matched it in elegance. But those same guests had no inkling of the chamber of horrors down below in third class where we were cooking. There was no real kitchen so we had to prepare our food in advance and finish off the cooking on the spot with the help of hired refrigerated trucks and gas burners. It was part of what was becoming a permanent learning curve!

Britain produces good-quality turkeys and we decided to make a *pavé de dindonneau en blanquette*. We took thick turkey escalopes, removed the skin, cut them into four even-sized slices and stuffed them with a turkey mousse. The meat for the mousse, taken from the trimmings and the rest of the bird, was mixed in a blender with egg whites, then double cream was worked in gradually to obtain a light and smooth consistency. We slit the even-sized slices and filled the cavities with the mousse and two prunes. The escalopes were cooked in a pan for two minutes on each side, removed, wrapped in aluminium foil and then finished in the oven for ten minutes before serving with an Armagnac and poultry stock sauce thickened with cream.

At this event, people like Rudolf Nureyev, John Cleese, Lord Olivier and Sir John Gielgud, as well as some of Britain's leading medical researchers, like Professor Sir Richard Doll, were called to the podium to receive Salvador Dali bronzes from Princess Alexandra. The evening turned into a huge surprise for us when Albert and I were unexpectedly summoned as well, for our work for gastronomy in Britain.

I used to prepare spring chickens or *poussins* for Cécile de Rothschild, her favourite being a *poussin crapaudine*. The spine and ribcage were removed, and the bird was opened into a butterfly shape, held in place with cocktail sticks. I used to egg and breadcrumb the *poussins*, then sauté them in foaming butter with herbs and serve them with thin slices of bacon. When Cécile de Rothschild sent me to the 1964 wine harvest at Château Lafite to cater for the family, I barbecued poussins over vine twigs. I was not used to cooking with the twigs, which made for a violent and strong fire, so I always brought extra birds with me in case some were charred. Nothing could beat the taste, however. I would usually end up with a couple of uncooked birds, and these I cooked for my *commis* chefs in the kitchen or the young women who came to clean up. For them, I brushed the birds with clarified butter and served them with a butter flavoured with tarragon and lemon juice, and a garnish of little south-western French tomatoes cooked in the oven with a drop of olive oil. Our wines, as might be expected, consisted of different vintages of Château Lafite, the leftovers in the decanters from the family table. None of us complained about the blend in our glasses!

Cold chicken needs special attention. When my brother Albert and I cooked our picnic chicken for our fishing trips in Kent, we did so the evening before. Once it was out of the oven, we turned it upside down so that the juices would flow into the breasts, to give them more taste and keep them moist. We left the chicken in the larder overnight, never in the refrigerator. The juices in a chicken always provide the clue to how cooked it is. When the juice is clear, the bird is ready; if there is no juice, it is nowhere near ready; if the juice is pink, the bird needs more cooking. We would make a mayonnaise to go with our picnic chicken or take some pickles then eat the bird with our fingers. The simplest foods are often the best, and the only secret is to start with a good-quality chicken.

In the mid-1960s, my mother-in-law used to raise chickens and rabbits in her village near Senlis in Picardy. We used to eat a lot of oysters and she would throw the oyster shells into the yard for the chickens to pick clean. Between that, vegetable peelings and, perhaps surprisingly, the cold ash from the fire, nothing was lost and the animals were eating proper, healthy food. The chickens not only pecked at the ash – which, like the oyster shells, was good for their egg shells – but they used to roll themselves in it with their feathers fluffed out so that they looked twice the size, apparently taking great pleasure in having a very dusty bath. My mother-in-law killed her chickens herself, and would pluck and draw them as well.

Her great pleasure was having all her children and grandchildren for Sunday lunches when she would cater for a dozen or more people, cooking her chickens or rabbits. These she kept in the same part of the garden – in much the same 'habitat' – in adjacent caged runs. She cooked her chickens and rabbits simply. She would also make rabbit pâtés, taking the less noble parts of the animal and putting them through her hand-mincer which was screwed to a corner of her kitchen table. She would throw in some parsley, thyme and tarragon from the garden, always too much garlic, and never weighed anything. She would lay some pork fat in the bottom of a terrine that she had inherited from her mother, a blackened dish that was probably about 100 years old, put the pâté mixture on top and cook it.

After these lunches, the adults would play *boules* on the road outside the house. It was just a hamlet and no cars ever came through. This helped us digest our meals while the children played in the farm buildings, or picked strawberries, raspberries and redcurrants. She was very upset when we had to leave for England – in those days, it seemed a long way – because she was going to see less of her grandchildren.

The happiest times that Albert and I shared were undoubtedly the first years of our work together at Le Gavroche. It was then that I realised that my brother excelled in cooking poultry. He used to make a *poulet poêlé mon coeur*, pot-roasted chicken. He took the breasts and thighs and cooked them in a cast-iron casserole on a very low heat so they did not brown. Then he added some dry Martini, a hint of paprika, and a dollop of the cream that he adored . . . *et voilà!* The dish was garnished with turned cucumber, peeled and de-pipped grapes, and a heart-shaped *croûton*. When we worked together in the kitchen, he would always suggest I get on with the fish or the desserts while he handled the poultry. His trick was never to let his chicken dishes boil, and to use only a little liquid. I had usually cooked whole birds up until then, and poultry in pieces requires a different technique and approach. Our poultry cooking styles were divergent, especially in portioning, and some of our regular customers could recognise the differences and guess accurately who had made their dish that day.

From the mid-1970s, I went to the Beaujolais in the spring of every other year to buy wine for our restaurants. This was when I discovered the full pleasures of *coq au vin*. Georges Duboeuf, the wine-merchant and grower whose name is synonymous with the region's wines, used to invite me to a different restaurant each time so that I could experience a variety of *coq au vin* dishes. These experiences prompted me to start making *coq au vin* myself. For me, it has to be made from a bird that has lived, a real tough cock with character, even a bit chewy, but not too old. (I always think that twelve months is too short a time to give enough flavour to my pot, two years old is superannuated, and eighteen months is just perfect.) The sauce should contain large mushrooms, button onions, and thumb-sized pieces of bacon that are not added too early in the cooking since this would overwhelm the sauce.

I serve *coq au vin* mainly for my lunch-time menus in winter because it is not regarded as a 'delicate' dish, rather something that warms the heart and fills the belly. I always have it with boiled potatoes, and a special treat is mashing the potato into the rich, copious sauce. Like many dishes in sauce, it is often better in terms of flavour to make it for ten or even twenty people, using at least three or four chickens. If I make it with a Beaujolais, I will use a Moulin à Vent or a Pinot Noir from Burgundy, like a Côtes de Nuit. You only get good sauces from good wines; when you use light, acidic wines, you get light, acidic sauces. One last hint: keep back a drumstick from *coq au vin* for a snack in the morning. This is delicious sliced on a piece of bread with some cold sauce (see p. 246).

In the 1960s, some modern Henri IVs decided there must be chickens for everyone, and they started churning out battery hens. You could buy them very cheaply in Britain and in France. I bought some for staff meals, but not for long. When they were roasted, instead of turning a golden brown, the skin would blister and burn; there was no juice and the flesh smelled and tasted of fish since many of them were reared on fish-based feed. You could almost eat the bones together with the flesh without noticing. Now, thankfully, the battery chicken has largely had its day.

The irony is that battery hens were produced on a continent where there are so many hygiene and public health regulations. I realised during a trip to Hong Kong that such concerns are not shared by all. There, when I was at the market choosing ingredients for meals I was to cook in the Mandarin Hotel, I came across a poultry 'slaughter-house'. Chickens were hanging by their feet in a line and a man decapitated them in turn with the jagged top of a tin. Blood was spurting everywhere, but this did not seem to bother the Chinese, who walked by without paying any attention. When the blood stopped flowing, the chickens were thrown into cauldrons of boiling water for a minute or two, then put into cold water in front of kneeling men and women who plucked them, ready for further cooking. They were full of flavour, so perhaps Brussels should go and have a look at Hong Kong. . .

Britain has never been very rich in poultry in terms of quality, although things are improving. However, there are now so many labels, in France and the UK, that it is confusing for the customer: we have red labels, superior quality labels, maize-fed, organic, semi-liberty and free-range labels. Today's housewife virtually needs a special dictionary in order to choose a chicken! After Britain's entry into the European Community in 1973, my brother and I began importing poultry from France. We brought in chicken from Les Landes, which have yellow feet, and have been fed on maize, and come with a label of quality and origin. We also offered France's most reputed chickens, those from Bresse near Lyons. With the latter we came up against some problems, though. Many of our British customers disliked them, claiming that the skin was tough and elastic, and even that the bones were too hard – which only goes to show how people can lose their taste for good things. Occasionally at both Le Gavroche and the Waterside Inn, our chicken dishes would be sent back, because the flesh near the bones was a little pink, rather than the pure white they were used to. Sometimes it was a bit like a tennis match, with the dish being carried to and fro from dining-room to kitchen and back again, backwards and forwards. However, I won the tournament. We decided to hold out, and our faith in our beliefs and in the ultimate (and belated) good sense of our customers has been justified. Many have returned to taste our chickens again, and chicken dishes remain central to our menus in both restaurants. Once more, we have been pioneers, and pioneers always have to take the flak.

After I obtained my third Michelin star in 1985, I took off with Michel Perraud, my chef, and Olivier Ferretjean, my restaurant manager, for a celebratory tour of three other three-star establishments in the Lyons area. We went to the restaurants of Georges Blanc, Alain Chapel and Paul Bocuse. We ate poultry, given that we were in the best poultry-producing region of France, for almost every meal. Paul Bocuse cooked a chicken in a pig's bladder, something that health regulations – or perhaps simply ignorance – would not allow us to do in Britain at that time. The chicken was brought into the dining-room in the swollen bladder and carved in front of us. As the bladder was cut open, a dense steam arose, enveloping us in a marvellous aroma of chicken, truffle and *foie gras*. Truffle had been thinly sliced and inserted between flesh and skin, and the bird was served with the rice, peas and *foie gras* that had been used as a stuffing. Those disparate flavours had united to a marriage of perfection, and that dish will remain one of the most vivid memories of my life.

At Bray, customers often tease me about the ducks on the Thames, asking if the duck on their plates came from the river. Every spring, we watch the arrival of the new ducklings; some of them even hatch in our flower-beds, where we do our best not to disturb them. In the evenings, it is not uncommon to see a duck leading her ducklings for a swim under the Waterside Inn's spotlights. What can ruin this charming spectacle is when a duckling suddenly disappears, snapped up by a pike, a sight that takes your breath away. The mothers see nothing and carry on swimming. This at least proves that pike like good things.

In 1976, I entered for my most coveted award, that of *Meilleur Ouvrier de France* – the 'best craftsman of France' – in two categories, cooking and *pâtisserie*. This was an unusual approach since it was a bit like entering the Olympics in two entirely different disciplines. I won for *pâtisserie*. In the cooking finals, we all had to make a *canard soufflé à la rouennaise*, one of the classic French recipes recorded by the great Escoffier, writer of the standard works of reference on French cuisine. This was a formidable task. The duck is first lightly roasted, remaining rare, then the breasts are removed. The top of the carcass is cut out with scissors to leave a hollow 'box'. The duck's liver and the raw meat from another half duck are used to make a *mousseline* in a food processor with an egg white to bind them. Some raw *foie gras* is added before the mixture is mixed and sieved. In a bowl over ice, double cream is worked in and seasoning is added to taste. This *mousseline* is then mounded up inside the carcass box to re-create the shape of the bird and smoothed with a palette knife. The duck, covered with buttered greaseproof paper, is then very lightly poached in a covered *bain-marie* in the oven. To serve, the duck carcass box is placed in the middle of a silver dish surrounded by some *croustades* of pastry, with slices of the duck breast placed on each. A *sauce rouennaise*, a bordelaise red-wine-based sauce to which a purée of the livers of two ducks and butter have been added, completes the dish and is served separately. It is a dish that requires exceptional skill as the fifty finalists discovered. Only a handful achieved top marks.

Magrets, or breasts, of duck comes from a particular species of duck that have been fattened up in south-western France to make *foie gras.* A *magret* is thick, like a steak. We introduced them into Britain in the late 1970s, but the idea was slow to catch on. At first, we pan-fried and then roasted them with garlic and served them with a blackcurrant sauce. It is a meat that has to be eaten pink, rare or medium rare because well done, it is dry, hard and inedible. If customers ask for *magret* well done, we advise them to order something else. This was another of our battles, to convince the customer that the duck we served was different from the Aylesbury duck they were used to, whose soft flesh is covered in a lot of fat.

I also used duck in a dish that, since the the early 1980s, has appeared to enchant not only the customers but many of my staff, who were surprised at the result of the mixing of unexpected yet simple ingredients. I cooked a challandais duck with cloves, in a honey and lemon sauce. The duck is boiled in water for twenty minutes and then chilled. At the moment of ordering, I stud it with cloves, brush it with honey and lemon, and roast it for about twenty minutes. This is a dish that Diego Masciaga, my restaurant manager always carves in the dining-room – magic to watch, he makes it look so easy. In general, we see plate service – arranging food on the plate in the kitchen – as progress, since it has the advantage of ensuring that the dish stays at the right temperature. There are some things, however, that provide extra pleasure when the final serving is done before the customer. Not only is it fascinating visually, but the tantalising smell when the bird is carved can really set the tastebuds tingling. Waiters might often seem to be little more than cooks' slaves, but service in the dining-room is the next act in what should be a sort of ballet.

This was a dish I was to offer at a rather manic event in 1991 at the Dorchester where I was instrumental in setting up a fund-raising auction for the Duke of Edinburgh's Award Scheme. Some 170 guests were seated at tables in the Dorchester ballroom, but a few of the tables just in front of a rather unusual stage remained empty. On the stage were two beautifully appointed kitchens donated by suppliers of mine and specially built for the evening. Michael Broadbent of Christie's proceeded to auction a few dinner menus accompanied by some great wines, the latter generously offered by well-known wine-merchants and growers. Half the menus –

variously for two, four, six etc. – were to be cooked in front of the assembled company by Albert, half by me. Our natural rivalry came to the fore as the bidding proceeded, with banter, compliments and some downright rudeness between us, as we both fought for the highest bids. The twenty eventual winners then moved to the empty tables to watch their dinners being cooked. While they ate them, the rest of the guests enjoyed a dinner devised by me but cooked by the hotel kitchen staff. At the end of the evening, even the kitchens on stage were auctioned. Frank Bruno was very instrumental in encouraging bids for 'cookers that have been used by the chefs of the Waterside Inn and Le Gavroche. . .' The end-result was £70,000 for the charity.

In the early years at Le Gavroche, we had to use Aylesbury ducks because nothing else was available. Once cooked, there would be three ladlefuls of fat left behind. Now many ducks consumed in Britain come from the Continent, including those sold by Marks & Spencer, to whom we introduced them. Albert and I pushed hard for this, force-feeding the British with quality poultry – like a south-western French farmer force-feeds his ducks for *foie gras* – until a majority understood and accepted it!

A less successful campaign was to introduce the *pintadeau*, the guinea fowl. We brought it in from Bresse, tried it with a classic tarragon sauce, cooked in champagne or just roasted and served with a macaroni *gratin* with *foie gras* and truffles in a cream sauce. The customers would eat the macaroni, truffles and *foie gras* but not the guinea fowl. I am stubborn so I keep going and have it on my menus from time to time, but I always know I am only going to sell a few portions.

On my first visit to Australia in 1983, I tasted a pigeon that was to become the classic turtle dove of romance. (I consider pigeon as poultry and not game in Australia, because traditional hunting is banned there.) I arrived in January after a tour of Asia, during the winter closure of the Waterside Inn, this had amounted to a series of visits to hotels, meetings with food and beverage staff, and little rest. Just after getting off my plane early in the morning, I called Leigh Herbert, one of my former cooks who had set himself up in Sydney. (That is one major advantage of training so many young cooks: I have contacts in most ports of call.) I told Leigh I wanted to eat that night in a good restaurant with someone, preferably female and attractive, who loved food and wine, and had a good sense of humour. There was a bit of a silence then Leigh said he would need to give this a lot of thought. He would call me back around lunch time.

When he did, he said he had found just the person. I was waiting in the foyer that evening when a white Porsche pulled up, driven by a young woman aged around thirty, a tanned brunette in a bright red dress. She drove me to Claude's, a small restaurant owned by Damien and Josephine Pignolet, who were the king and queen of Sydney cuisine. It had a distinctly European feel in terms of smell and decor. It was then that I was introduced to BYO – bring your own – wine. Robyn Joyce, my companion for the evening, had taken care of that and had brought a Petaluma, an Australian Chardonnay, and two vintages of Grange Hermitage, 1960 and 1971, which she had already decanted. One of the dishes we tasted was roast squab, or pigeon, with a golden skin, served on a bed of lentils. It came with a sauce that was rich and powerful (it must have been made from one or two other pigeons). For dessert, we had the most delicate passionfruit soufflés.

After Robyn dropped me off at my hotel, I could not sleep. My first marriage had broken up several years before, and I had no particular desire to become permanently involved again. However, the girl, the food and the wine had me hooked. Taking a cigar, I wandered through Sydney until three o'clock in the morning.

The feeling was mutual, and two weeks after my return to England, Robyn flew to join me. Then I was to discover, amongst other things, her own large repertoire of culinary talents. She was at ease cooking Thai, Indian and Chinese dishes, and one speciality is a Chinese-style duck. She takes an Aylesbury duck, puts it in an oven bag with hoisin, plum and soy sauces, chopped ginger and chopped garlic. She leaves this in the refrigerator overnight, then cooks it for ninety minutes in the oven. The smell when she cuts open the oven bag is fantastic. She serves it with Chinese vegetables and rice. It has always been a huge pleasure for me to eat things from outside the disciplines that I know and practice, and Robyn does this particular type of dish so well.

It was with poultry that I ushered in the third millennium. Planning to spend New Year's Eve at our house in the south of France as usual, I ordered a Bresse capon from my Saint Tropez butcher two weeks ahead of time. He was excited to hear that I was calling from England. I spent ten minutes on the phone as he made sure he had the exact weight and other details. I had truffles sent from the Rhône valley by special delivery post. I picked up the bird on 29 December 1999, and slipped slivers of truffle under its skin. I placed the truffle peelings inside, wrapped it in a cloth and left it for twenty-four hours in the refrigerator. I finally poached it in a chicken stock in a low oven for two hours. I accompanied it with a gratin of macaroni and truffles. When I carved the bird at the table, there was a black layer of truffles and creamy-white flesh. I made a simple sauce of chopped truffles in cream and poaching stock and served three vintages of Château Latour, 1978, 1982 and 1985.

The capon melted in the mouth, it hardly needed to be chewed. That meal marking our passage into the new millennium was like a firework display for the palate. It was the ultimate in gastronomy despite its simplicity: fine rich products simply prepared, and served with the greatest wines that France produces.

Game

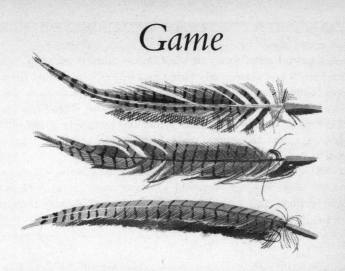

I FIRST REALLY began to hunt, and to understand the pleasures and *esprit de corps* of hunting, when I came to Britain. My hunting previously had been mainly limited to bizarre expeditions with army rifles in the Sahara to bag gazelles (and the occasional bustard) to feed my fellow soldiers during my military service.

Game is one of Britain's most important culinary resources, both big and small, feathered or four-legged. Britain has quality, quantity and variety, and all have a place in my heart, in my kitchen and on my plate. British game includes wild duck, hare, rabbit, wood pigeons, venison, woodcock, snipe, pheasants, partridges and, of course, grouse. Grouse is virtually unique to Britain, rivalled only by cousins that live in small numbers in the Pyrenees and Scandinavia. I marvelled at the choice of game when I arrived in London. We featured it a lot at Le Gavroche in the season, always as a speciality of the day, depending on what was available.

I discovered the pleasures of hunting in Norfolk the year after I settled in London. Hunting, in every country in the world, began as a necessity for survival, but now, when properly organised, it is classified as a sport and not at all as a killing spree. The main participants are country folk, people who respect the environment, tradition and the animals themselves. City-dwellers who think hunting should be abolished or controlled would be better employed dealing with the pollution in their cities, and with the life on the streets where they have chosen to live, and let those in the country carry on as they always have.

The first game I actually ever ate was Garenne rabbit, which is found all over the French countryside. My father poached rabbits during the war, using snares, and we ate them with great relish because meat was so scarce. I even had a rabbit-fur coat when we left Charolles for Paris. I must have looked as though I was from another planet, but I was very proud of that coat. It eventually disappeared, and I never really knew what had happened to it.

I also had some Garenne rabbit at the farm of the Girards, where I was sent for my health as a nine-year-old. That was about the only meat we experienced there, and I would suck the bones and even swallow the leadshot since I did not know what it was.

As a *pâtissier*, I had no experience of preparing game in the early days of my career, so my first proper introduction was at the British Embassy. That was when I also learned that all young cooks dread the game season. It is always the most junior who has to pluck and clean the game in any kitchen and at the Embassy we might have to pluck, for one meal alone, about thirty brace for 120! The down in the feathers gets everywhere and sticks to clothes and skin. A special knack is needed, twisting the feathers at the moment of pulling, to avoid tearing the bird and damaging the skin. I used to tell my cooks that plucking was an art. Now, however, we use machines that do a very good job, and all that is needed is a final, human check to ensure that every last feather stub has been extracted.

One game dish commonly served at the Embassy was pheasant or partridge *en chartreuse*. This involved braising curly kale, a tough but tasty cabbage, for several hours, with an old, tough or damaged bird, first browned on all sides, in the middle to give it taste. Once cooked, the kale was drained. Some blanched Savoy cabbage leaves were used to line a special mould – a pudding bowl would do if not many servings were needed. The kale was then laid in layer by layer, with thin strips of belly of pork separating the first two layers, then pre-cooked and sliced *saucisson* between the next two, then fillets of flesh from a lightly roasted pheasant or partridge on the next. Particular attention had to be paid to the quality of the *charcuterie* used, ensuring that it came from a good craftsman, since poor *saucisson* could ruin the dish. This layered mould was then put in a gentle oven for around one and a half hours, so that the flavours would combine to become a *chartreuse*. After that, it was drained, then turned out of the mould, brushed with clarified butter and served with a sauce made from the carcasses of the game. Accompanied by a fine, full-bodied Burgundy, this was a very high-class dish. It was only ever made for a service of up to ten people since it was not practical for greater numbers. To make it look more imposing, it was served in a dish resting on a *socle* of hollowed and baked loaf with a decoration of pheasant feathers that tickled guests' noses. The waiters were forbidden to sneeze as they served, for had they done so, it would have been a disaster!

In my army days in the Sahara, Foreign Legionnaires at my base used to organise hunting parties to kill gazelles every two weeks or so. Apart from the frozen hindquarter of beef we received every month, this was our only meat. I used to dry the skins, treat them with salt and send them to my mother as carpets. They were not properly treated, however: they lost their hair, and my mother finally asked me to stop sending them!

I went hunting with around a dozen legionnaires in open-topped four-wheel-drive army trucks, and we would shoot with our service rifles. These expeditions were usually good-natured and pleasant but, on occasion, a legionnaire would get carried away, leaving his gun firing on automatic, for example. This would tear a gazelle to pieces, making it useless for cooking. Our hunting expeditions were often quite hair-raising as well. As soon as the drivers saw gazelle in the distance, they would lose all notion of caution and charge after them, which meant the rest of us had to hold on or risk falling out as we bounced over rocks and dunes. It might be hard to believe, but I once saw a driver push down the accelerator with his hand, block the steering wheel with his feet and use his free hand to discharge a round of automatic fire at the gazelles we were following. One of his bullets even grazed my head, leaving a mark at the roots of my hair! (For this behaviour, the driver was punished. His officers made him dig a hole in the middle of the camp and live in it for three days, shielded from the sun by a tent, with only one water bottle a day. He then spent a week in hospital recovering.)

We usually bagged around ten gazelles. Most were killed instantly but, of those that were just wounded, I would always slaughter one by cutting its throat to conform to Islamic butchery laws. This blood-letting enabled

Chougui, my Algerian assistant and a good Moslem, to join our meals. This ritual sickened me and I did it with a heavy heart, only out of friendship for Chougui. Back at the base, I would use the gazelle for a different dish every day, roasted, jugged or barbecued in a North African-style *mechoui,* cooking a whole animal on a spit. I kept the best legs and salted them to make a sort of raw ham. This was not exactly Parma, but I was pleased with it. We would eat this several weeks later or I would give it to friends who were going back to France at the end of their military service. I grilled the liver, a very tasty part of the animal, on the spit, or cut it into chunks with peppers and onions and barbecued it on a skewer. I would turn the meat into *goulash* or cook it like *boeuf bourguignon,* in a rich, Algerian red-wine sauce. I could have written a gazelle cookery book by the end of the ten months I lived in the Sahara, but I would have had little chance of winning the Glenfiddich Award for doing so. . .

As in so much of my career, it was with the Rothschilds that I really got to know game. There, the game served was never bought in a shop but arrived in the form of gifts. The Comte de Paris, the pretender to the French throne, used to bring game or send it with his chauffeur after a hunting party. Most often, he gave Cécile de Rothschild pheasants or partridge. Her brothers, Elie and, occasionally, Alain, did the same. I used to hang the game for between three and five days in the cold store. Cécile de Rothschild, rightly, did not like it too high in taste.

One of the dishes I used to prepare was saddle of hare interlarded with strips of back fat and roasted. I brushed it with clarified butter and put it in the oven with diced carrots, shallots and thyme. I cooked it very lightly for five to seven minutes in a very hot oven so that it was still pink, took the meat out and let it rest, covered in foil. I then deglazed the roasting pan with a dash of cognac and made a sauce with the other parts of the hare and the bones, mixed with a drop of cream. I served the fillets cut lengthwise and re-formed in the shape of the saddle. I put spinach on one side and little butter-tossed mushrooms on the other. As in all cuisine that is truly excellent, it was simple.

It was Cécile de Rothschild who taught me that the best pheasant to cook was a hen; as a result she was only ever offered hens. They had to be young and she always reminded me 'to slip a *petit suisse* [cream cheese] *dans le cul* [in its arse],' which kept the flesh moist and tender. Venison I used to buy young so that it did not need to be marinated, and I would interlard it with pork fat, add some bay leaves and thyme, then leave it for a day in the refrigerator wrapped in greaseproof paper (now we would use clingfilm) before cooking. I often served this with braised chicory ('Chef, chicory cleanses you, like a glass of water'), a slightly runny chestnut purée and a *sauce grand veneur*. This is a classic sauce for game, made with trimmings of the game, shallots and red-wine vinegar, veal and game stock to which some redcurrant jelly and a little cream are added just before serving.

Albert and I had never done much in the way of hunting until 1968, a year after we opened Le Gavroche, when we were invited to Wensum Farm at Elsing in Norfolk. Our trips were soon to become a regular event, and we started bringing along friends such as Tony Batistella, our Italian restaurant manager, or Guy Mouilleron, our chef from south-west France who was a specialist at home in hunting *palombe,* or wood pigeon. We quickly made friends in Norfolk, joining up with Peter Jones, the owner of the neighbouring Hall Farm. We soon formed a hunting syndicate together that kept going for some twenty years.

We would all bring something for our picnics. Jean Cellier, chef at the Mount Royal Hotel, would bring cold leg of lamb or chicken. Tony would bring half a Brie cheese and some crusty French *baguettes*. Albert and I would bring some *bourguignon* ham and *pâté de campagne* from our delicatessen, Le Cochon Rose, and bottles of Georges Duboeuf's Brouilly. I would always make a huge apple tart. We ate all this near the gamekeeper's lodge when the weather was fine and huddled inside our cars if it rained or was too cold.

Later, as our numbers grew, we would take lunch at the local pub, the Mermaid. We often had tinned tomato soup and a dish like Irish stew or a Lancashire hot-pot. With the landlord's agreement, we brought our own wine from Le Gavroche. The hunters, their families, the beaters and the local farmhands, with their weather-beaten faces, all enlivened these mealtimes with their conversation and jokes, which took me a little time to understand because of their strong Norfolk accents. At the end of the day's hunting, before Albert and I had to rush back to London to open Le Gavroche, we would have tea with scones, apple or mince pies made by Peter Jones's wife, Joan, and their three daughters.

Albert used to bring his two labradors, the golden Sultane and black Gavroche. Our friend, neighbour and regular customer of Le Gavroche, Anthony Stanbury, brought Conner, his red setter. Albert's labradors were not too well behaved, but Conner was much worse. He ran everywhere, making the game fly away before a shot was fired. Perhaps, as a result, our bag was usually modest – about thirty pheasants, a few partridges, some woodcock and a couple of rabbits – but these days out were extremely salutory, allowing us to get some fresh air and to relax. At first, none of us except Anthony was really well equipped. I wore a suede jacket, until I traded it in for a Barbour, and my old army shoes on my feet. The latter had been all right in the desert, but were useless in the damp. My first gun, a double-barrelled Falcor that I had bought at the La Samaritaine department store in Paris, looked decidedly amateurish alongside British Purdeys or Holland & Hollands.

I never grew tired of that flat Norfolk countryside, with its ever-changing skies and those high, thick hedges where wild pheasants liked to hide. On the frequent days when winds were high, partridges were pushed along at the speed of tennis-balls, giving the slip to many a shotgun. Reluctantly, the pressure of work began to mean that I cancelled my visits to Norfolk more and more frequently, and I stopped going altogether in the mid-1980s.

In 1970, I was on a wine-buying trip to Alsace when I called in un-announced at L'Auberge de l'Ill at Illhaeusern, a Michelin three-star restaurant some forty miles from Strasbourg. Jean-Pierre Haeberlin, the brother of the chef and the man running the dining-room, told me the restaurant was fully booked but he set up a small table just for me. He told me he would choose my menu. First, I had a *mousseline* of frogs' legs, an Haeberlin speciality, and then he brought me a slice of hare, a *lièvre à la royale*. The hare had been prepared for a party of about a dozen people there that evening. The stuffing in the hare was sensual, rich and powerful, and this marvellous dish was accompanied by a Chambertin Clos-de-Bèze that was about twenty years old. My only regret was that there was no-one with whom to share this meal.

There are about as many individual recipes for this particular hare dish as there are cheeses in France. It used to be a favourite in aristocratic houses but, like some other old recipes, time has killed it. It simply takes

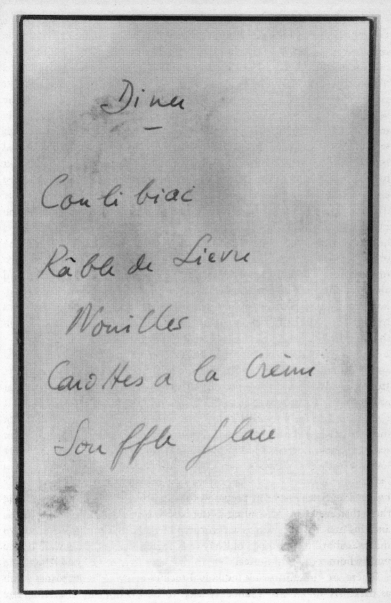

A menu handwritten by Cécile de Rothschild

too many hours and too much work to be viable. Thus it was to be twenty-five years before I would eat another, when Alain, my son, who was then in his late twenties, got hold of a hare and decided to cook it the same way. It had to be a big hare, about six to eight pounds in weight, and ideally one that had been shot in the head, so that its body had not lost any blood and its flesh was not riddled with lead. Alain removed all the bones, working from the inside, and cleaned the cavity out with a little wine vinegar (taking care to keep the vinegar and blood mixture that resulted to one side in a bowl). The hare was then marinated for twelve hours in red wine – a full-bodied Burgundy like a Hautes Côtes de Nuits is ideal – with orange peel, herbs, onions, pepper, carrots, chunks of celery and a head of garlic.

Then, Alain filled the hare with a stuffing which required twenty-one ingredients, including pork fat, fillet of pork, loin of pork, and the liver, heart, lungs, tongue, cheeks and feet of the hare, with herbs, cognac and port. This was all minced and put inside the hare in layers, with a fine slice of calf's liver laid between each layer. The hare was then re-formed and sewn up. Wrapped in a cloth like a sausage, the hare was lightly simmered, never coming to the boil, in its marinade in the oven for around two and a half hours. After that, the marinade was reduced and, once off the boil, the mixture of vinegar and blood added to thicken the sauce.

Alain's expertise at making this dish convinced me that he had stamina and true culinary talent, and he has now been working with me at the Waterside Inn for the past eight years. The time will come soon, I fear, that my job as chef-patron will be under siege. . .

In an old recipe I found for this royal dish, for presentation, the skin of the animal should be stuffed and seated on a throne in the dining room with a crown on its head!

I have a somewhat simpler recipe for hare, a form of *civet*, or jugged hare, cooked in red wine. Albert and I have always loved this dish, *l'estouffade de lièvre quercinois*. We always worked on the basis that when we drew up menus we really were making dishes for ourselves, even if we were happy to serve them to customers as well. In the early days of Le Gavroche, some things were difficult to sell, such as dishes containing lamb brains. Hare was another. Albert and I might sell one or two portions in an evening but would console ourselves with the thought that there would be enough left

A Historic Wine Tasting

(for the wines tasted see pp. 211–12)

Les plus grands chefs du monde chez Louis Jadot
6 April 1992

The Chefs were photographed here separately from the Masters of
Wine - but they were there! here I first met Robert Parker, in the
days before he struck terror into wine-growers' hearts.

On the front row from left to right:

Georges Perier
Albert Roux
Michel Roux
Roger Vergé
S. Vrinat
André Gagey
Paul Bocuse
Pierre-Henry Gagey
Jean-Claude Vrinat
Pierre Troisgros

On the 2nd row from left to right:

Jacques Lameloise
Jean-Pierre Haeberlin
D. Bouley
Alain Ducasse
J.L. Palladin
Marc Meneau
Georges Blanc
H. Ishinabe
F. Jyo
Jacques Pic
P. Guillou
Emile Jung

On the 3rd row from left to right:

Raymond Blanc
Michel Lorain
B. Pacaud
J.C. Bourgueil
S. Maccioni
H. van Raust
F. Santin
Gualtiero Marchesi
Alain Senderens

September 1977
Les 40 Ans d'Alain Chapel

1 Roger Roucou (Lyon)
2 Marcel Kreusch (Brussels)
3 Fredy Girardet (Crissier, Switzerland)
4 Hans Stucki (Basel)
5 Michel Guérard (Eugénie-les-Bains)
6 Alain Chapel (Mionnay)
7 François Bise (Talloires)
8 Mme Mado Point (Vienne)
9 Louis Outhier (La Napoule)
10 Gérard Vié (Versailles)
11 Michel Roux (Bray)
12 Mme Gaston Brazier (Lyon)
13 Jean Troisgros (Roanne)
14 Charles Barrier (Tours)
15 Paul Haeberlin (Illhaeusern)
16 Jacques Pic (Valence)
17 Jean-Claude Vrinat (Paris)
18 Michel Lorain (Joigny)
19 Roger Vergé (Mougins)
20 Rémy Krug (Reims)
21 Louis Vaudable (Paris)
22 René Lasserre (Paris)
23 Michel Chabran (Pont-de-l'Isère)
24 Paul Bocuse (Collonges-au-Mont-d'Or)
25 Pierre Troisgros (Roanne)
26 Gaston Lenôtre (Paris)
27 Emile Tingaut (La Ferté-sous-Jouarre – Président des Maîtres Cuisiniers de France)
28 Emile Jung (Strasbourg)
29 Pierre Wynants (Brussels)
30 Lucien Ogier (Pontchartrain – Président-Fondateur des Maîtres Cuisiniers de France)

...he greatest and the happiest ...hering of 3-star chefs I have ...in my life; alas some of them ...longer with us.

...with Michel Guerard trying to identify a few half-obscured faces in the photographe on the previous page.

Hommage à Alain Chapel

Mionnay 15 Septembre 1977

A l'apéritif
Krug, Private cuvée
et petite friture de goujons du lac d'Annecy.
❦

Jeunes poireaux à l'huile de truffes
CHASSAGNE MONTRACHET 1976 - Les Ruchottes - P.Ramonet - Prudhon
❦

Rouelle de langouste bretonne à la vapeur de verveine,
aux girolles et chicorée
CHASSAGNE MONTRACHET 1976 - Les Ruchottes - P.Ramonet - Prudhon
❦

Foie de lotte au vinaigre
et petit ragoût de bettes nouvelles.
PULIGNY MONTRACHET 1974 - Les Pucelles - Domaine Leflaive
❦

Poule faisanne à la crème et aux chicons,
poêlée de champignons des bois.
CÔTE ROTIE 1967 en magnum - Cave personnelle de M. Chapoutier
❦

Petit pâté chaud de lapereau de Garennes, son beurre.
Salade de roquette, reine des glaces,
et feuilles de chêne à l'huile de noix et chapons
MUSIGNY 1967 - Leroy

Saint Marcellin, vieux gruyère, reblochon,
Citeaux
CHAMBERTIN 1937 - Leroy
❦

Glace crème de noisettes,
Pêches de vignes de Thurins rôties au four,
Brioche parisienne grillée,
Fruits rouges déguisés et confits,
Bugnes et mignardises.
Château d'YQUEM 1937
❦

Moka, Brésil, Colombie.
❦

Marc et Fine de Bourgogne,
Quetsche et mirabelle de Lorraine,
Tarragone et Liqueur de framboise,
Poiré de la Vallée du Rhône,
Grande Champagne Louis XIII de Rémy Martin.
❦

Mes cigares.
❦

Le verre de l'Amitié.
Krug, Private cuvée.

In everyone's opinion this was a meal to remember for a life time.

Seated from left: Jean Troisgros, Paul Bocuse, Madame Bocuse, Jean Pierre Haeberlin and myself

A pre-wedding party for Michael Harris of the Bell, Aston Clinton

Yeltsin seizing his cake

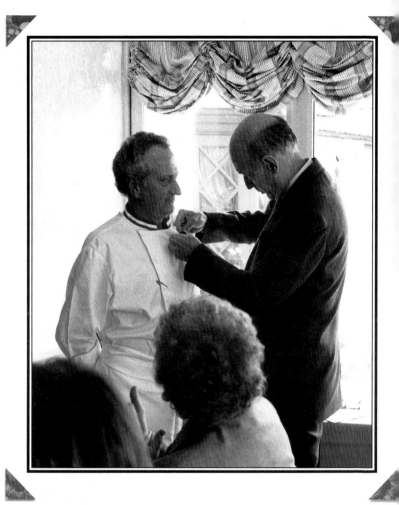

Giscard d'Estaing pinning on the medal of the Chevalier dans l'ordre National du Mérite, at the Waterside Inn 1990.

Early days - waiting at the Crillon in 1971 for the result of the European Taittinger Competition.

Presentation of the Egon Ronay Restaurant of the Year, 1982 - first time for the Waterside Inn.

Local wine, local food in the Perigord with
Roy Ackerman

Trying to relax at home. And what shall I do next?

over for us to lunch on the next day. Now, out of a sitting of seventy or so, I can expect about ten customers to take hare.

The hare's liver, with the gall removed, should be placed in a bowl with the hare's blood and a little vinegar, covered with clingfilm and left in a cool place. The hare, cut into portions, goes into a bowl with carrots, shallots, herbs, garlic and crushed peppercorns, olive oil, wine vinegar, some marc or Armagnac and a bottle of red wine, preferably a Graves. This is left to marinate for twelve hours. The hare is then cooked in its marinade together with some veal stock. The blood and liver are passed through a sieve and added to the reduced marinade to thicken and give more depth to the sauce just before serving. I like to garnish this with Agen prunes that have been soaked and cooked in half a bottle of the same wine (see p. 248).

One of my most successful, and simpler, game dishes is breast of pheasant in port. This has the advantage of being served without bones for those who do not like grappling with them. Preparation time is only fifteen minutes, and the actual cooking of the breasts interlarded with pork back fat takes just three to five minutes. The port is used to deglaze the cooking pan, stock from the game carcass is added and then reduced to make a sauce. I serve this with wild rice and onions, mushrooms and rings of *choux* pastry filled with a leek purée.

Eating the first grouse of the season has become a family tradition. Alain brings some with him to my house near Saint Tropez at the end of August each year for a get-together with his sisters and me. Personally, this is the earliest I like to taste grouse, even if the season does open on the twelfth. Alain makes the bread sauce, my elder daughter, Christine, makes fresh potato crisps, and my other daughter, Francine, looks after the Brussels sprouts which she browns in butter while my son-in-law takes care of the wine. I cook the actual birds, roasting them simply in a hot oven. This summer custom reminds the children of when they first tasted grouse in England, when they lived together *en famille* in Tooting and, later, Wimbledon.

Many of my friends in France are eager for me to bring them grouse because it is something about which they have heard a lot but know little. So when I go to France between August and November, I take grouse when I am invited somewhere, just as other people might take chocolates or flowers! Jean-Pierre Fava, who ran the Bas-Bréau restaurant in the Fontainebleau forest, south of Paris, for many years, told me that his friends used to ask him if his 'contact' from England was on his way. Grouse can now be found on markets in France but it is still rare.

I also take grouse to Château Loudenne in the Bordeaux region, a vineyard owned by IDV-Grand Metropolitan and run by Britons. Nothing can give British exiles in the Bordelais more pleasure than a few grouse. The Loudenne cook, Josette, prepares grouse exactly as I would, slightly pink on the bone, never overcooked. Like all other game, it should be young and not hung for too long.

In 1985, when grouse was scarcely known in France, Albert and I had just published our book *New Classic Cuisine,* and we were invited to prepare a press lunch at Fouquet's on the avenue des Champs-Elysées to promote the French edition. Albert had hated the whole book project and left me to do the writing – which took about two years – and, when we were invited to cook, retorted, 'I would rather go to France to eat than to cook.' I promised him the whole episode would be easy and said we would take as much food as we could prepare in advance. 'When you say there'll be no problem,' he said, 'that's when I begin to worry.' In the end both of us cooked grouse for the main course, and he insisted on making the bread sauce. We got a series of highly positive reviews and, to our great pleasure, were awarded a prize by the Veuve-Clicquot champagne house as 'ambassadors of French gastronomy'.

From the mid-1980s, I began going to France to buy my truffles directly every January rather than going through the Rungis market outside Paris or through agents. I chose Carpentras in Provence where I always stay with my *pâtissier* friend, Frédéric Jouvaud. I would go round the market, inspecting, feeling, smelling and bargaining for the 'gold nuggets' that truffles represent. They are brought into town by local men who have searched for and found them in the woods near their smallholdings or farms. With their trophies in small hessian bags, their business is conducted surreptitiously, considerable amounts of cash changing hands. I take great pleasure in buying in this way, dealing directly with the supplier – much more immediate and exciting than going to Fauchon or Harrods.

After that Friday morning of buying, Frédéric and I always have the same lunch. He prepares a pan filled with thrushes. He removes only the gizzards and cooks all the rest larded and sealed in olive oil, mixed with Provençal herbs and chunks of carrots. After about an hour, the thrushes start singing in his *pâtisserie* oven, which is when he throws in some cloves of garlic and leaves them to cook for another thirty to forty-five minutes. Then he fries slices of *baguette* in the fat of the birds. There are never more than six of us and we usually drink either a Châteauneuf-du-Pape or a Côte-Rôtie. I eat the lot, the bones and even the head. Then Frédéric brings his dessert, always a new creation, and I recall with sorrow that I have to head off to take my flight from Marseilles that evening. Then comes a moment of great tension: I check in my forty to fifty kilograms of truffles, worth up to £15,000, cross myself and pray that I shall be re-united with my suitcases at Heathrow before the day's end. Seeing my fervent gesture, the girl at the check-in asks. 'Are you a first-time flyer, sir?'

My favourite game is the woodcock. Since Australians do not have much in the way of game, I prepared a woodcock for Len Evans, the gregarious ambassador for Australian wine, when he came to Bray in 1997. I like the woodcock's strong taste and the fact that nothing is wasted. It does not need to be drawn because, since it evacuates everything every time it takes off, its intestines are totally clean. Once plucked, it is singed over a gas flame and the eyes removed with a sharp knife. I tie the feet together and pull the long beaked head of the bird between the thighs. It is then browned in clarified butter before being roasted for just five to eight minutes in the oven. I fry *croûtons* from a *baguette* in its fat. I remove the bird's intestines and, after crushing them with a fork, add a little mustard, salt and pepper and a drop of Armagnac or Cognac and spread this on the *croûton*. I serve the bird on top.

I prepared this for a special dinner of the 'Bray Chapter' of Len's Single Bottle Club, a wine-tasting group of his friends in Australia to which each guest brings along wines to taste blind. One of Australia's greatest wine makers, Brian Croser was in Bray. It was an occasion too for the chef Rick Stein to break away from the fish he cooks in his own restaurant. I served the woodcock with a Romanée-St-Vivant Les 4 Journaux Louis Latour 1978 and a Griotte-Chambertin Pernot Fernand 1969.

One particularly famous bird in France is the ortolan or bunting. This is caught alive in special nets in the forests of the Landes and Gascony. It is too small to be hunted with guns since gunshot would ruin it. The bird is killed by immersing it in Armagnac; it dies instantly. For some years, ortolan trapping has been banned in France. But just a week before his death in 1996, the former Socialist President François Mitterrand, despite his pro-European views, sought out and obtained some ortolan for what he rightly thought would be his very last New Year's Eve.

I have tasted ortolan only once in my life, at a huge clandestine chefs' dinner. The birds were roasted in little white bowls in their own fat. We ate them with napkins over our heads to take in all the flavours. There were around 150 of us, all with two or three Michelin stars each. Our mouths were open, but our lips were sealed ...

Vegetables and Salads

ONE OF THE most chilling experiences of my life was discovering the British pea. I happened on this fluorescent green object, almost the size of a quail's egg, when I passed a Lyons Corner House near Marble Arch soon after arriving in London. Through a steaming window, I saw plates with these peas, a dollop of tomato ketchup and bleached-white Mother's Pride bread smeared with deep yellow salted butter. I was appalled not only by this sight, but also by the fact that people seemed to be tucking in with such gusto. It bothered me that millions in the British Isles were eating in such a way. Like a witness of an atrocity, I told myself I had to put this out of my mind as quickly as possible.

It was also in Britain that I came across the worst ways of preparing vegetables I have ever encountered. Boiled vegetables were served swimming in water, with no seasoning and no taste. Everything – potatoes, leeks, carrots and Brussels sprouts – all seemed to have the same flavour and texture. Then there was a sudden switch to the new fashion of eating vegetables crunchy. Asparagus as rigid as a pencil found its way on to dinner tables, and carrot rings were so hard that they flew off the plate when you tried to cut into them. Vegetables, when cooked, should generally be firm but not crunchy. Leave that for uncooked vegetables, like *crudités*. The only vegetable that should ever stay crunchy is the mangetout.

I also encountered my first vegetarians in London in the early 1970s. We were obliged to serve vegetarian dishes at Le Gavroche, and sought to create new ones, but making them annoyed me. Albert used to laugh at my frustration, and would say, 'Vegetables are the cheapest thing we have. Think of the profit margin. I wonder if we shouldn't have more vegetarians.' That drove me mad.

Perceptions, however, change. In recent years, the Waterside Inn has occasionally offered menus that are entirely vegetarian. One of my Indian clients, Rajesh Mehta, whose family has represented the De Beers diamond merchants in Antwerp for generations, took the restaurant over for an entirely vegetarian evening for eighty-five people in 1999. He came twice in the weeks before the event to test the dishes, and he proved to me that some vegetarians have very developed tastes. When he and his guests finally sat down for the dinner, some of the Europeans questioned the menu given to them, asking what was available for non-vegetarians. They were told there was a set menu and no alternative, and I believe that all of them finally left contented.

The menu began with a cream of watercress soup, followed by a Provençal vegetable terrine with a few drops of a red pepper *coulis*. All the ingredients – the main ones aubergines, courgettes and tomatoes – were cooked separately and then layered before being pressed to firm up the terrine. For the next course, I placed green and white asparagus tips with tiny softened leeks in little clumps on a bed of pan-fried, wilted rocket from my garden, seasoned with a truffle vinaigrette. There were several different textures to the dish: the leeks were tender; the asparagus was *al dente;* and the rocket was soft but its stalks still firm. Then I served a grapefruit and strawberry sorbet, which was both a pleasure to behold and refreshing to eat.

This was followed by a *tourte de légumes* from the Loire Valley, using a few mushrooms and other vegetables, the former bringing a moistness to the whole. Again they were all sautéed separately, then mixed with herbs. They were wrapped in a pancake to hold in the juices, then in puff pastry. Each individual *tourte* was decorated with a knife-point to look like marquetry after baking. The sauce was made from a reduced vegetable stock flavoured with tarragon, and I served the golden *tourtes* with a spoonful each of wild black rice and basmati rice.

The meal ended with my *péché gourmand,* a plate containing miniature versions of my most famous desserts, up to eight of them, all very 'sinful'! The meal was accompanied by wines that included a Chassagne Montrachet and a Château Latour 1983 (which married perfectly with the *tourte*), and followed by coffee and *petits fours*. Some of the guests even suggested I should write a vegetarian recipe book. Albert would have laughed to see how far I had evolved from when I used to fulminate against our non-meat-eating clients. . .

In my childhood, buying vegetables was fairly straightforward. Things came in season, and you saw what you were buying. Enormous, crude and ugly crates were strongly built to be used and re-used time and again, and for different products. They brought the seasons with them, potatoes and cabbages in winter, asparagus in spring, and leeks in the late autumn. Now, greengrocers' displays are as colourful as florists'. We have seasonal vegetables such as broad beans and asparagus, and all sorts of salads and mushrooms, all year round even when they're not in season, and they no longer look as if they come from the earth. There are posies of smooth, clean carrots with fluffy green leaves; cherry tomatoes come in bunches like grapes; root vegetables are all the same size and shape, all washed, brushed and good to look at. But now, instead of washing them to get rid of earth, we have to scrub them or even peel them to clean off the pesticides. Sometimes they have the beginnings of mould caused by lengthy storage, which can carry carcinogenic mycotoxins.

With an over-use of pesticides and fertilisers, and now the introduction of genetically modified vegetables, I am beginning to worry about health, quality of life and taste. I believe that organic production should be encouraged and not treated as a health fad. I am not alone, since in France there are now 1,500 shops serving only organic fruit and vegetables. I know we cannot turn the clock back, but I should like to try and recover some of what we have lost. In recent years, we have seen a growing fashion for the vegetarian way of life, for both moral and health reasons. Whereas 1 or 2 per cent of my customers might have been vegetarians twenty years ago, now it is more like 5 per cent. I wonder how safe many vegetables are, however, and whether we are not soon going to be exposed to the 'mad carrot'.

In the world, there are three vegetable products used as a basic food: rice (the cultivation of which covers one-third of the world's land mass), potatoes, and grain flour, transformed into bread and pasta, etc. As a child, my mother would send me to the market to buy potatoes and other vegetables. The potatoes were misshapen and could be little, large, medium or fat. They were covered in earth and I would dirty my hands when I picked them out. I bought cabbages as well, and my mother used to tell me that two or three slugs on a cabbage meant it was a good one. I loved presenting my mother with leeks, their muddied white roots uppermost, like a bunch of flowers. In the kitchen, I liked helping her, scraping twisted carrots, and cutting away the hard skin of the turnip to unleash its strong, pungent smell. If we had some belly pork, my mother would put this with the vegetables in a big stewing pan to make a *potée.*

I am anything but a vegetarian but I nevertheless like to have one meal a week of vegetables alone. I feel this cleanses me. My only sorrow is that in today's vegetables, although I find all the colours of times past, there is little of the taste. Sometimes when I am in France, peasants bring baskets of funny-shaped vegetables to market that only a few people like me want to buy, and I happily rediscover some of those old, strong flavours. For France is blessed in its vegetables. Two regions, Provence and the Loire Valley, are actually in competition to supply the best. Most of their production is sent to Rungis in Paris, the biggest fresh food market in the world, where 11,000 people, one-fifth of them handling fruit and vegetables, are employed.

In the south of France, far from that Rungis ballet of thousands of manoeuvring trucks, I find huge pleasure in the wonderful Provençal vegetables, especially those that are cooked in olive oil, to go into a *ratatouille.* When I want to make a *bouquet garni,* I simply walk ten or so yards from my house and pluck wild thyme and cut bay leaves from the small bay trees growing in my wood of oaks. Early in the mornings, I wander through the Cogolin or Saint Tropez markets, looking for round courgettes, white or violet baby aubergines, young onions, fennel bulbs and bunches of new season garlic heads that need a hearty scraping to get the skin off. I like to cook this garlic for around twenty minutes in the oven and, when it is soft, eat it on a bed of coarse sea salt. I sometimes press the separate cloves with a fork to extract the softened purée, season it with a little pepper and drizzle with a little olive oil. This makes a good accompaniment for lamb chops or it can be spread on a piece of country bread.

Another way of eating whole garlic is to cut the head in two horizontally, season it with some sea salt and sprinkle it with some thyme and olive oil. The two halves are then put back together, wrapped in aluminium foil and cooked in the oven or on the side of a barbecue. This is ideal with *brochettes* of lamb. The *caieux* of garlic, the cloves that go to make up a head of garlic, should be plump and regular. I like garlic with a mauve skin, particularly that from Lautrec in the region of Albi. It should be kept hanging in a larder that is well aired, when it can last for eight to ten months.

When my mother made us chips as children, she used potatoes like Cara, Maris Piper or Désirée, which all remain firm when fried. The King Edward, for example, is fragile and, although it is ideal in a purée, it crumbles in hot oil or fat. My mother would start her chips by rendering beef suet, the fat from around the kidneys. She cut the suet as fine as possible, put it in a pan with a little water, and cooked it slowly until it dissolved. She then poured the fat carefully from the pan into another container, leaving behind a residue of nerves and other impurities. This rendered fat was excellent for frying because it did not penetrate like oil, thus the chips were less fatty. It also cost nothing because French butchers gave suet away free in the 1950s. And of course the chips also tasted very good!

My mother cut the chips, patted them dry, then plunged them into the fat heated up to around 160 degrees centigrade for about five minutes. Then she took them out and placed them on a cloth. At this stage, they were softened and two-thirds cooked. When it was time to eat, she would heat the fat up to 180 degrees and put the chips in again to obtain a golden, crunchy and crisp exterior with a soft, tender centre. (When oil is used, the temperature at each stage must be a minimum of twenty degrees higher.) A peculiarity of oil and fat is that, when taken off the heat, the temperature continues to rise and, if the temperature was high to begin with, it can even ignite. If the fat grew too hot, my mother would quickly clean a whole potato and cut it in two, or scrape a carrot, and drop these in the fat to cool it down.

There are more than 400 varieties of potato, and if I had to choose just one vegetable that should survive, it would be the potato. From mid-April I really enjoy them, especially *la Reine de Benotte*, which comes from the French Atlantic island of Noirmoutier and is grown on beds of seaweed. It is ready about three months after being planted, which is very fast. Another favourite is the Jersey Royal which is ready about the same time (and I believe is grown on fields which are fertilised with seaweed). Both these types of potato, to borrow the *Guide Michelin* formula, are 'worth a special journey'. I brush them lightly, cook them in their fine skin with a little salt and some mint leaves, and serve them with a little farm butter with some Guérande salt. They should never be kept more than a few days after picking and should be kept out of the light, otherwise they start to turn green. And as for potato salads, these should never be too cold. The potatoes should be cooked in their skins, peeled after cooking and served tepid in slices with a mild vinaigrette or mayonnaise, or with a little fresh cheese, *fromage frais,* and snipped tarragon. This is ideal with a cold fish like salmon.

In winter, when potatoes are more rustic, old rather than new, I like to serve them *à la lyonnaise,* sliced and sautéed, with sautéed onions added, about one-third onion to two-thirds potato. I also love potato purée, almost as much as I relish chips, and I can't resist telling a couple of little stories. The Belgians are the butt of many French jokes, and their love of chips and other substantial food has led to the French defining 'a Belgian fondue' as chips dipped in mashed potatoes. I love both so much that I must admit this is a dish I could easily grow to love (although I'd hide away to eat it). More usually, however, I would eat a potato purée with a Toulouse sausage or black *boudin*. Because my grandchildren love chips or *frites,* my eldest daughter has developed a 'little white lie'. She has convinced them that green beans, *haricots verts,* are green chips, *frites vertes,* and as a result, they really love their greens now. A good ploy for reluctant vegetable eaters!

During my time in the kitchen of the British Embassy, one of the worst chores was preparing *artichauts Clamart*. First we broke off the stalk by hand. This way, the fibrous or hairy strings attaching the stalk to the heart were pulled away; cutting would leave the fibres attached. Then we stripped the artichokes of their first two layers of leaves, taking care to twist each leaf individually to leave the edible part still adhering to the heart. We cut the top of the rest of the leaves away, leaving a two-centimetre thick base which we cut into a smooth shape with all the hard, inedible parts removed. At this point, we rubbed all the cut surfaces with lemon juice to stop them going black. After that, the artichokes were cooked, either in water containing a little salt and vinegar or in a *blanc*, water mixed with flour and vinegar, which is used to keep artichokes or salsify white.

We took the cooked artichokes and plucked out the soft, fibrous 'choke' in the middle to make a hollow that we filled with peas. We had three bowls in front of us: one for little peas, one for medium-sized peas and one for big peas. We had to empty each pod and find about two spoonfuls of little peas only to go in each artichoke. The worst was to open a pod and find it contained several different sizes that had to be sorted. It was then, by dint of *hours* of work, that I learned that the ideal pea comes from an immaculate, unspoilt, smooth and plump pod containing five well-formed and equal peas.

If the Embassy chef saw one big pea in an artichoke, there would be hell to pay. This was a real test of patience and devotion. I must say I was glad to get out of the Embassy just so that I would never again have to calibrate peas for 160 people!

I generally like my vegetables to be cooked quickly so that they preserve their taste and texture. Seasoning is extremely important as well. I often put in a few snipped *fines herbes*, like tarragon and flat parsley. Sometimes I will add a few drops of lemon juice to bring out the taste. If and when I feel this is necessary, I add these ingredients just before serving, almost intuitively, like a painter putting the last touch to a finished canvas.

After that, the arrangement on the plate is important, deciding on the juxtaposition of a crunchy vegetable like the mangetout and of a tender, soft potato. Colour is another element to be taken into consideration. As a rule, I avoid peppers; these are over-used in my view, partly because they are cheap. They are too strong for the palate, difficult to digest, and they overpower other vegetables in a dish. One exception was my creation in around 1980 of a red pepper *sabayon* sauce. Ripe red pepper is cooked in vegetable stock with thyme, then puréed, and made into a *sabayon* emulsion with egg yolks and butter. The peppers are less aggressive cooked like this and, served with vegetables or fish, bring colour to the plate.

I also like light *coulis* of vegetables that must be in the same spirit and taste as the vegetables already on the plate. This improves the presentation, and accentuates the taste of the vegetables, just as a *coulis* of fruit enhances a dessert. A typical *coulis* is made of tomatoes, but I also make one from asparagus, with butter, chopped shallots, thyme, chicken stock and double cream as well as seasoning. Passed through a blender and with some asparagus tips added, it makes an ideal accompaniment for my vegetable *lasagne*.

As for salads, my first memory was of a winter leaf, *mâche* or lamb's lettuce, that my mother also called *la doucette* (from the adjective *doux*, sweet or tender). Unlike the clean, hygienic variety of today, that has been grown under glass, our *doucette* had firm roots concealing a lot of earth and sand. My mother would scrape the roots a little first, making an almost surgical cut in the middle to help get the sand out. I would then wash the leaf clumps three or four times in ice-cold water from our single kitchen tap until my fingers were blue. We had to keep the crunchy heart of the salad intact. My mother liked to serve this leaf with fresh walnuts sprinkled on top. I used to peel the walnuts with the point of a knife and soak them in milk to give them more taste. If we had had roast pork or chicken just beforehand, a little of the meat juices added to the salad made it a pure marvel.

Each salad leaf is different. It might be crisp, or more delicate and smooth in texture. It might be spicy, bitter or sweet. There are as many tastes as colours, and the vinaigrettes that go with them should be adapted to suit. They should be more subtle and delicate for sweeter leaves, stronger, with more mustard, pepper or herbs, for coarser leaves. I always tell my young cooks that olive oil or peanut oil with a vinegar made from old wine makes the seasoning *par excellence*.

As with so many other things, Cécile de Rothschild had fixed ideas on vegetables.

Her favourite vegetable was fennel, in season from late May or early June until September. She liked it raw, thinly sliced in salads or thickly sliced, blanched, lightly grilled and brushed with olive oil; it could also be braised with a fresh tomato *coulis.* As I like the look, colour and flavour of the ferny fronds on the top, I used to sprinkle them on salads or on grilled mullet or sea bass (in fact fennel is a delicious accompaniment to many fish).

Cécile de Rothschild always wanted big Marmande tomatoes from the south of France, or the small, firm and meaty tomatoes from Languedoc-Roussillon. She liked them fully ripe, always peeled and only in season. They were never kept in the refrigerator, and were often presented raw in slices with just a few leaves of basil as garnish. I might cut them into thick slices and fry them very quickly in olive oil, and serve them as they were, or with some fresh, raw anchovy fillets.

She liked her courgettes and French beans cooked firm; she used to say she did not want them soggy or crunchy like *crudités.* Vichy carrots were eaten *al dente,* cut in rounds and cooked in just a little water with a knob of butter, some sugar and a pinch of salt. To serve, I used to sprinkle them with chopped hard-boiled egg and snipped parsley, and use them as a garnish for grilled lamb cutlets or *piccata* of veal. 'Carrots,' she intoned, 'are healthy.' So was new season, small-leaved spinach which she also adored, especially raw as a salad.

Cécile de Rothschild particularly liked three potato dishes. *Fondant* potatoes, firm potatoes peeled then cut into circles of about two to three centimetres thick, are cooked very quickly in lots of butter until golden. They accompanied leg of lamb or sirloin of beef. They are so butter-rich that they are a very 'naughty' dish – but delicious. I brought the idea to England after learning it from the Rothschilds. *Pommes boules*, small balls cut out of potato using a melon-baller, which I blanched in a little water and then sautéed in butter and oil. The third was what she called the 'weekend potato'. This consisted of slices of potatoes, blanched and drained, which were then cooked in a lot of butter in a frying pan, and stirred with a fork until they broke up into uneven large and small pieces. I added lots of snipped tarragon and parsley from the garden and generous seasoning. It looked a mess but it was delicious.

She loved asparagus, usually eating it as a vegetable after the main dish rather than as an *hors d'oeuvre*. She wanted the white variety from Les Landes or the Loire Valley. She hated green varieties, like the *verte du Perthuis*, saying she did not like the colour, taste or finesse. Personally, I find green asparagus delicious. It is simply different from the blanched white asparagus found in most of France. Asparagus is best when freshly picked, and you can check for freshness by pushing your thumbnail into the

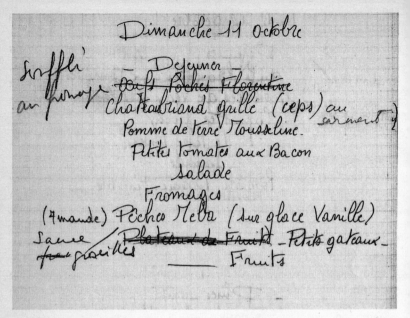

Dimanche 11 Octobre

Souffle
au fromage
— Déjeuner —
~~Œufs Pochés Florentine~~
Chateaubriand grillé (ceps) au sarment y
Pomme de terre Mousseline
Petites tomates aux Bacon
Salade
Fromages
(Amande) Pêches Melba (sur glace Vanille)
Sauce framboises ~~Plateau de Fruit~~ — Petits gateaux —
_____ Fruits

A vendange lunch at Château Lafite, 1964

centre of the stalk. If it gives way, then the asparagus is fresh. If the bottom of the stalks are still damp, this is another hint that it has recently been picked. There is also a wild asparagus, which looks like little ears of wheat. It does not have much taste, but I like to serve it around other asparagus spears as decoration.

I like asparagus when it is in season (in spring, and not usually after late June), served firm and lukewarm with a delicate sauce, like a *mousseline* or a *Hollandaise* flavoured with orange, (which adds both the colour and taste of the fruit). Or I might serve it with a *sauce gribiche*, a mayonnaise with capers, herbs and chopped hard-boiled egg. A really gourmet sauce for a special occasion is a mayonnaise mixed with a little fresh cream, a drop of lemon juice and a few generous spoonfuls of Sevruga caviar. That gives asparagus a completely new dimension.

Most mortals would consider truffles in champagne a small luxury garnish, even a decoration. But for Cécile de Rothschild, it was a regular vegetable, especially around Christmas and New Year. 'You either eat something or you don't, Chef,' she would say, 'and if we can't do it properly, then we don't do it at all.' Our servings were between 100 and 150 grams per person, appropriate to the Rothschild fortune.

There were some aspects of vegetables that appealed less to her. Once I was chopping and cooking onions in the country, as she sat in the garden. She called out to Marcel, the butler: 'Tell Chef his onions are in conflict with my lilac.' As she heard a window slam shut, she added: 'Don't bother, he heard me.'

Until the mid-1970s, we used to serve vegetables separately at the Waterside Inn. I was helping out in the restaurant one weekend on a day the waiters were having difficulty keeping up because we had more than 100 customers. At that time, weekday trade was sluggish and we took as many covers as we could at weekends to make up. I took a dish on a silver tray held above my head. Suddenly, I heard a customer say 'I didn't order vegetables!' I had tilted the tray and he was covered in carrots and peas. Fortunately, he was a regular customer and remained one. The incident taught me that, while I might be an accomplished cook, I still had a lot to learn about waiting.

When I am not pouring vegetables over customers, I might be developing vegetable dishes. Over the past thirty years I have created quite a few, and always work with the seasons. I have made purées of cooked vegetables with olive oil, basil and garlic, introducing them in the early 1970s. I have made Russian-style *blinis* and served them as a multi-layered *millefeuille* with vegetables between the pancakes: puréed carrot, shredded leek, a few peas. I topped the stack with snipped chives or parsley. There is also my *subric de légumes,* a mousse made in *dariole* moulds from spinach, watercress or carrots. The puréed vegetables are mixed with eggs, seasoning and a little cream, and the moulds are poached in a *bain-marie* as you would a *crème caramel.* This makes for a light, melting texture that is particularly good with fish. I was the first to cook vegetables in this way.

From aubergines, I like making aubergine 'caviar'. The vegetable is baked whole on a bed of salt then opened and the soft flesh spooned out. This is then seasoned with some olive oil, garlic, lemon juice, salt and pepper. It can be eaten on little *croûtons* of country bread on its own, or as a garnish with firm-fleshed fish.

To garnish game, I blanch cabbage leaves in salted water. Then I fry diced potatoes. I place the potato dice on the cabbage leaves, add some pieces of *foie gras*, fold the cabbage over to make little parcels and finish them in the oven with a little poultry stock. Customers have told me that this garnish alone made their meal.

Perhaps the only sort of vegetable dishes I don't cook are Indian in concept, cooked with lots of spices – although I love to eat them (if not *too* spicy)! I was invited by the Taj Mahal hotels to explain my philosophy and approach to gastronomy to their chefs. The head chef then asked what I wanted them to make for me, and I told him of my love of vegetables, which I can eat endlessly out of pure greed. His cooks then brought me dish after dish of their vegetable specialities, among them *paneer muttar*, feta cheese and pea curry, and *subzi kochar*, with cauliflower, pumpkin and ginger – an over-indulgence.

Caesar salad is a dish that I appreciate when I am in the United States, but it is not something I would ever think of putting on my menus since it is not part of my cultural repertoire. And yet, for one customer, the late King Hussein of Jordan, I used to make it as a special favour. He came to the Waterside Inn several times with Queen Noor and their son. The first time, he asked if we could make him a Caesar salad, and I did so without a recipe and from memory. After that, an aide would call, with little warning, to reserve a table, and I would hastily prepare my ingredients for the same meal each time – Caesar salad followed by Châteaubriand steak. The second time he came, though, he asked if he could possibly have his salad without anchovies. King Hussein of Jordon did not like anchovies. It is a thing I rarely do, cook something unfamiliar to me, but I did it not so much for a king, as for a gentle and unassuming man. For King Hussein was always charming, greeting those who recognised him, and would stand up to shake my hand when I went to the dining-room to see him. Two or three months after his death, Queen Noor made a reservation and ordered exactly the same meal as before. Somewhat wistfully, she asked, 'May we have the same so it will be as though he was still with us?'

In 1989, the ship-owner John Chandris asked me if I could cater for a family wedding in Athens. Assuming at first that this would be for about 100 people, I agreed. Then it dawned on me that I would be catering for between 700 and 800. Chandris owned a hotel in the city so had a kitchen available, but the catch was that the actual wedding dinner was to be served at a yacht club in Akrotiri by the sea, a good three to four miles from the hotel. The club had no refrigeration and its somewhat inadequate kitchen needed industrial cleaning before I could use it. Yet again, I was obliged to order a refrigerated truck for a meal that was to be served on a day when the temperatures reached almost forty degrees centigrade.

I decided on a seafood starter followed by chicken in basil surrounded by three stuffed vegetables, *petit farcis à la provençale* (see p. 250). Ahead of time, I sent faxes to Athens ordering various ingredients, like 600 chickens of between one and one and a half kilograms each, 1,000 courgettes, 1,000 potatoes and 1,200 mushrooms. I specified the sizes of the vegetables too. The courgettes had to be fourteen centimetres long, the mushrooms had to weigh fifteen grams and be four to five centimetres in diameter while the potatoes had to weigh around 260 grams and measure eleven centimetres. I received a fax in reply saying there seemed to be something wrong in the transmission of my order, and could I repeat the figures. My return fax confirmed the original details.

I set off with nine staff, six for the kitchen and three to serve, with 550 kilograms of extra material for the meal, such as sherry vinegar, thirty kilograms of *foie gras*, truffles, ninety vanilla pods, twenty sides of smoked salmon and a battery of vital kitchen equipment. I was worried that the language barrier with local cooking and serving staff would be a problem. So, ahead of time, I drew a diagram of my main dish with the vegetables arranged round the chicken. I had the instructions and names of the ingredients translated into Greek and faxed all this to Athens. This was then posted up around the kitchen with photographs of the finished dish so that the Greek staff knew what the final result should look like. I wanted it, through the different colours and shapes, to look like a mosaic or a garden planted on the plate.

The night before the wedding, I and my cooks from England worked through the night while our Greek colleagues went off to bed. I led my team from the centre, staying with them throughout. As soon as I saw one of my cooks begin to flag, I would take him a lemonade or a Coca-Cola to keep him on his feet. The potatoes and courgettes were cut in barrel shapes, then emptied out with a spoon, leaving a thin casing. The flesh was then finely minced, sweated in a pan with some olive oil, chopped onions and thyme and put back inside the casings. The mushroom stems were removed and minced with flat parsley, onion and thyme. I packed this on to the underside of the head. The three vegetables were then dusted with some chopped parsley, breadcrumbs, a little Parmesan and some olive oil. The chicken was cooked at the last minute, as were the stuffed vegetables. The whole dinner was a great success, served to tables of ten to twelve in the open air in very elegant and beautiful surroundings.

This meal so impressed John Chandris that he decided I could probably apply that same engineering precision to boats and cruises. Not one ship had yet been built for Celebrity Cruises, but I was brought in as consultant, and had a hand in designing the galleys, cold rooms etc. Now I am looking after six ships, and have gone on more than sixty cruises in the last eleven years. And all because of one (although not so small) wedding party. . .

We flew back to London from Greece by Olympic Airways. My staff clearly thought I was a bit mad to have taken on such a challenge, but their fatigue was beginning to give way to elation at the success of the venture. Suddenly during the flight, we hit an air pocket and the plane fell so sharply that a hostess fainted and the oxygen masks dropped down. My colleagues all turned to me and I tried to look reassuring. One, Marco Avitabile, who was of mixed French, German and Italian origin, recovered his poise first. Smiling, even though the captain said he had obtained permission for a priority landing at Heathrow and was therefore commencing his approach immediately, Marco wrote a few words on a card. He handed this to me and said he had not been afraid because he felt safe flying with me.

He had written down a German proverb: *'Es ist noch kein Meister vom Himmel gefallen'* – 'Masters don't fall from the sky.' I still have the card.

Desserts

ALL MY LIFE I have faced a dilemma that the French sum up as being 'between the hammer and the anvil', a sort of 'between-the-devil-and-the-deep-blue-sea' situation. In my case, the two poles of this dilemma are savoury and sweet. I refuse to allow the more celebrated savoury cuisine to be considered in any way superior because, for me, with my beginnings in *pâtisserie*, desserts are an affair of the heart. They should be the apotheosis of the meal, the last, lingering taste that defines the final impression.

The savoury part of the meal, of course, requires a variety of disciplines: handling the huge array of possible starters, making sauces and soups, and dealing with meat, poultry, fish and vegetables in all their forms. But *pâtissiers*, if anything, probably have to develop even *more* skills. They must learn oven techniques to perfection, or see hours of preparation put at risk. They must be able to manipulate flour in different ways, making all the dough for tarts, puff pastries, croissants, *brioches* and *choux* pastry as well. They must master the techniques of ice-cream and sorbets. They must learn the intricacies of chocolate: *ganache* cream, chocolate sauces, gâteaux, mousses and a host of other hot and cold variants. They have to learn how to craft and to sculpt their chocolate. (And when I speak of chocolate, I refer, of course, to real chocolate, not to the scandalous new substances now permitted by the European Union. These use up to five per cent of vegetable fats other than cocoa butter, a measure that leads to an inevitable drop in quality and which benefits no-one but industrial manufacturers obsessed by profit.)

Pâtissiers have to make sweets, nougat and other confectionery. On top of all this, they must be visually creative and have artistic skills to decorate their work, especially when making elegant or stunning *pièces montées* for grand occasions, like the *pièce bretonne,* made of *biscuit* or *génoise* sponge, the *pièce montée croquembouche,* a tower of cream-filled *choux* buns, or a traditional wedding cake covered in icing. They have to learn to make a host of different desserts and gâteaux, that might use any number of fruits, passionfruit or blackcurrants, for example, as their main ingredient and flavour. They also have to perfect moulded *bavarois,* desserts made with a variety of different cream fillings, iced dishes or delicate *millefeuilles,* rum babas, mocha cakes or round, hollowed-out *choux puits d'amour* filled with mousse or cream.

They will make tiny *petits fours* to be served with coffee. At the Waterside Inn, there is one person in my kitchen who does nothing but make *petits fours* all day. This *pâtissier* starts in the morning for the lunchtime service. After lunch, all the remaining *petits fours* are fed to the ducks on the Thames and the cook starts work again for dinner.

Of the four basic ingredients of *pâtisserie* – butter, eggs, flour and sugar – sugar is the most complex. To the consumer, sugar is a simple everyday ingredient. In fact, it is an incredibly diverse product. Chemically, it is a mixture of carbon, hydrogen and oxygen. In terms of physics, it can be viscous, crystalline, absorb fluids or be soluble itself. It has crucial nutritional qualities, being one of the body's main sources of energy. It handles differently when hot and cold. In cooking, it can be used alongside fruit or dairy products, or to caramelise a sweet or savoury dish. In its natural state, it is found in sugar-cane, sugar-beet, maple, palms, sorghum and honey as well as in fruit. Without sugar, there would be no *pâtisserie*.

Pâtissiers work sugar into many shapes and forms. From pulled sugar, they can make edible roses, dahlias, lilies of the valley and sugar baskets holding sugar flowers. To make pulled sugar, the first requirement is a small and spotlessly clean, pure copper saucepan that has been scrubbed with vinegar and coarse salt to remove every hint of dust or grease. Sugar lumps are gently heated up in a little water with a small amount of cream of tartar and a little liquid glucose. As this boils, impurities rise to the surface, and this 'foam' must be skimmed off. Then what I do is dip my fingertips into a bowl of cold water, and clean the inside edges of the saucepan with a swift and repeated sweeping motion, cooling my fingers after each stroke in the cold-water bowl. This process averts crystallisation and the formation of grains. It could be done with a pastry brush, but I love to feel the heat, to feel the transformation of the sugar.

When the temperature rises to exactly 156 degrees centigrade – a degree or two over is too much – small samples of the sugar, pulled out with the fingers again, are plunged into cold water to harden. This must be done extremely quickly otherwise fingers will be burned. At this stage, after hearing a 'crack' as the hot sugar hits the water, I then bite the sugar to gauge its readiness: it should crack but not stick to the teeth. Too hard, it cannot be fashioned; too soft, it can be worked but, very quickly, the petals or other objects made will droop.

At the right moment, when the sugar is ready, the pan is placed on a wooden board to arrest the heat, and to allow all the bubbles to disappear. After that, the sugar is poured on to a cold marble slab that has been greased, preferably with Vaseline (this is purer than oil). The sugar is then pulled from the edges to the centre repeatedly to make a ball, using a palette knife. Then it must be worked with the fingers, without squeezing to avoid burns – it will still be around 80–100 degrees centigrade! This sugar shape then begins to shine like satin. Kept under a heating lamp or another heat source, it is now worked with the thumbs and fingertips into the desired shape. Hands must be dry with no hint of sweat. If the end result is too thick, it looks heavy and devoid of finesse. Too thin, it will be brittle and break. For roses, sugar petals – up to twenty for a competition – are assembled one by one on a cone-shaped rose centre, also made from sugar. For a carnation, the leaves are cut with scissors and joined by heating the base of each petal on a small lamp and then assembling them.

Blown sugar, blown by a hand pump or by mouth through a tube, can make swans, fish or vases. To blow sugar, more glucose is added to the original mixture, and it is cooked at a slightly lower temperature. Otherwise, the operation is much the same. After it is folded into a ball, I create a hollow with my thumb, take a bulb or blowpipe and fill the ball very slowly with air, working it into the required shape of bird or fish. It is exactly the same as glass-blowing. The ambient temperature must be warm, neither too cold nor too hot, and draughts are anathema. During the final stages, the creation is held near a fan to enable it to harden quickly. Edible colours can be added during the cooking, or painted on afterwards if I don't want to keep it in its original pure white state.

On the other hand, my son Alain has been experimenting, and has chosen a slightly different recipe for his sugar work. He uses bought fondant instead of sugar cubes, along with liquid glucose and cream of tartar. There is no water in it at all. He cooks it at a lower temperature, 142 degrees centigrade, and argues that he can get a better shine on his sugar than he can with my recipes!

Working with sugar, using it for small single portions of desserts or fashioning it into something decorative and evocative, has been a source of great pleasure and fascination for me. So, too, has the whole world of the *pâtissiers*. Both my brother and I started our working lives as *pâtissiers*. It delights me that my son, Alain, and my nephew and namesake, Michel, have followed in our footsteps and decided to start their careers as *pâtissiers* too. Through my contacts in the trade, they were apprentices under some of the finest craftsmen in Paris. Neither has remained in the discipline, though, and both have moved on through the various sections of the classical kitchen. Their *pâtissier's* grounding was important, nevertheless, for in my view, a truly excellent chef must be able to understand, oversee and control the standards of workmanship in *all* the sections of his kitchen. He or she must be able to encourage innovation while still respecting classical standards.

The *pâtissiers'* world has thus far been basically French, and is one of shops rather than of restaurants. Largely unsung, *pâtissiers* enjoy little of the public adulation and glory of the great chefs whose dining-rooms are frequented by the rich and powerful. They are a brotherhood of craftsmen who labour hard and long hours, working in isolation but sharing their expertise and discoveries with each other. I am proud to have come from the *pâtissiers'* world; it is one to which I love to return and where I have some of my closest friends.

Pâtissiers have to use other ingredients apart from sugar, like almond paste for modelling. They have to learn to write, anything from names to good wishes for a birthday or anniversary, using paper cornets filled with royal icing or chocolate cream in different calligraphic styles. In the same way that cooks making savoury dishes use herbs and spices, *pâtissiers* have to learn to use vanilla, cinnamon, cloves, liquorice, orange blossom, caraway seeds, mint, lavender or pistachios. Like herbs, these should be fresh and of the best quality. A vanilla pod should be swollen and supple, not thin and dry. Good vanilla, which should smell like a combination of roasting coffee and browning sugar, is the ultimate dessert spice.

Attention to detail is of the essence. I can tell by just looking whether things have been done right. My own recipe for a *pâte sablée* – the result resembles shortbread – insists that the preparation should all be done by hand. My wife Robyn sometimes considers my methods fastidious but, one day, even she was surprised when, as she pulled this dish from the oven, I told her she should not have used a food processor. I had not been present during the preparation, but I could see without tasting that the consistency was not quite right.

I first handled pastry as a small child. I can still see myself in the kitchen at our little wooden table. I would climb on a stool and watch my mother make tarts. She would give me the trimmings of pastry, and touching it used to make me very calm and reflective. Instinctively, I worked it with just the tips of my fingers, being careful not to crush it. I would use it to line the little moulds my mother gave me, and then put a little bit of fruit in the middle, often damaged fruit which can be good for cooking – a plum, apple or apricot. I used to think that my fruit looked like a baby in a pram. I was anxious to get my little tarts alongside my mother's in the oven. I was not allowed to go near the oven myself but I would wait in the kitchen, savouring the different smells as the baking progressed. My tastebuds were effervescent. As soon as the oven was opened, I would rush over to smell the result. Sometimes I would catch the full blast of burning-hot vapours, but this didn't deter me. I always wanted to get my first tart out of its tin and sample it immediately. I soon learned that greed was unwise when my mother, who usually restrained me, would occasionally let me go ahead and burn my lips.

Saint-Mandé, where we lived when we moved from the country, is on

Soufflé milanois : 150 gr de gruyère 75 gr de parmesan
2 cueillère de crème et 2 noix de beurre faire fondre ajouter
4 jaunes, monter 4 blancs, 12 a 15 minutes de four moyen.
enroulé

Saumur : 750 gr de sel, 3 gr de salpêtre,
150 gr de cassonade, 5 litre d'eau faire bouillir 10 minutes
(Ajouter herbes aromatiques, thymun laurier menthe
clous de girofle ect...)

○ Sauce diable ; échalotte v.in blanc tombér a sec, mouiller
au Fond ou glace de viande incorporer carcasses de
volailles, Piler au mortier (un soupçon Worrster sauce).

Sorbet : pour 1l de Fruit passé 300 gr de sucre
glace.

Sablés Vendéens: 125 gr de farine, 90 gr de beurre, 60 gr sucre
sel, 4 jaunes d'œuf dur Haché, 3 est citrons Haché
Couper grand emporte, pièce rond fini couper en quatre
glacer d'une glace citron (sucre glace)

Souvaroff : 200 gr farine - 125 gr sucre semoule -
100 gr beurre - 1 cueillère a café ou a soupe de lait
une fois cuit superposer les abaissent avec groseille au milieu
un trou au centre - poudrer sucre glace

Sablé chocolat: 200 gr farine - 60 sucre glace - 100 gr beurre -
30 gr cacao - 1 œuf - (Coller une fois cuit par deux abaisse) beurre
chocolaté Menier + crème fraîche.

Sultanes ; 300 gr farine - 150 gr sucre semoule - 1 œuf + 1 jaune
185 gr Beurre - 8 gr canelle (coller une fois cuit a la confiture)

● Sablé Noir et Blanc: 500 gr Farine - 450 gr beurre - 135 gr
de sucre glace - Pincée sel - (Pour le noir 100 gr de cacao)

● Sablé Noir de Coco: 125 gr Sucre - 125 gr Farine
125 gr coco Râpé - 125 gr beurre - 3 jaunes -
semoule

Some of my favourite recipes from my apprenticeship, both salty and sweet

the edge of the Bois de Vincennes, the huge forest and park on the eastern outskirts of Paris. My mother used to take the family on walks round the lake there and treat us to freshly made waffles bought from stalls. I would go for a ride on the merry-go-round, competing ferociously to capture the rings that would entitle me to a free ride, then have my waffle. It was made in a cast-iron mould – modern moulds simply do not produce the same result – and sprinkled with icing sugar that would make us sneeze if we ate it too quickly. It was crusty on the outside and tender inside. On special occasions, or when my mother thought we deserved a treat, we would have Chantilly cream – whipped cream flavoured with vanilla – instead of icing sugar.

In those post-war days, my mother used to offer desserts that would fill our stomachs. She made thick pancakes, sometimes adding water to the batter if she didn't have enough milk. These were served with sugar or jam. They were guaranteed to weight my brother and me down, ensuring that we would not fight at bed-time and would go straight to sleep. She also baked big cooking apples in the oven. She cut out the core, put in some butter and sprinkled sugar on the top to form a layer of caramel. During cooking, there would sometimes be a hiss as one of the apples burst. Our treat was to be allowed to scrape the tray once it had cooled. The scrapings were half firm and half liquid, and they had a taste of apple I have never experienced since, not even in the most sophisticated apple dishes I have eaten. Perhaps they were wild apples.

When I was a teenage apprentice with about six months' experience behind me, my boss, Camille Loyal, was called into the shop to deal with a customer one Sunday just as he was in the process of making Saint-Honoré gâteaux. This required the preparation of a *chiboust* cream, which, because it contains a little gelatine, had to be piped immediately while still warm, otherwise it would set. It was used to decorate the top of the gâteaux, piped through a special nozzle attached to an enormous piping bag which Loyal held under his arm. He squeezed the cream out little by little with arm pressure. After he had been gone about five minutes, I became worried that the cream would be spoilt. Another apprentice, Guy, who had been there about a year longer than I, refused to try anything without his boss's go-ahead. So I picked up the piping bag and began to decorate the Saint-Honorés myself, something only a professional should do. I must have completed about half a dozen before Loyal came back. When he saw what I had done, he changed colour. I thought I saw an expression of contentment rather than anger, but he said nothing. After that, he made a point of making his Saint-Honorés in the early morning when he would not be interrupted.

A little later, when I was fifteen, I created my first *pièce montée,* a *croquembouche,* for my little sister Martine's first communion. I made this at home with a mould borrowed from Loyal, on our coal range. It involved making a *nougatine* base, which was topped with some cream-filled *choux* buns. These were decorated with caramel and assembled in the shape of a pyramid with the help of the borrowed mould. My family were astonished and delighted. I was very proud of myself too!

Later, as a qualified *pâtissier* in the British Embassy kitchens, my head chef, Emile Rouault, handed me two traditional Christmas recipes, for mince pies and Christmas pudding. I thought it was a joke. Not only was I obliged to work with margarine, rather than with pure butter as I had been trained, but now I had also been given two dessert recipes that included beef fat! I went to see my brother, who assured me that it was a genuine recipe and that millions of people across the Channel ate such a suet pudding every Christmas. I was really shocked. Little did I know then that I was going to join those millions and that, within a few years, I would actually be taking mince pies and Christmas puddings abroad as presents...

It was at the British Embassy that I also made my first wedding cake, for Stella Gladwyn Jebb, the ambassador's daughter. I took ideas from a few books and I found myself working evenings and even some nights getting this huge iced cake ready. On the actual wedding day, when I had finished assembling the cake, Rouault came to inspect my work. He looked at the cake from side to side and up and down. A short man, he took a stepladder to place the sugar flowers that I had made on the top. He climbed back down, took a step back, puffed out his chest, took one more look and then walked away. An outsider watching this scene would easily have believed that it was all Rouault's own work!

Shortly after that, I found myself cooking in the Sahara, during my military service in Algeria. The mess kitchen didn't have much for dessert-making, either in terms of raw materials or utensils. Sometimes I would make croissants, *brioches* or *pains au chocolat* for Sundays to break the monotony, until I had the idea of using the one thing we did have in abundance – dates. With these, I made an *île flottante aux dattes,* a variation on the traditional floating islands of poached egg whites on custard. The whipped egg white, flavoured with chopped dates and a pinch of ground star anise, was baked in a large mould, its sides lined with whole dates. It was then unmoulded on to a sea of *crème anglaise* and topped with warm caramel which quickly set to a crisp crust. This I introduced later to my menu at the Waterside Inn, and it became one of my signature recipes.

Another dessert I still serve is the one I devised for my daughter Christine's christening in 1965. I took white peaches from the garden, peeled them and poached them for a minute in a 1955 Veuve-Clicquot pink champagne. When cool, I added a dash of sugar to stop the champagne becoming too sharp. Given that it was the strawberry season, I crushed a few and mixed them with some whipped cream to make a strawberry mousse. I put a peach and some mousse in individual bowls, and served the champagne liquor separately – simple, but so good!

Cécile de Rothschild more or less left me alone so far as desserts were concerned. She would advise guests 'to go easy on the cheese because my chef is a *pâtissier* without equal'. I found this out from Marcel, the butler, who would come to me anxiously, saying 'Chef, I hope your dessert is ready and as good as usual because she's been singing your praises again.'

According to what was available in her garden in Picardy, I would make iced soufflés, usually with strawberries in early summer and raspberries later in the season. She also liked sorbets, but would deliberately never put them on the menu. As she did with canapés to go with an *apéritif*, she would call me around six in the evening to discuss these last-minute menu additions. 'What fruit do you have in store for sorbet, Chef?' she would ask. 'I'll call you back in five minutes when you've had a look.' Then she would decide. It was all tactics, though, simply to ensure that her sorbet was freshly made, and had not been hanging around in the freezer. I used to make it in an old wooden ice-cream-maker, and it took about half an hour of hand-churning for the sorbet to set.

Cécile de Rothschild liked variety, and she often asked me to make things that were out of the ordinary. Once I made a Camembert ice-cream. I mixed the cheese with untreated milk, which you could still find in Paris dairies at the time, passed this combination through a sieve, seasoned it with a little cayenne pepper and some salt, and set about churning it. I used to serve it with little shell-shaped pieces of puff pastry that I cooked at the last minute. Another iced dish was a gingerbread ice-cream served with a compote of oranges.

I also made *coeur à la crème,* a 'heart in cream'. I packed cream cheese, with 40 per cent fat, into a little mould in the shape of a heart. I would put single cream on the top, and often served it with wild strawberries when we were in the country. One day, Cécile de Rothschild called me in and said, 'This dessert is marvellous but, next time, use a richer cream cheese or else give me some more cream. I like your desserts to be unctuous, I'm not on a diet.'

From the moment Le Gavroche opened, our desserts became famous. Albert excelled at *brioches* and puff pastry. I recreated my Rothschild *roulé marquis au chocolat,* which is similar to a Swiss roll: the sponge is made without flour, though, and filled with a red fruit *coulis,* lightly whipped cream and fresh raspberries. This combination and the lightness of the dessert made it an extremely popular signature dish of mine for more than thirty years.

Albert and I used to fight over one of my specialities, *la rose du chef.* This involved making a pulled sugar rose, something that helped me keep my *pâtissier's* hand in. Making one rose alone took me twenty minutes. The heart of the dessert was a *quatre quarts* cake, made with equal parts of butter, eggs, flour and sugar. This was soaked in Maraschino syrup, then it was topped with a mixture of Chantilly cream and *crème pâtissière.* The rose was placed on top, and then the whole dessert was transferred to a very thin *nougatine* base. It became extremely popular and we would run out of it almost every evening. There were only three or four cooks in the kitchen in those days, compared with twenty now – including four *pâtissiers* at the Waterside Inn – and eventually *la rose* became too time-consuming to keep on the menu. Frankly, this was a relief. When we had enough roses to go round and the customers were complimenting my work, Albert was annoyed, demonstrating clear sibling jealousy. When there were not enough roses to go round, he was annoyed at their absence and, while I was making them, he was annoyed that they were taking up all my time! The issue had become so contentious that it was a no-win situation.

Albert's skill at making the *omelette soufflé Rothschild* was breathtaking, so much so that it was difficult to believe that it was I and not he who had actually worked for the Rothschilds. This was a vanilla soufflé mix cooked just like an omelette in an omelette pan and then covered with apricot jam. Another omelette soufflé, prepared simultaneously in a second pan, was immediately placed on top and sprinkled with icing sugar. It was served with a side helping of fresh cream. The customers had to be very greedy to eat it all, but they usually did!

At the beginning of the 1980s, my desserts were inspired more and more by fruit. These could be figs, apricots, fresh almonds, mangoes, blackberries or bilberries, anything except kiwis. I had come to loathe kiwis! In the 1980s we saw the kiwi everywhere, even on fish and lamb. Once I was due to give a demonstration at the Grosvenor House Hotel for around 500 people when I received a call from a New Zealand farm marketing board official. This young woman asked me if I could use kiwi fruit in my demonstration. In return, she offered me a year's free supply of kiwis. I replied, 'I hate kiwis because you have pushed them too far. I don't even like their shape.' Although I do quite like its taste, as with *nouvelle cuisine,* we had seen too much of it.

During the 1980s, I could sense I was becoming influential in the *pâtisserie* field because of the number of cooks asking to come on study visits, a few actually from France. I was also pleased that some of the confirmed savoury cooks on my staff wanted to give desserts a try. This prompted me to come out with my first book on desserts, *The Roux Brothers on Pâtisserie.* I put everything I had into that book, everything that the discipline, balance, weights and measures aspects of being a *pâtissier* – together with the lighter creative side – had given me. Because I wanted Albert to be involved – we did everything together at the time – I asked him to be in the jacket photograph, taken at the Waterside Inn. Albert arrived some time after nine o'clock and told me to tell him where to sit and when to smile. 'I have a driver waiting outside and can give you an hour or two, no more than that.' That irritated me a bit since I had spent six months on the book. Albert hated writing, and could not understand why anyone would take so much time on a project like that. He was, however, pleased with the result. We sold 250,000 copies in five languages, and the book was even reprinted in France. Over the years, I have come across it in restaurants or in people's homes, and it is extremely gratifying to see that it has been used, that the pages are soiled. It is anything but a coffee-table book.

In January 1986, I had a 'gastronomic week' at the Intercontinental Hotel in Sydney. I took along five cooks, including a *pâtissier*. We had to get started immediately but found there were hardly any of the usual tools in the desserts corner of the kitchen, not even a mixer. I had to borrow my mother-in-law's Kenwood, spatulas, whisks, and a lot of other utensils, even scrapers. That revealed how desserts were viewed in Sydney at the time; they simply did not interest people. However, once I left, sales of the Roux brothers' book took off in Australia, and I think desserts have now earned their rightful place on menus down under, partly due to my influence.

I always have a tart on my menus, from a lukewarm and delicate *tarte fine* to a more generously filled tart. The one I am most often asked to produce, however, is my *tarte tatin*. When my fellow chef and friend, Nico Ladenis, comes to see us in France, he always asks to have this, a generous, caramelised apple tart served with a vanilla ice-cream (see p. 252).

One of the most delightful desserts I have ever eaten was that prepared by Michel Guérard, before he moved to Eugénie-les-Bains, in 1969. He was still then at his highly reputed restaurant in Asnières in the northern Paris suburbs, Le Pot-au-Feu. There, after eating his marvellous *pot-au-feu* with *foie gras*, I was stunned by the quality of his pears in puff pastry. This was served warm, and was as light as a feather, with a smooth cream that just melted in the mouth. The fruit was juicy and had a clear taste of pear. The pastry looked as if it were varnished a tempting golden colour. It is not often that a dessert attracts me both visually and by taste, and that remains one of the most memorable meals of my life.

Guérard is the chef that I consider most like myself. He is a *pâtissier* by training as well, and he has three Michelin stars. After that Christmas meal, he came to our table and we talked late into the night. He showed me some photographs of his work and explained why he had decided to go in for the *Meilleur Ouvrier de France* competition in 1958. This conversation led me to enter the contest myself in 1976. Guérard had become an example for me to follow.

At the age of twenty-eight, I became a member of the *Relais et Desserts* association of master *pâtissiers*, the youngest ever to join. It was then a purely French organisation but is now European. The beauty of this association is the way its members share everything: there are seminars where they demonstrate their work, showing their tricks of the trade, and

Xcigarettes : 250 gr de beurre pommade, 300 gr d
sucre glace, 6 blancs, 225 gr de farine, Vanille.

cake royal : 250 gr de beurre pommade, 300 gr de sucre
glacé, 6 œufs, 1/4 de lait, 600 gr de farine, 30 gr de beurre
sèche, 500 gr de fruits confits, 250 gr de raisins.

cake : 375 gr de sucre, 375 de beurre, 375 gr de
fruits confit et raisins, 400 gr de farine, 6 œufs, + Rhum.

crème patissere : 1 l de lait, 8 jaunes, 300 gr de sucre, 80 gr
de farine, Vanille.

Anglaise : 1 l de lait, 8 jaunes, 300 gr de sucre.

crème au beurre : 1 kg de beurre, 13 jaunes, 250 gr de
sucre cuit au petit filet.

crème au beurre Italie : 750 gr de sucre cuit au petit boulet, 9 blancs
montés, 1 kg de beurre (1 l d'eau, 3 kg de sucre)

crème d'amande : 1 kg de pâte d'amande, 400 gr de beurre
pommade, 8 œufs (Rhum).

crème Flanc : 6 œufs, 1 l de lait, 250 gr de sucre, 250 gr
de farine, fleur d'oranger.

crème Marquise Roth. : 4 jaunes 1/4 de lait, 100 gr de sucre
Vanille (crème anglaise) faire fondre 250 gr de chocolat,
laisser refroidir les deux Appareils avant de mélanger.
(3 ou 4 Heures de Frigidaire)

croissants : 1 k de farine, 1/2 de lait faible, 12 gr
de levure, 12 gr de sel, 20 gr de sucre (beurrer la détrempe
à 200 gr au Kilog de détrempe.

chesterkake : 150 de farine, 150 gr de beurre,
75 gr de chester, 75 de parmesan (Cayenne)

crème caramel : 1/4 de lait fort vanillé, 3 jaunes, 2 œufs
150 gr de sucre versé dans moule caramelisé, pocher au
bain marie (Four moyen)

Classic recipes of Monsieur Loyal from the 60s, many of which I still use they exchange recipes. From *Relais et Desserts* I have received as much, if not more, than I have given, and I still love attending its meetings and mixing with my fellow associates. And it was with their help that I finally prepared for the *Meilleur Ouvrier de France* contest. They watched me at work, criticising and analysing, and I watched them.

It was wonderful to see a man like Jean Millet take a cornet and write a name that looks like lace on the top of a gâteau. At that time he was one of the leading figures in *pâtisserie* in France. In fact, I went to his *laboratoire* in Paris where I was to work for four or five days before the competition in 1976. It was August and his chef, Denis Ruffel, who is about fifteen years younger than me, came back from his holidays a week early. 'If I just gave you the keys you wouldn't find anything,' he said. 'And you know, Chef, working alongside you is worth more than a week of holiday.'

At one point during those few days, we had an unexpected visit from Jean Delaveyne, another of the giants of French *pâtisserie* and cuisine. Delaveyne had become *Meilleur Ouvrier de France* many years before in 1952, and at his restaurant in Bougival, south of Paris, had trained such renowned French chefs as Guérard and Joël Robuchon. Seeing that the Millet *laboratoire* was open, he dropped in, expecting to meet the boss. He watched me work a bit and then asked, 'Are you trying to prepare for the *Meilleur Ouvrier de France*?' When I told him that I was doing just that, he replied: 'You have to start somewhere.' The remark did not sound unkind or discouraging coming from him.

Among those I have most admired is Gaston Lenôtre, the famous Paris *pâtissier* and restaurateur who, in my view, was responsible for the renewal of French *pâtisserie* between the 1960s and 1980s, both through his own work and through his school where he inspired and trained new generations. With a company of 1,000 employees, with dozens of shops inside and outside France, from Berlin to Kuwait, he is for me the Paul Bocuse of *pâtisserie*. In Britain, only Francis Coulson, the chef and *éminence grise* of the Sharrow Bay Hotel in the Lake District until his death in 1998, demonstrated what I considered total mastery of *pâtisserie*. Just the sight of one of his puddings made guests, including myself on several occasions, smile with pleasure and anticipation.

I entered the contest for the title of *Meilleur Ouvrier de France* in 1976, and gained the highest marks, in *pâtisserie,* securing me the title. I was overwhelmed, and the following words, taken from the introduction to *The Roux Brothers on Pâtisserie,* sum up most precisely how I felt.

Desserts

My body trembles as though I have been beaten, my throat is tight with emotion, my eyes brim with tears – they have just announced my name; my work as a *pâtissier-confiseur* has received the ultimate recognition and I have been honoured with the title '*un des Meilleurs Ouvriers de France 1976, Pâtissier-Confiseur*'; in other words, I am considered to be one of France's finest craftsmen in pâtisserie. Drained by the physical effort of the hundreds of hours of work and the nervous tension of the past few weeks, I hardly dare believe it. All I know is that I am here and I have succeeded. I stagger, I lurch forward as though in a dream to collect that gold medal on its red, white and blue ribbon, the first to be presented by the President of the French Republic, Monsieur Valéry Giscard d'Estaing.

I am burning hot. I am consumed by that fire which burns in every craftsman who cares passionately about his work. This is the strongest emotion I have ever felt in all my thirty-five years. I feel intoxicated. My mind flashes back, as in a film, to the master whose apprentice I was, who awoke in the adolescent I was then that most precious love for this work. I can see the craftsmen who guided me, my colleagues and my friends, the MOFs who gave me good advice – I see everyone who has helped to teach me my wonderful craft. To them I give my joy, my pride and my gratitude.

Pâtisserie, in many people's minds, is about cakes, and I have made quite a few in my time! In the 1970s, I found myself succumbing to the persuasive talk of Lord Weinstock, the chairman of GEC, when he wanted a six-foot-high cake in his racing colours, carrying a horse's head and a Star of David for the marriage of his son, Simon. This eight-tier cake, involving hundreds of hours of preparation, cost more than £1,000 even that long ago. In 1980, Weinstock asked for another for his daughter Susan. This was much smaller, about half the size of the first, and more tasteful aesthetically, but it still involved sixty man hours.

Perhaps most impressive was the ten-tier wedding *pièce montée* I made for the daughter of the Lebanese industrialist, Michel Klat. This weighed 240 kilograms and stood over two metres high. Michel Klat collects and breeds pheasants, and his collection includes forty of the world's forty-eight known species. His wife secretly took photographs of the birds so that I could put a row of sugar pheasants around the base of the cake. There were sugar roses with twenty petals each on some of the lower tiers. The roses grew smaller on the higher tiers to be replaced by different sorts of flowers nearer the top. It took me and two assistants three weeks to make, and our clothes became stiff with sugar. I worked from the photographs and I cut out the pheasant forms in *pastillage,* a special sugar gum paste, from models I made in cardboard. When the paste set, I smoothed it down with glass-paper and painted it with edible colouring agents. For the wedding itself, we hired a van and transported the cake, its separate parts wrapped in foam material. I also took along a cornet of royal icing to repair any flaws, and the end result looked as polished as porcelain. When the wedding couple cut the cake, I had very mixed emotions. I was pleased to see their happiness at this poignant moment, but at the same time, I was distressed to realise that this thing of beauty, that had taken so much effort, would soon disappear into several hundred stomachs.

To celebrate one of my own personal milestones, my fiftieth birthday in 1991, my chef Mark Dodson produced a dessert that I sometimes used to make for the Rothschilds, an Austrian *Salzburger Nockerl.* A mixture of egg yolks and icing sugar was flavoured with fresh vanilla, then whisked egg whites were folded in as if making a soufflé. Poured on to a silver tray, it was baked for two to three minutes only until just set. It's like a flat, fluffy omelette, which trembles as you move it. We had it with raspberries (but wild strawberries, not then in season, would have been even better).

That was not all, though, for Robyn decided to spoil me with another birthday celebration. For this special dinner at John and Susie Boeckman's house, Jane Asher, the actress turned accomplished *pâtissière,* made a novelty cake showing a duck dressed as a chef – representing me – stirring a saucepan in which were the twelve heads of the twelve people around the table, including my wife, brother and sister-in-law.

Over the years, I have invented and perfected a huge number of desserts. My signature *tarte au citron* has probably inspired the most imitations (rather like the salmon with sorrel developed by the Troisgros brothers, that now turns up, in markedly inferior versions, in plates all over the world). Over the last twenty years, *crème brûlée* has always been near the top of the hit parade of my desserts. By popular demand, I have developed over twenty different variations. In autumn and winter, I might add white or dark chocolate, with raspberries in September and October, or bananas toasted in caramel and flavoured with white rum. In summer, I might use wild strawberries or the most delicate white peach. I even use fennel bulb for a most unusual flavour not to everyone's taste. Those who do like it are total enthusiasts! But the *crème brûlée* that is most people's favourite is the one flavoured with pistachio, which sells and sells. When making a *crème brûlée,* it must always be lightly cooked, almost runny in the middle, not quite set. The sugar caramel glazing should be so thin and brittle that it cracks like a mirror under the spoon. The surest way to achieve this effect is with a blow-torch just before serving.

But it is without doubt my raspberry or yellow plum soufflé that arouses the most emotion. Several comments in my visitors' books – different books so no one has been copying! – have made sexual comparisons.

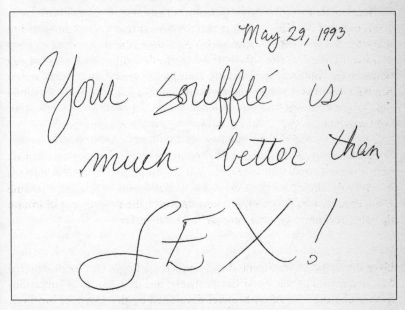

An entry in my visitors' book

However, there was one woman who really used to irritate me. She and her husband came to the Waterside Inn two or three times a year for lunch, and they would always have the same table by the Thames. On each occasion, she would analyse and dissect her soufflé as if she had just eaten it for the first time. One evening, when they were complaining that their usual table had been taken, I'm afraid I was less than polite, and told them in no uncertain terms what I thought of them. My rudeness was repaid about two years later, when I was looking for garden furniture. I found some I liked, and was put through to the managing director of the company. 'Well, Michel,' I heard, 'you don't like us talking about your soufflé, but you want me to talk about our furniture. I wonder if I should since you were so nasty to us on our anniversary. . .' For once, I was speechless.

One of the more unusual of my ventures into 'desserts' began in 1993. The British branch of the *Académie Culinaire de France,* the Academy of Culinary Arts, was anxious to ensure the proper development of young British palates, and took inspiration from the French *la semaine du goût.* This was a week in which chefs go into French primary schools to explain and demonstrate different ingredients to children, and invite them to taste their specialities. Under the British 'Adopt-A-School' programme, we started at the Waterside Inn to invite junior-school children to spend a day in our kitchens and sample different ingredients. We had to do this in a way that was familiar and easy to understand. My chef, Mark Dodson, is particularly good with children and takes over the whole show. What we do is to make them jellies, some flavoured with coffee, others with lemon or vanilla, some with unusual or downright unpleasant tastes, but the colours do not relate to the flavours. It is fascinating to see the reactions of the children who frown or smile when they suddenly find bitter or acidic where they anticipated sweet, or the completely unexpected taste of fish in a pink jelly! By this, we aim to help them learn to taste with their palates as well as with their eyes. Hopefully, this introduction of new flavours, of the ability to *discern* flavours, will develop future gourmets, something that is crucial for our profession.

Wines

THE FRENCH like to say there is no good meal without wine – *'Il n'y a pas de bon repas sans vin.'*

Wine goes back to the beginning of time. The oldest wine-press ever found, near Damascus in Syria, has been dated back to a full six millennia before Christ. The Pharaohs drank wine as did the Persians, Greeks and Romans. The Phoenicians, from what is now Lebanon, and the Greeks are credited with introducing the first vine-growing into France in the sixth century BC. In the New Testament, wine symbolises blood and therefore life itself.

When I was a child, only my father ever drank wine in our household, just a glass from time to time. Even then, he was so often absent that wine did not really play a role in my upbringing. My mother, as she did her shopping, would take an empty bottle to the local Monoprix store and fill it up with red table wine from a cask. Now there are just one or two places left in Paris that still sell wine on tap, but the practice is still common at *coopératives* that act as clearing houses for small producers in wine-growing areas.

As children, we were not allowed to taste wine. My mother, who was from Normandy, told me that she had painful memories of her father who, after drinking too much cider and Calvados, would fly into uncontrollable and violent tempers. She kept us away from wine and other alcohol during our early years out of a fear that we too might acquire an unhealthy taste for it. The only exceptions were New Year, or other occasions like a first communion or a christening, when we were allowed just a tiny drop of Italian Asti Spumante. It was so fizzy that it made me sneeze. I had this with shop-bought pink *boudoirs,* sponge fingers, that I would dunk in the wine.

Later, during my apprenticeship, Monsieur Loyal would give us a drink at Christmas. When most people are celebrating, *pâtissiers* are hard at work, and Christmas Day was one of our busiest times. At lunch the next day, Loyal poured us each a glass of a sweet Vouvray with a slice of a *bûche de Noël,* the traditional chocolate yule log, that had not been sold. 'Go easy, children,' he used to say, 'taste it, savour it.'

Things changed radically when I was nineteen and began working for Cécile de Rothschild. Not only did I get the occasional glass of wine at the end of the day, but it was a truly great wine. Marcel, if he was in a good mood, would bring to the kitchen what remained in the decanter and my first introduction to red wine was the Rothschilds' own Château Lafite. For someone who had never really drunk wine, this was a real culture shock, to start with one of the very best wines in the world.

This awakened a fascination in me and I borrowed a book Marcel kept in his office. An old volume dating back to the 1920s, it described how wines were made, the differences between the regions and between the various grapes. I devoured this rather complicated book very fast. I was discovering a new world and a new passion. I began to develop my taste by going to wine fairs and exhibitions in Paris, passing from one stand to another. Remembering my mother's fears, I used to tell myself that I was there to taste, not to drink. I quickly became very selective. I learned to differentiate between the different wines, regions and varieties of grape. With a *penchant* for luxury, my favourites were *premiers* or *grands crus.* I realised there were aspects of science, some of chemistry, some even of alchemy, and many parallels with cooking. As there are bad cooks serving bad food, there are also bad wine-makers turning out plonk.

After my military service, when I went back to work for Cécile de Rothschild, I began to put aside a little money each year to buy two or three cases, mainly Burgundies but also some Bordeaux and champagne. Since I had neither a house nor a cellar I laid this down in Picardy, at the house of my parents-in-law. They had a wonderful dark cellar below ground with a constant cool temperature all year round, and I installed racks on the walls. The only other thing in the cellar was a pile of sand where my mother-in-law grew chicory. Over time, my several dozen bottles turned into a couple of hundred. The thought that I was collecting great wines to share with my family and friends in the years ahead gave me great satisfaction.

Naturally, I was obliged to keep my acquisitions of Burgundy secret from Cécile de Rothschild. For her, a Pinot Noir was simply not a wine. Only Cabernet Franc, Cabernet Sauvignon, Petit Verdot (all of which coincidentally went into family wines) and, 'maybe', the Merlot grapes made a good wine. And wine, of course, had to come from Bordeaux. 'Then, *mon vieux,*' she told me, 'they should be not just a Bordeaux but a Rothschild.'

It was in Britain that my knowledge really began to broaden, thanks to the expertise of the excellent wine-merchants who offered their services to Le Gavroche. I began to discover wines from Alsace, the Loire and the Rhône that I had not known before. I even started to discover the merits of some of the simple *vins de pays*. These were things that I would never have found either in the Rothschilds' cellar or my own. Thanks to merchants like Gerald Asher, I came across *vins de soif* – 'thirst wines' – that are to be found everywhere in Europe, reasonably priced wines which are made with great love and attention. Just as you should not have great cuisine all the time, but simple, light or country cooking as well, it is the same with wine. There are great wines for great occasions and simpler wines for everyday consumption.

I looked after the wine-purchasing for Le Gavroche and all our group until 1985. Albert considered I was better suited to this than he was and that I also had the right negotiating talents to extract the best deals. Over the years, I learned to surprise merchants with my gifts for blind tasting when I could almost always identify the grape, the vintage and sometimes even the exact origin. (Like a golfer, I like to remember the good hole, and try to forget the bad one!)

Life is a Menu

As soon as Albert and I opened Le Gavroche, I wanted to offer the best possible wines to our customers, wines that would be in complete harmony with our cooking. Our lists at both Le Gavroche and Le Poulbot were rich in French *grands crus classés,* and our suppliers were both surprised and pleased at our rapid turnover. No other London restaurant sold so much fine and up-market wine as we did, and it represented 40 per cent of the average Gavroche bill. Our *sommeliers,* the wine waiters, reporting on a very favourable customer reaction, encouraged me to keep my standards high. I was constantly courted by new wine-merchants who were anxious to see their products on our lists. I usually had around ten regular suppliers. I asked them to guarantee the supply of the vintages I had chosen and at the prices agreed for the six-month duration of the wine-list.

At the time, we had very little room at Le Gavroche and we used to stock our wine in the most unlikely nooks and crannies, even under the bench-seating along the walls. Our customers, without knowing it, were sitting atop a liquid treasure with some great names: Pétrus, Lafite, Mouton, Yquem or La Tâche. The capital we invested was substantial but there was no alternative. We sometimes had to ask wine-merchants for a delay in payments. One day, Ronnie Sichel, one of our most faithful suppliers, stopped by at Le Gavroche and, in passing, mentioned to Albert that one of his bills had been unpaid for more than three months. Albert, without a hint of humour, asked me to bring my chef's *toque*. 'Ronnie,' he said, holding my hat, 'in view of the fact that you did not make this request until the middle of the month, your bill cannot be considered for the usual drawing by lots from this hat now. Perhaps we can put it in at the end of next month.' This episode soon did the rounds of the whole London wine trade.

Because of the pressure of work in the kitchens, I could not accept the multitude of invitations I received to wine-tastings, usually followed by a lunch. These tastings were, however, useful since they allowed me both to expand my knowledge and to test new wines and vintages for our own lists. In a city where I knew no other professionals, the tastings I did manage to attend put me in touch with other buyers like George Potts, a refined, educated man, and a director of the Savoy group. As the buyer for the Savoy, Lancaster, Berkeley, Connaught and Claridge's hotels, he was an *éminence grise* of the British wine trade, a position which guaranteed him a red-carpet reception at any tasting. I used to compare notes with him to benefit from his judgement and experience.

The generosity extended was huge. Morgan & Furze, in Brick Street, which used to supply more than half the wines listed at Le Poulbot, was especially hospitable. Typically, there would be between six and ten guests from the restaurant and hotel trade, all seeking new bottles to add to their lists. The quality of the food was rivalled only by the quality of the fine wines served in their private dining-room in the basement of their headquarters. The atmosphere was at its best at the end of the meal when the decanter of port went round the table. It was up to the guests to try and guess the vintage and it was there that I tasted 1935, 1945, 1955, 1960 and 1963 ports as well as my first Havana cigar. I remember leaving there in the late afternoon and returning to Le Gavroche with my cigar still in my mouth. Albert greeted me with a somewhat equivocal smile. . .

Gerald Asher was a wine-merchant who fascinated me enormously. He only imported *vins de pays,* everyday wines that he was trying to introduce to the British. Like Albert and myself, his mission was to educate the British. He believed that wine was something that should be available for all budgets and classes but, unfortunately, he was well ahead of his time. The middle and upper classes preferred more structured wines like the better Bordeaux and Burgundies while the working classes remained faithful to beer. The public was not ready for him and he ended up bankrupt. Now, figures testify to the change in British drinking habits, with wine – the international choice the British have is phenomenal – drunk throughout all layers of British society.

It was Gerald who introduced me to Quincy, a tasty, light white from the Loire that he served as an *apéritif.* He invited very small groups to his tastings, offering them fifteen or so wines from the Jura, Languedoc, Roussillon, Corbières or Hérault, often with a country-style meal. I particularly remember meeting Elizabeth David, the *doyenne* of British food writers, at one of Gerald's tastings. This allowed me to get to know a bit better a Gavroche customer who was extremely reserved, even shy. Her personal preference in food was for sunny Mediterranean cuisine and for regional and *bourgeois* cooking, much like Cécile de Rothschild.

Once or twice a year, I was invited to tasting lunches at J.B. Reynier, a family business run by Peter Reynier. Peter once described to me in French with a touch of English accent his love for Pinot Noir, and his eyes shone at the mention of this vine. Peter represented all the great names of Burgundy: Drouhin, Faively, Rousseau, d'Angerville, Gouges and Sauzet. His firm was one of the few in Britain to start buying in bulk, as well as by the case, importing barrels to bottle in its cellars in London.

We would begin with a Perrier-Jouët champagne – which he represented in Britain – in his office. Then we would taste wines chosen to go with each dish, like poached Scottish wild salmon served still just warm, with a succulent mayonnaise and a glass of Clos de Sainte-Catherine, Côteaux du Layon, Domaine Jean Baumard, from the Loire. Peter, above all an outstanding ambassador for Burgundy, was one of the first Britons to gain French recognition as an authority and to be named *Grand Officier de la Confrérie des Chevaliers du Tastevin*.

When I was thirty-six, in 1977, I joined a club of fourteen members, whose aim was to seek out good food and wines, at the instigation of Leonard Denis, one of the great British authorities on wine. The Benedicts' Club, whose members are leading figures in their speciality, ranging from medicine to banking, visit a different region every year, sometimes venturing beyond France to Penedes or Xeres in Spain, to Portugal or Italy. This also helps me make new contacts who sometimes become suppliers.

Travelling outside Europe, particularly in my capacity as an adviser on food to British Airways, I came across New World wines, from California, Oregon, Australia, New Zealand or South Africa. Although there were some very honourable exceptions, I often found that these wines lacked structure and complexity. They often had a good floral bouquet but this was not followed up in taste, and the flavour of wood in whites was frequently too strong. At home, however, where Robyn and I often eat ethnic food, we drink wines from the New World or from elsewhere in Europe other than France.

In the 1970s, I had between 150 and 200 wines on my list, compared with 750 and thirty suppliers now. When I look at those old wine lists, I can hardly believe what I read. In 1971, we had a 1945 Château Haut-Brion, the year of the century for this Graves, at just £15.50 and a 1937 Château Latour at £10.50!

Those figures look somewhat weak compared with the prices obtained at some recent wine auctions. In September 1997, Christie's told me one of its clients had asked for me to prepare a dinner for just over 100 guests in advance of the auction of his cellar. All I knew of the vendor was that he knew my name! A Christie's director suggested, not to my displeasure, that having me organise the dinner was a way of ensuring that the right buyers would all be in London for the occasion.

At the end of the meal, I was called into the hall and asked to say a few words. I noted that, usually at Christie's, I was a buyer, adding that 'While you have been tasting my food, I have been enjoying your wine.' The mystery vendor had offered six wines for the dinner. The main course, a rolled saddle of lamb, was served with three Bordeaux, a Château Latour 1964, a Château Calon-Ségur 1947 and a Château Pétrus 1990. This was followed by Château d'Yquem 1983 and a 1955 Taylor's port.

The vendor put his wines up for auction during the next two days, and succeeded in keeping his identity secret throughout. According to press reports which speculated that he was a Norwegian millionaire, none of those present, bidders from as far afield as Japan and the United States, recognised him either. Christie's called him 'Monsieur X'. The total raised by the auction was £7.04 million. A single jeroboam of Mouton Rothschild 1945 fetched £71,500. The *Daily Telegraph* calculated that this amounted to the equivalent of £1,702 a glass!

Now I look for wines for all occasions and all wallets because I believe everyone nowadays should be able to enjoy wine. My choice, as far as supplying my restaurants is concerned, has always been a simple one. I have chosen to be a purist and buy only French wines for the Waterside Inn. French wines fully complement my cooking. My financial stake is substantial since I buy *primeur* wines. These are wines of the last vintage, which will remain in cask at the château for two to two and a half years. After being bottled, I will still have to wait five to ten years before I can put them on my list. This is not to say that there are not wines from elsewhere that would be suitable for many of my dishes. It is just that I know there is always a French wine to go with everything.

Nowadays I take part in fewer tastings than before and leave it to my *sommeliers* to do a pre-selection and learn to take responsibility. I come in for the final choice when we change our wine-list, which is about every six months.

An interesting phenomenon of the past few years has been the change in philosophy concerning the marriage of food and wine. There are classic formulae such as asparagus with a muscat d'Alsace, roast leg or rack of lamb with a Pauillac, or roast sea bass and fennel with a Puligny Montrachet. All of these combinations are excellent and free of risk. Now there are novelties like a chocolate dessert served with a late harvest wine, a *vendange tardive,* from Alsace, or with a Banyuls from the south. My red mullet dish *rougets en bécassine*, cooked woodcock-style with its liver and blood in a wine sauce, is excellent with a Volnay, a red Burgundy. This marriage would have been inconceivable a few years ago.

For myself, I abstain from all wine and alcohol a day or two each week, in the same way that I have one day of eating just vegetables. This precludes the need for dieting, which I hate, and gives my system a chance to breathe. And of course, when I take my first glass of wine after these little 'fasts', I appreciate it all the more!

Away from my own cellar, I rarely choose my own wine in a restaurant. I ask the *sommelier* to find me something out of the ordinary, off the beaten track, a wine I am not likely to have tasted before. They often love the challenge, and my request leads to heated debate between colleagues about the possibilities.

As for the service of wines, especially in these days of central heating, it is an absolute heresy to serve a wine at room temperature. At my house in the south of France when I am selecting the wine for a dinner, I choose it as I choose ingredients in the market. I look around my cellar and select the bottle for that day. Then I move it up the stairs gradually to let it pick up a degree or two in temperature, but no more. I would sooner drink it at its cellar temperature, however, than over-warmed by modern heating. Decanting is usually a must for the reds, as is carafing for whites.

When I prepare a celebratory meal, I like to offer a wine for a *mise en bouche*, to get the tastebuds tingling. This will be a lighter and younger wine from the same region as the grander vintage chosen for the main course. So a first growth from the Bordeaux region should be preceded by a third, fourth or fifth that is just four to five years younger. I think it is wrong to expect the palate to appreciate a really great wine immediately; it needs preparation, just like an athlete needs a warm-up before a big race (although a lot less strenuous!). Just a glass of this first wine will do, the rest can be kept for the following day or used to make vinegar – the best wines make the best vinegar. That is my policy with sauces as well: the best wines must be used.

Appreciating wine is a complex and exciting speciality and, in my view, *sommeliers* have the best job front of house. It is their role to educate the palate and the senses. They have to keep their own tastes alive as well as manage the cellar, the stocks and the accounts.

I discovered the Burgundy region properly thanks to a Tyrolean, Joseph

Berkmann. He had five restaurants at the time and was also the British agent of Georges Duboeuf, the man who made Beaujolais famous all over the world. In the 1970s, I started going to the Beaujolais every two years with Joseph and we would progress northwards to Burgundy. In the Beaujolais, we tasted the Gamay grape, which is very simple and has nothing of the complexity of a Pinot. The Gamay, however, produces a wine which is good to start with, as a precursor to nobler wines.

I took the precaution of taking a spoonful of olive oil in the morning to line my stomach and absorb what was to come as we did blind-tasting of between thirty and forty different Beaujolais wines in a day. In between, we ate *charcuterie*, like *andouillette* sausages or *caillettes,* little individual pâtés, from Bobosse, the king of Lyons *charcutiers.* Then we would have a siesta.

In Burgundy, I met the three Moreys, Albert and his two sons, Bernard and Jean-Marc. Their Chassagne-Montrachets were among the best and were, like them, generous and opulent. My preference was divided between their wines and those of Michel Colin-Deleger who, in his own image, produces something more austere. Everyone, whether in wine or cuisine, makes something that comes from within. For me, the greatest pleasure is to taste a wine when I know who made it. It resembles his character.

In 1992, I had the privilege of attending one of the great wine-tastings of the twentieth century. This was held to celebrate the forty-fifth anniversary of the career of André Gagey, the director of the Louis Jadot Burgundy house. The fifty guests, from as far afield as New York and Japan, included a number of two- or three-star Michelin chefs, among them Raymond Blanc of the Manoir aux Quat' Saisons near Oxford, and others from France, Germany and Italy. And then there was Robert Parker, who was just then beginning to make his way in the world of wine. He can now make or break the fortune of a wine-maker through reviews and comments in his wine guide.

We tasted twelve wines of which the youngest and, in most opinions, the best, was (perhaps surprisingly) a white, a 1904 Montrachet. In his tasting notes published in *La Revue du Vin de France,* Michel Bettane wrote: 'The first nose is of *brioche* or butter of an exquisite finesse, evolving very quickly towards citrus/grapefruit (was a proportion of the grapes perhaps affected by *pourriture noble* [noble rot]?), and after five more minutes, towards quince jelly.' The oldest wine tasted was an 1865 Romanée and others included a Richebourg 1877, a Pommard 1875 and a Clos Vougeot 1898. About the Romanée, Michel Bettane said it had a nuance of cocoa bean, which is a characteristic of the *terroir.* He said it was impossible to transmit in words the miraculous impression which this floating and spiritual wine leaves in the mouth. After the tasting, we were treated to lunch in the King's Chamber at the Hospices de Beaune, the first time this room had been opened for such a celebration, testifying to Beaune's belief that this was a truly historic occasion.

I had a unique tasting of what I first assumed was just one wine in Australia four years later. There, at the Hunter Valley home of the Australian wine guru, Len Evans, a large decanter of wine was brought out to accompany the lunch-time cheese. Len asked me to taste it and guess what it was. I said immediately, on the first sip, that it was a Romanée-Conti, DRC (Domaine de la Romanée-Conti). It had extraordinary finesse, complexity, and so much concentration. It was a silky mouthful that had more length than any other great Burgundy I had tasted. The flavour of tart, over-ripe wild fruits went on and on, ending up in the famous 'peacock's tail', a marker of Romanée-Conti. Len looked stunned, and asked me to identify the vintage. I said this had stumped me, since the colour and nose suggested it was between thirty and fifty years old, but something in the taste put it at more like seventy years old. Len turned white and confessed that it was a blend of seventeen Romanée-Contis, whose vintages went from 1917 to 1978, that he had re-bottled from what remained of a tasting given five years before to celebrate his sixtieth birthday. He described my judgement as a *coup de grâce,* and was very quiet for the rest of the meal (which is very unlike him).

I experience enormous pleasure every time I open a bottle of wine. The most exciting thing, however, is to present it, to explain it and to serve it to those who are about to taste it.

Cheese is an excellent companion for wine, especially a farm cheese. Since I do nothing with cheese except choose it and serve it, and since there are so many cheeses, I have not presumed to discuss their richness and variety. I just offer a prayer that Brussels' efforts to pasteurise Europe's soft cheeses do not destroy them.

If just one cheese were left in the world, I would choose Roquefort. If I had to choose just one last wine to go with it, I have no hesitation. That would be an Yquem.

Buffets

T HE GREATEST meal of my life was without doubt that offered by Alain Chapel, a three-star Michelin chef, for his fortieth birthday in 1977. At his restaurant in Mionnay near Lyons, Alain made lunch for 110 people, all two- and three-star chefs. All of us, revelling not only in the food but also in the spirit of comradeship, were to encounter new tastes. For me, it was eating monkfish liver for the first time ever. Alain, who was sadly to die at fifty-two, killed by a heart attack, demonstrated his extraordinary culinary skill with great simplicity. Drinking only Krug champagne and excellent wines chosen to match the food (some dating to the year of his birth), and ending the meal with Havana cigars, we, his fellow chefs, did not get up from the table until early evening. It was an extremely pleasurable and memorable exception to one of my rules: meals should never drag on for hours.

That is why I am a fan of the buffet. A buffet allows guests to sample what they want, with whom they want and for as long as they want. It allows them to move away from other guests who are not to their liking and to stretch their legs. It has built-in informality. If a guest is late at a buffet, he or she can join in with no ceremony or embarrassment. If someone needs to leave early, this, too, goes unnoticed. The buffet allows the gourmet to hop from one food to the next, tasting delicately, or eating to excess, depending on his or her mood.

In my life I have prepared few buffets, but I have sampled many. They can vary from the ordinary and banal to the spectacular. The best buffets should offer a huge choice like a market. They should be colourful and diverse like a theatrical production or a painting. Buffets, when first seen, should take the breath away like the opening scene of an opera or ballet. A designed arrangement, as for flowers, is crucial. You can have good materials, but if they are not shown to their best advantage, the result can be too fussy and overloaded or too light.

Among the most attractive buffets I have known are those made for the annual Congress of *Relais & Châteaux,* the voluntary organisation that unites top hotels and restaurants from all over the world. The 700–800 members and guests meet in a different country each year, and one of the events is always a buffet organised by local chefs for their colleagues. It includes the best of regional specialities from all corners of the host country, and those that serve often wear local costume.

A particular advantage of the buffet is that you can walk around it and reconnoitre before deciding what is best. On the second time round, you can home in on what you want. A master of this technique was France's late President, Georges Pompidou, who, when still working for the Banque Rothschild, was a frequent guest of Cécile de Rothschild. It is said that the Rothschilds leave their mark on everyone who associates with them, and Pompidou – described to me by the long-time Elysée chef Joël Normand as the president with the finest gourmet taste – almost certainly refined his palate in their service. Marcel, the butler, used to describe to me how Pompidou, staring intently from under his bushy eyebrows, would circle the buffet table like a predator before swooping.

On a simpler, less formal level, my favourite sort of buffet is the French country-style buffet served in the open air. I sometimes have one at my home in southern France, with *charcuterie*, pâtés, terrines, ham and salads like *tabbouleh*, followed by large tarts, ice-cream and fruit, with simple *vins de soif,* wines to quench your thirst, served from small barrels.

The first buffet I ever worked on was for the British Embassy in Paris to celebrate the Queen's official birthday in June. In far-flung British missions all over the world, the event is known as the QBP, for Queen's Birthday Party. I was at the Embassy for two QBPs. For the first, I remember the chef, Emile Rouault, standing on a stool to make up for his short stature and clapping his hands to bring us together. He told us there was to be a garden party for 2,000 people ten days later. I was then eighteen and my job was to make 5,000 *petits fours* of eight different kinds. I thought Rouault was going to give me recipes but he told me to dig my own out of the book that I had started compiling as an apprentice. My contribution included *langues de chat, petits rochers noix de coco, macarons, palets raisins,* and *petits sablés.* Other Embassy cooks had the daunting task of making 10,000 savoury pieces of which there were sixteen different sorts. Before going home each night, I put my *petits fours* in sealed boxes to keep them fresh. When the day of the garden party arrived, it took me more than five hours to arrange them on silver dishes.

Cécile de Rothschild used to organise buffets during the *Saison de Paris* in May and June, two to three a month, for up to twenty people. Guests would arrive at eleven in the evening after the theatre and stay until about one. She preferred buffets to seated suppers because 'Suppers are boring, *mon vieux*. I either know the guests too well or not well enough.' She wanted nothing laid out on the buffet table before she returned home and 'nothing in the fridge either'. She often liked a half-cup of *gazpacho* to start with 'to keep them calm'. This allowed each guest to sit down with a starter and a glass of wine, heading off an undignified rush to the buffet.

Then there would be lightly cooked lobster, bean salad with a sprinkling of watercress and a dressing made with lemon juice rather than vinegar, cold fillet of beef, with little sticks of carrot preserved in olive oil and a horseradish sauce. Sometimes I made a cold ham soufflé. This I made from the best-quality pork that had already been cured in salted water or *saumure*. It was slowly cooked thereafter to a melting tenderness, and when cut into, gave off a light smell of hazelnuts. The soufflé was pink in colour, made with the ham, whipped cream, poultry stock and a little gelatine with spices. The trembling jelly garnish made from the ham-poaching liquid was flavoured with a drop of dry sherry. There would be a whole wheel of Brie cheese, followed by macaroons, of different flavours and colours – vanilla, lemon, chocolate and raspberry – then perhaps a strawberry tart. If I had not made a ham soufflé, then I might make a cold strawberry soufflé. (There was no question of serving both a savoury and a sweet soufflé in the same evening.)

In 1976, when we were well established in London, the club of two- and three-star chefs, *Traditions et Qualités*, invited the Roux Brothers to join. Although Albert said he did not care whether we did or not, dismissing the association as a purely French outfit with no relevance to Britain, I set about filling in the forms on my own. Le Gavroche became a member and the year after, we hosted their annual spring outing, for colleagues like Paul Bocuse, the Troisgros brothers from Roanne, and Jean-Pierre Haeberlin of the Auberge de l'Ill near Strasbourg. I prepared massive sugar set-pieces for the entrance to the bar, and we opted to have a buffet lunch. One of the hot dishes was an enormous pillow-shaped puff pastry, filled with layers of quail breasts and a forcemeat of veal and quail flavoured with pistachios and truffles. The other was a *navarin d'agneau printanier,* a rich lamb stew with spring vegetables. We also poached about twenty Aylesbury ducks wrapped in napkins for twenty minutes. We served the breasts cold, pink and juicy, finely sliced, with a port-based Cumberland sauce and a bean salad. I have never seen ducks disappear so fast! For dessert, I made huge arched *tuile* biscuits flavoured with orange, lemon tarts and a passionfruit and blackcurrant mousse. The first guests arrived at half-past twelve, and although the eating had finished, the *camaraderie* kept everyone at the tables until just before five, leaving us very little time to prepare the dinner service.

As the only *Meilleur Ouvrier de France* living in Britain, I was later asked to organise a huge buffet at the Royal Pavilion in Brighton to celebrate the bicentenary of Antonin Carême. Carême was a *pâtissier* who worked as a cook for Napoleon, Talleyrand, the emperor of Austria and the Tsar of Russia before he was tempted away from Saint Petersburg by the Prince Regent to take charge of his kitchens. Carême worked in Britain from 1816 to 1820 and then he returned to Paris to work for the Rothschilds until his death in 1832. He was the author of many classic books on cuisine. According to a contemporary account, the Prince Regent once told Carême his food was so tantalising that it would kill him. The chef replied: 'Your Highness, my duty is to tempt your appetite; yours to control it.'

The 1984 celebration, whose principal sponsors were G.H. Mumm Champagne and Diners Club International, brought together about thirty chefs from top London hotels and restaurants, British, Swiss, German and French, all prepared to pay homage to their patron and mentor. Among the guests from abroad, mainly France, were Georges Blanc, Paul

Haeberlin, Louis Outhier, Gérard Pangaud, Alain Senderens and Roger Vergé. We had a formal dinner one night, the courses cooked by different chefs based in England (among them Anton Mosimann, Bernard Gaume, Peter Kromberg, Michel Bourdin, Albert and myself), but the star of the show was the aforesaid buffet. Much of it was for the eye rather than the palate, much as Carême himself used to do. Other *Meilleurs Ouvriers de France* brought some pieces of blown and pulled sugar. Some of the displays were made with vegetable fats and *pastillage,* a gum sugar paste. One of my *pâtissiers* made a life-sized harp from sugar. Also present was John Huber, then senior lecturer in *pâtisserie* at Slough College of Higher Education. He and his brigade of students made the centrepiece of the buffet table: a hollow column of *pastillage,* Carême's portrait painted in the middle with edible colours, with a flag on either side, one French, the other British.

The guests sipped champagne and marvelled at this spectacular display of sugar work, something that is rarely seen by the public outside a competition room. In fact the buffet table was open to the public for two days after its first appearance. We had actually arranged for BBC Television to get a preview and immortalise the scene before the guests arrived, but suddenly the technicians started rolling up their cables. The producer told us they had been called out on strike, which infuriated me. Because the BBC had an exclusive, we had not organised any other professional recording or photography of the event, which was the result of literally thousands of hours of work.

The following year, I was among a group of chefs who went to Morocco with the *Club des Chefs des Chefs,* a club for chefs who cooked for the world's heads of state. King Hassan II had invited the club, then including the chefs of the French and American presidents, King Juan Carlos of Spain, the Grand Duke of Luxembourg and Prince Rainier of Monaco. The king also invited a handful of three-star chefs to accompany the party.

When we arrived, invited to his summer palace for afternoon tea, the king had decided to play golf and therefore could not receive us. We were put in two coaches and driven to a beach where rich Moroccans were enjoying their *cabanas.* Within minutes, they had been evicted and we were installed. A buffet consisting of snacks like nuts and pistachios, appeared from nowhere, and was served with Dom Pérignon champagne. After a couple of hours shuffling in the sand, we were taken back to the Royal Palace – Hassan was now ready – and treated to a huge buffet of desserts in a marquee. I had never seen so many pastries and sweetmeats. They were still warm and soft in the middle. The Moroccan chef said he had been told to prepare this at the last minute and that more than thirty *pâtissiers* had been put to work with no more than an hour's notice.

That night at dinner, we were entertained in small groups in the private houses of friends of the king. We sat cross-legged around our tables, Moroccan-style. My wife Robyn and I were seated with the host and hostess, cousins of King Hassan. Fellow guests Gilles Bragard, the world-renowned maker of chef's clothing, and the two French restaurant critics Henri Gault and Christian Millau. Gault and Millau had done much to promote *nouvelle cuisine* in the 1970s, and had founded a restaurant guide that still carries their names even though they have both since retired. They were controversial figures in the world of cuisine, with some chefs accusing them of favouritism in their judgements, and of accepting free meals and other perks. I was among their detractors and could never bring myself to even shake their hands. The atmosphere was further deadened as Gault and Millau had split up their business interests and spent the evening pointedly ignoring each other! With three guests not speaking to each other, it was an especially memorable dinner for Gilles, his wife and Robyn...

In the early 1990s, the recession that followed the Gulf War prompted a tightening of belts all round. A client had asked me to arrange a wedding buffet at the Waterside Inn for his daughter. He explained that, while there would be seventy guests, it would not be necessary to cater for more than sixty, as the children coming would eat very little. This turned out to be a miscalculation. Other guests, knowing they were going to eat at the Waterside Inn, seemed to have starved themselves in anticipation and ate for two. I had prepared salmon in aspic, lobsters and crayfish, and arranged them on the buffet tables with platters of cold meats, and bowls of salads. All the noble dishes went first, leaving the meats and salads untouched. The buffet looked a little bare, but even worse was that the newlyweds, while circulating with their guests, had not eaten at all. I went back to the kitchen, and started to cook fish and grill lobsters all over again, and all this was soon wolfed down too. Some months later, I repeated the wedding buffet experience, and the result was the same. That was the last buffet I served at the Waterside Inn. It is not a restaurant for buffets.

Among the most spectacular buffets I have seen are those organised on Celebrity Cruises ships. There is a magnificent, surreal gala midnight buffet, the immensely long table dominated by a huge ice carving in the form of a swan or bear. There are dancers made from blown sugar, and dragons and eagles carved from different vegetables (Filipinos and Latin Americans are very talented at these sculptures). Some fifty chefs from different continents work for several days, and their work gives a flavour of each country and continent. When the buffet is unveiled, passengers start by taking photographs and filming the scene for an hour or so before the protective rope barrier is removed and they can begin their feast. There are lobsters, saddle of lamb and beef, terrines and desserts like gâteau Saint Honoré, gâteau Paris–Brest and, *croquembouches*. The end result looks like an international culinary exhibition, a feast for the eyes and the palate.

Once when I returned to Bray from a Monday in London, my wife Robyn had laid out a very special buffet. Marks & Spencer had asked me to test pies and steak and kidney puddings. I asked them to send the samples on a Monday or Tuesday when the Waterside Inn was closed. I had forgotten all about this but I could smell something unusual as I entered my house. Robyn welcomed me to 'the kingdom of buffets'. Knowing the time of my train, she had warmed up the pies, made by some twenty existing and potential M & S suppliers, and arranged them in best buffet style on a white-clothed table. In truly professional spirit, she had put spoons in water bowls for tasting, and other bowls for spitting out as in a wine tasting, papers and pencils for notes.

Some of the pies were very good, others edible but some were barely edible (I have a particularly bad memory of a minced beef pie). The meat in the pies varied in quality, quantity and texture; the sauce in some was too thin, too glutinous or thick in others; some were too sweet, some too bitter. I had to get up twice during the night to take medicines for indigestion.

When I woke up the next morning, I could still smell the mixed pie odours. I sent a fax with my findings to Marks & Spencer. I had learnt a very important lesson: food is just like wine, and you should no more taste twenty pies in one sitting than you should sample 100 wines.

After-dinner Speech

CRYSTAL BALL–GAZING is not a common pastime of mine. However, nearly two decades ago, I was persuaded to publish my predictions for cuisine in the year 2000. In 1967, when others thought we were wasting our energies in a land of culinary Philistines, my brother Albert and I brought across the Channel our unrevolutionary ideas, based on quality and tradition with a healthy dose of innovation. We gambled on a change in Britain's eating habits. The rest, as they say, is history. When we first arrived in England, food and sex were treated in the same way: they were taboo subjects never to be mentioned. Now, the reverse is true and everyone is an expert on both food *and* sex.

In my excursion into fortune-telling in 1983, I predicted that a thirty-five-hour working week in Europe would force restaurants to change their methods and bring a decline in standards. In the event, as the year 2000 dawned, France introduced a mandatory thirty-five-hour week, causing gloom among my colleagues in many of the world's finest restaurants. They simply do not see how they can maintain quality with the constantly changing kitchen team that shift-work must inevitably bring. I also forecast, all those years ago, a drop in the production of organically grown fruit and vegetables and the increasing pasteurisation, homogenisation and sterilisation of dairy products.

My powers of clairvoyance did not, however, extend to the arrival of the e.dot.com generation. In the 1990s, the genteel elegance of my early customers gave way to the jeans and trainers of gold-card holders. The main similarity between their business world and mine is timing – for success in any start-up, one must be in the right place with the right idea at the right time. In my early years, 600 of our customers had accounts at Le Gavroche in London. Many just left a card and we would forward the bill. The system never failed and our reservations book used to look like pages out of *Who's Who*. Now we often do not know who our customers are.

Gertrude, a German girl at reception, was a stickler for the requirement of those times that all men must wear ties. She steadfastly barred the way one evening to a mild-mannered man because he was under-dressed. 'My child,' the man pleaded, 'I am a priest.' Finally, I escorted the poor man into the restaurant and explained to an unrepentant Gertrude that a clerical collar was ample dispensation. 'For the Pope maybe,' she muttered, 'but for a priest?'

I wonder how Gertrude would make out now. Even if the customer is always right – a point that I drum home to my youngsters – I do wish he or she would take the trouble to dress decently and not come to the Waterside Inn in garb more suited to gardening than a smart night out.

My first months in London were a time of constant astonishment.

I remember driving to our first restaurant, Le Gavroche in Chelsea, and seeing what looked liked a crowd of refugees, with backpacks, on foot or in cars, all flocking towards the same spot. It reminded me of pilgrims converging on Lourdes. The crowds were in fact horticultural enthusiasts heading for the Chelsea Flower Show. In the evenings, they would pour into the streets, virtually ambushing taxis and looking for sustenance.

The next year, not to miss out, we opened Le Gavroche early each evening. Occasionally, we got insults for not serving either tea or sandwiches. Some customers, however, stayed on for dinner and at the end of the week others arrived, hidden by the huge plants they had bought, stacking them behind the bar for safekeeping as they ate.

Now the flood comes in Ascot Week, though in a more structured fashion, when some people book a table every evening at the Waterside Inn and the same customers return year after year. Their mood-swings depend on the weather, what they have eaten or drunk at lunch time and whether or not they backed the right horse. The women in their colourful hats and the men in more sober grey top-hats all arrive at the same time, and they all want to eat, drink and pay at the same time. This creates minor mayhem while my kitchen goes on a war footing to make 100 dinners a night.

The British public got its best view of the much talked about Roux Brothers in the late 1980s when my brother and I were the stars of a BBC television cookery programme. This was somewhat ironic because, after more than ten years of almost idyllic cooperation, relations between the two of us had become very tense. I had even taken the decision to end some of our joint enterprises and concentrate on the Waterside Inn, leaving Le Gavroche entirely in Albert's hands.

Fraternal rivalry had always played its part in our relationship; it had pushed each of us to ever greater culinary exploits. But I had begun to feel that Albert was cutting me out of decision-making. In the early years, because of his fluent English, he had led the way, but as plans were laid to move Le Gavroche from Chelsea to Upper Brook Street, I found I was not consulted on the new site for the restaurant, its decoration or on the planning of the kitchen, my specific role in all our other restaurants. Then in 1982, when Le Gavroche became Britain's first Michelin three-star restaurant, my brother claimed the credit; until then we had always shared everything. It was time for a parting of the ways, and our 'de-merger' was finally complete in 1986, a year after the Waterside Inn became Britain's second three-star restaurant.

It was two years later that the BBC suggested the thirteen-programme cookery series, which eventually reached an audience of around two million people. All the old tensions resurfaced and the first day of recording in Cardiff was torment for me. As in all our publishing ventures, Albert left the script-writing to me, but just as work began he insisted on swapping scripts. The poor cameramen were quite lost since our musical chairs totally disrupted the plans they had been given. Subsequent weeks produced more rows. The banter that spiced the programmes prompted the press to compare us with Morecambe and Wise, but the resentment between us was real enough.

For the sixth programme, I invited our mother from France. During a pause, she descended from the producer's box to give us both a piece of her mind. She told us we spent more time quarrelling than cooking and that she was ashamed of us. Frances Whitaker, the producer, was livid that she did not have a camera team on hand to film her.

Despite the tensions and the difficulty of working together, that series had a positive effect: it brought Albert and me back together and effaced some of the bad feeling of previous years. A few weeks after the last programme, Albert even said he missed the series as he was just beginning to get interested in it.

Where the Roux Brothers have triumphed is in training native British chefs and giving them opportunities they never had before. In the 1970s, when most of our staff were French, a few young Britons, attracted by our success, sought work in our kitchens. At the time, it would have been inconceivable for a British cook to work on the Continent. In Europe, British cooks were a laughing stock. But we began to persuade colleagues in some of France's best restaurants to take in British chefs for a couple of weeks – and not just those who worked for us. One of the very first to go, to Roger Vergé's three-star restaurant near Cannes, was Nico Ladenis, who then had his own restaurant in Dulwich. Nico, never a Roux employee, soon had one Michelin star and he went on to win the top rating of three.

Later, Nick Rowe from Diners Club, himself a *bon vivant*, suggested that the Roux Brothers should introduce a more structured system that Diners Club could sponsor. Thus was founded the annual Roux Brothers' Scholarship for a promising chef. Entrants must be in full-time employment, at a particular level in their culinary careers, and between the ages of twenty-two and twenty-eight. They progress through a series of regional heats, culminating in a national final, with six regional winners vying against each other, in April of each year. The contestants have fun, I think, but we judges enjoy ourselves even more – each time it's like one big party. The judges in 2000 were almost all top chefs and cooks – Rick Stein, Brian Turner (a particular favourite of Robyn's, and vice versa), Simon Hopkinson, Gary Rhodes, Frances Bissell, Sally Clarke, my nephew Michel, my son Alain, myself and Albert, with Victor Cesarani, our vice chairman. The star prize for the ultimate winner is to spend three months in a three-star restaurant on the Continent, working closely with the individual chef. The merit of the scheme is that Roux scholars not only bring back new expertise but also enhance the reputation of British cooks abroad. Perceptions have changed to such an extent that in 1999 I managed to place three of my British staff in responsible posts in three top restaurants in France. Thirty years ago we could not even have dreamt of such a thing.

That said, I sometimes feel that there is an innate British complacency. Some chefs – behaving too much like starlets for my liking, slamming doors, expelling customers and even physically abusing their staff – seem to think they have now understood everything. They think they have arrived. In my view, if you think you have arrived, then you should retire, because I firmly believe that the battle for good, innovative food is a constant one, and a chef can never rest on his laurels however many Michelin stars he may have.

Ever since Albert and I earned our first stars, I have been aware of sniping press comment that Michelin is not up to much, that it is outdated and that it is a French guide unsuited to British needs. I am hardly likely to attack an institution that has honoured me for so many years, but to me, given the mix of nationalities putting it together, it is a European guide and the one that remains the most professional. And what is marvellous to me about my fellow three-star chefs, is that these men and women are all so different. There are just thirty-seven of them at the time of writing on a continent of 380 million people and their cooking may be modern, imaginative, classical, eclectic or eccentric. Each is an individual, and as there is not just one tenor in the world, nor just one painter, there is not just one chef. What they have in common is what is primarily recognised by Michelin – that their cooking is superb and that it is superb every day.

I do not, however, cook for Michelin. I cook what I like to eat, and I am delighted that my customers like what I like.

For that I need staff, and around me are staff who put on a show every night, a fireworks display that ends, without fail, with a grand finale for the customers. Yes, the staff. What a staff I have been blessed with!

One of Britain's greatest assets, from my selfish point of view, is its language. Another is that it is only just off the coast of France and the rest of Europe. A mastery of English is now essential for any ambitious youngster anywhere in the world. This single fact, together with my three

Michelin stars, makes it easier for me to recruit the highly qualified cooks and waiters I need and to bring them from some of the finest restaurants in the world. Although I have a staff of only around forty-five now, literally thousands of different people have worked for me in my various restaurants, from those who stayed just a day or two before walking out in a huff to those who stayed for years and became close friends.

I have had staff of whom I am immensely proud: those who went on to set up and run top-class restaurants of their own as well as those, like my chef, Mark Dodson, or my manager, Diego Masciaga, who have stayed by my side helping me maintain the highest standards day after day.

And there have been others . . .. I had a manager who left with the restaurant's takings in a bag, never to be seen again. This was not a case of dishonesty, since the bag containing the money and cheques was found intact by the roadside, but one of mental disorder. His disappearance happened to coincide with that month's full moon. He not only abandoned his job and the money that day, he also walked out on his wife.

I had a *voiturier* looking after customers' cars who grandly handed over the keys to the wrong Jaguar when a client left the restaurant. The client drove away in style with the real owner watching in horror from his bedroom window. He rushed down in his dressing-gown. My *voiturier* shouted reassuringly one of the few English expressions he had mastered: 'No problem!' (The car was subsequently restored to its rightful owner.)

I had an absent-minded *commis* waiter who mixed up orders, taking pigeon to a customer who had ordered rabbit and rabbit to a man who had ordered pigeon. Alerted by an agitated *maître d'hôtel*, I left the kitchen to seek a peaceful solution to a highly embarrassing mistake. The customers turned out to be no brighter than my *commis* and, before I could begin my hand-wringing apologies, they congratulated me in turn on the quality and originality of both my rabbit and my pigeon. The would-be pigeon-eater apparently thought nothing of the rabbit made of bread perched at the head of his plate, while his gastronomic rival saw nothing odd in the wing-stub, protruding from his saddle of rabbit! I retreated to the kitchen, preferring, for all our sakes, to leave these good people in blissful ignorance.

In the early days, crossing the Channel to work was an adventure. Among our first was Raymond Langlois, an engaging young man. Raymond's mother kept ringing me up to complain that she had no news of her son. Each time, I told Raymond to write home and he assured me that he was writing regularly. Finally, the mother's calls became too insistent. I taxed Raymond with the problem and asked him exactly when he had written to his mother. He replied that he wrote twice a week and posted the letters in Sloane Square, in the red letter-box as he had been told. I went with him to check. He pointed me towards a large red iron container full of grit for icy roads. I furtively put my hand inside and pulled out four or five soggy letters.

The people who work for me are by nature ambitious, sometimes very ambitious. There are Britons, French, Italians, Austrians and Australians and at times there can be tension between them. Acting like the head of the family, I try to resolve their differences. Of those who come to learn English, the Italians and Germans apply themselves the most assiduously. Up early on Mondays to go to classes, in two or three months they can see the results. The average Frenchman, on the other hand, is more talk than action and as often as not finds excuses not to take lessons. Sometimes some of them are overwhelmed, even those who come from other big restaurants, because there are few places that do things from A to Z as we do. But most of those who leave the Waterside Inn stay in touch for years. Every Christmas, I get hundreds of cards; there are wedding invitations, birth notices for their babies, and – best of all – the first menu from their very own restaurant.

One lesson I brought with me from the Rothschilds, a lesson taught to me for once not by Cécile de Rothschild but by Marcel, her butler, is what I now call *'l'appel du menu'*. Marcel always used to ask me exactly what I planned to serve, so that he had a full picture of how the meal should proceed. Before each meal at the Waterside Inn, all the serving staff – from the most junior *commis* to the most experienced *sommelier* – are given a rundown of everything on the menu, with the ingredients of each dish explained in detail. They take notes so that they can describe the dishes to clients and, in the case of wine-waiters, make the most intelligent suggestions for what should accompany them. Diego then carries out an inspection of their clothing, shoes and their fingernails to ensure that they are clean and fresh.

People sometimes ask me to recount my catastrophes. The truth is that, though there have in the past been fires and floods in the kitchens and cuts and burns to the staff, when you have three Michelin stars and keep them, it is because catastrophes have been extremely rare.

People also ask me how I come to create a new dish and how many I invent in an average year. This is not something any serious chef could do on a regular basis; I can't just sit down and decide to create a new recipe. It may happen at home or when I am travelling, and is greatly dependent on my mood – all five of my senses have to be ultra-sharp. But it is always the ingredient that triggers the idea; that and my greed to discover something new. I see something at the peak of its perfection, something crying out to be eaten, and I am fired up, single-minded, focused, selfish – I can't stop until I can surprise myself with the final dish. I look at its shape, I touch it, smell it, cut it, feel its grain. Should it be filleted or should it be left whole? Steamed, poached, grilled, pan-fried, roasted? Then the sauce – should it be full bodied or a clear *jus*? Any herbs or spices? What garnish most naturally complements it? And, finally, how should I present it so that the visual effect makes my own mouth water? The success of the dish – and I can claim to have created some 250, from savoury to desserts, in three decades – rests on achieving perfect harmony between the components, so as to extract the maximum flavour from the original ingredient.

Over the years, I have occasionally reflected on what I might have done if I had not become a chef. Each time, I come to the conclusion that if I had my life all over again I would not change anything. I believe that Albert and I brought Britain the best gift France could offer. Britain was in a receptive mood. Nevertheless, I offer a sincere 'Thank you for having me'.

And, just in case I am allowed to choose where I shall eat my very last meal in this life, please note that it should be in south-west France, at the restaurant of a man who, before me, was a *pâtissier* and then went on to become a three-star chef, Michel Guérard.

TWELVE SPECIAL
RECIPES

Croûte Genevoise
Swiss Cheese Toast

A satisfying canapé which is not dissimilar to Welsh rarebit. If this is your only canapé, though, and you are feeling generous, I would double or treble the recipe.

THIS RECIPE SERVES 4 PERSONS

Preparation and cooking time: approximately 15 minutes

2 slices white bread	1 large tablespoon double cream
200ml clarified butter (optional)	1 dessertspoon Kirsch
1 large egg	a pinch of cayenne
100g Gruyère or Emmenthal cheese, freshly grated	a pinch of freshly grated nutmeg
	salt and pepper

Preheat the oven to 200–220°C/400–425°F/Gas 6–7.

Remove the crusts from the bread and cut the bread into four. Fry until golden brown in the clarified butter, or toast on both sides.

Mix the egg with a fork and blend with the remaining ingredients to a smooth paste. Check the seasoning. Spread generously on the toasts so that the mix is slightly peaked like a pyramid. Place in the preheated oven on a baking tray for approximately 6 minutes until slightly souffléd and golden brown. Serve immediately.

Note: I prefer to cook the bread in the clarified butter as it becomes crisper and richer, but if you are on a diet the bread can be just toasted.

Crème de Potiron au Parfum de Curry
Cream of Pumpkin Soup Flavoured with Curry

Although I didn't like pumpkin soup as a child, I do now! I frequently serve this pumpkin cream soup at the Waterside Inn. The quenelle of curry cream complements the flavour of the pumpkin very well.

THIS RECIPE SERVES 6 PERSONS
Preparation and cooking time: 40–45 minutes

500g diced pumpkin flesh	*Curry cream*
100g diced carrot	50g finely diced carrot
50g diced white of leek	40g finely diced celery
50g diced celery	60g finely diced onion
250g diced potato	30g unsalted butter
50g unsalted butter	2 tablespoons mild curry powder
2 litres chicken stock or milk	250ml vegetable or chicken stock
1 small *bouquet garni*	1 small *bouquet garni*
250 ml double cream	200ml double cream
salt and pepper	

Cooking the pumpkin soup

Sweat all the vegetables, with the exception of the potato, in the butter without colouring. Add the stock or milk and the *bouquet garni* to the saucepan, and bring to the boil. Add the potato and simmer until it is cooked, about 20 minutes. Then add the cream and bring back to the boil for a couple of minutes. Season with salt and pepper. Remove the *bouquet garni*, then liquidise the soup for a minute. Pass through a fine *chinois* sieve. Check the seasoning.

Making the curry cream

Sweat the vegetables in the butter until they are a light golden brown. Add the curry powder and sweat for a minute. Add the stock, bring to the boil, then add the *bouquet garni*. Let it boil for 20 minutes to reduce by two-thirds. Season and pass through a fine sieve. Allow to cool, then store in the fridge. When ready to serve, mix this curry reduction into the double cream to taste, and whisk until ribbon consistency (when the cream is thick enough to drop off the whisk and form 'a ribbon' on the bulk of the cream).

To serve

Pour the soup into piping hot soup bowls. Using a tablespoon, make a *quenelle* of curry cream and place on top of each portion of soup. Serve at once, as the *quenelle* of cream will slowly start to melt.

Note: If you like, you could serve a few grilled flaked almonds separately to sprinkle on the top of the soup.

Rillettes de Canard
Duck Pâté

Rillettes is a classic French speciality, but I have added a few little 'notes' of my own. You could make the *rillettes hors d'oeuvre* more substantial by serving with some salad leaves seasoned with vinaigrette.

THIS RECIPE SERVES 8 PERSONS
Preparation time: 45 minutes   Cooking time: 3 hours

1 oven-ready duckling, about 2.2kg in weight
32 shelled hazelnuts
300g barding fat, cut into very small dice
100g pork fillet, cut into 4 pieces
1 garlic clove, unpeeled
1 medium carrot, cut in half lengthways

1 medium onion, halved horizontally
1 small *bouquet garni*, containing 10g fresh sage
salt and pepper
275ml dry white wine
1 teaspoon soft green peppercorns

To serve
2 grapefruits, segmented

Preparing the duck and hazelnuts

Remove the skin from the flesh of the duckling. Cut 150g fat from the fattest part of the skin and reserve in a cool place. Discard the skin. Remove all the meat from the bones and cut into strips about 3–4cm long. Keep in a cool place.

Toast the hazelnuts under the grill until the skin is lightly burnt. Remove from the grill and rub in a cloth to remove the skins. Cut each hazelnut in half. Put to one side.

Cooking the *rillettes*

Place the barding fat and the duck fat in a casserole. Add enough water to barely cover the fat. Set the casserole over a medium heat, cover and cook gently for about 30 minutes, stirring occasionally with a spatula, until all the water has evaporated. By this stage, the fat should have melted.

Add the pork fillet, the duck flesh, the garlic clove, carrot, onion and *bouquet garni*. Season with a little salt, pour in two-thirds of the white wine, and bring to the boil. Cover the casserole and set over a very gentle heat, so that its contents are barely simmering. Stir with a spatula from time to time to prevent the mixture sticking to the bottom of the casserole. Leave to cook for 2H hours, then remove from the heat.

Remove the garlic clove, carrot, onion and *bouquet garni*. Add the remaining white wine and green peppercorns to the casserole, and cover with a damp cloth, making sure that it does not touch the meat. Put the casserole in a cool, airy place.

To finish

When the duck and fat mixture is lukewarm, work the meat together with your fingertips until all the shredded flesh and fat are thoroughly mixed together. Correct the seasoning with salt and pepper. Add the halved hazelnuts. Put the *rillettes* into an earthenware terrine and cover them with greaseproof paper or clingfilm. Keep in the refrigerator for at least one to two days before eating.

To serve

With two large tablespoons, place three quenelles of *rillettes* on each plate. Arrange three or four segments of grapefruit next to the *rillettes*. Serve with some plain or toasted country-style bread.

Note: The *rillettes* will keep for three or four weeks in the refrigerator, in airtight containers, handy for a quick snack or a starter to a meal.

Oeufs Brouillés aux Pointes d'Asperges et Tourteau au Naturel
Scrambled Eggs with Asparagus and Crab

This dish is simplicity itself, as nothing involves complicated techniques, and it uses three of my favourite ingredients – eggs, crab and asparagus. However, the timing has to be just right!

THIS RECIPE SERVES 4 PERSONS
Preparation and cooking time: 20 minutes

120g brown crabmeat, cooked
4 crab claws, cooked
1 teaspoon *harissa*
a pinch of paprika
salt and pepper

18 asparagus spears
12 medium free-range eggs
60g unsalted butter
100ml double cream
1 large bunch fresh chives

Preparing the crab

Put the brown crabmeat in a liquidiser or pestle and mortar with the *harissa*, paprika and a pinch of salt, and blend until smooth. Pass through a fine sieve.

Crack the shells from the claws gently, making sure there is no shell remaining on the meat. Cut the claws in half lengthways, cutting either side of the cartilage in the centre, which you should discard.

Have ready a steamer with boiling water in the base, and preheat the oven to 180°C/350°F/Gas 4.

Preparing the asparagus

Peel the asparagus up to 2cm from the top, cut into lengths of 6cm, then lightly cook in boiling salted water. Cool rapidly in a bowl of iced water.

Cooking the eggs

Break the eggs into a bowl, season to taste and whisk lightly. On a low heat melt the butter in a pan and tip in the eggs. With a wooden spatula stir the eggs continuously. When the eggs are cooked to your taste, add the cream and cook for a further minute.

To finish and serve

Place the asparagus and crab claws in the steamer for 2 minutes. Spread the brown crabmeat in four deep serving plates and put them in the oven for 30–60 seconds. Pour the scrambled eggs into the plates over the brown crabmeat, and place the crab claws on top in the centre with the asparagus around the edges. Snip the chives into batons about 3cm long, using only the tips, and sprinkle over the top. Serve hot.

Tronçonnettes de Homard Poêlé Minute
au Porto Blanc
Lobster Medallions in a Port Sauce

The idea for this recipe first came to me when I was in China, and it is cooked in a way that is very Chinese in technique, with elements of eastern spicing as well. You could also serve this as a main course, using four 675g lobsters with a little extra vegetable *julienne*.

THIS RECIPE SERVES 4 PERSONS AS A STARTER
Preparation and cooking time: 40–45 minutes

4 x 450g live lobsters
salt and pepper
10g cayenne pepper
100ml extra virgin olive oil
200ml white port
300ml veal stock
400ml fish stock
100g unsalted butter, cold and diced
10g fresh chervil

Vegetable julienne
1 carrot
1 leek
5g fresh root ginger
30g unsalted butter
1 tablespoon redcurrant jelly

Preparing the lobsters

To kill the lobsters, blanch them in boiling salted water for 30 seconds, then cool in some iced water, or, using a sharp knife, pierce the lobsters between the eyes.

With a chopping knife, cut the end of the tail off at the last segment. Then remove the rest of the tail and cut into three pieces. Cut the tip of the head off with the two antennae, and remove the claws and elbows from the head. Crack the claws with the back of the knife across the middle. Remove the gritty sac from inside the head. Chop the rest of the head and put to one side for the sauce.

Mix 20g of the salt and the cayenne together and season all the lobster pieces.

Preparing the vegetable *julienne*

Cut the carrot, leek and ginger into *julienne* (hair-like strips). Melt the butter in a pan and sweat the *julienne* until soft. Add the redcurrant jelly to moisten, and keep warm on one side.

Cooking the lobster and the sauce

In a large, deep frying pan heat the olive oil until very hot, then sauté all the lobster pieces on all sides until nearly cooked. Remove everything from the pan except for the chopped head pieces which will give extra flavour to the sauce. Keep warm in a low oven.

Discard the oil from the pan, carefully add the port and reduce. Add the veal stock and the fish stock, and reduce to a light sauce consistency. Remove the chopped pieces of head. Add the butter dice to the sauce, stirring continuously until it has completely dissolved. Season to taste.

To serve

On four plates arrange the vegetable *julienne* in four equal piles. Remove the membrane from the base of the tail segment with scissors. Place the head of the lobster at the top of the plate. Cut the knuckles in half lengthways, remove the flesh from one side and put on top of the other. Place either side of the head. Arrange the three tail segments across the middle of the plate with the tail tip at the base of the plate. Pull the lower half of the claw back on itself, which will pull out the centre membrane from inside the claw. Remove the lower half of the shell and place the claw in between the tail pieces, forming a rough lobster shape on the plate. Reheat in a hot oven for a minute. Strain the sauce and pour over the top of the lobster. Sprinkle with plenty of chervil.

Note: For vegetarians the veal stock in the sauce can be replaced by vegetable stock. This is a three-star Michelin dish, one of my most successful, and certainly not for beginners.

Goujonnettes de Sole au Sauternes
Strips of Sole Poached in Sauternes

This dish is simple, light, colourful and full of flavour. I used Sauternes because a slight sweetness is needed, but you can replace it with a Vouvray made from the Chenin Blanc grape.

THIS RECIPE SERVES 4 PERSONS AS A MAIN COURSE
Preparation and cooking time: approximately 40 minutes

2 x 600g Dover sole
2 large potatoes
2 large carrots
30g unsalted butter
salt and pepper
pinch of caster sugar
18 small button mushrooms
4 shallots, chopped

200ml fish stock
300ml Sauternes wine
250ml double cream

Pistachio butter
70g shelled pistachio nuts
70g unsalted butter

Preparing the sole

Using a filleting knife, fillet the sole and remove the skin, or ask your fishmonger to do this for you. This gives four fillets from each fish. Cut each fillet into three strips lengthways (*goujonnettes*) and keep in the refrigerator.

Preparing the vegetables

Peel, wash and cut the potatoes into four slices lengthways, about 1cm thick. Peel and wash the carrots then cut them into 3cm lengths and 'turn' into small barrel shapes with a vegetable knife. Put the carrots into a shallow pan with half the butter, and a pinch each of salt and sugar. Cook until tender.

Remove the stalks from the mushrooms, then wash and dry them. Cook the mushrooms in the same fashion as the carrots, with butter and salt. Keep warm.

Making the pistachio butter

Pour boiling water over the pistachios, then drain and peel them. Blend to a fine powder in a blender. Add the softened butter and purée again to a smooth paste. Pass through a fine sieve, and chill. When ready to use, cut into dice.

Cooking the sole and the sauce

Preheat the oven to 190°C/375°F/Gas 5.

Twist a *goujonnette* and insert a cocktail stick through each end to hold the shape, sticking the cocktail sticks into a slice of potato. Do the same with two other *goujonnettes*. Each potato slice should have three twists of fish on them, held in place by six cocktail sticks altogether. Butter a sauté pan or gratin dish. Sprinkle the shallot in the pan, then add the potatoes with the *goujonnettes* on top. Pour over the fish stock and Sauternes. Season with salt, place on a medium heat and bring to simmering point. Cover with a buttered piece of greaseproof paper, and place in the preheated oven for 2 minutes. When cooked, remove from the pan and drain the fish and potato well. Discard the potato and cocktail sticks. Arrange the *goujonnettes* on plates and keep warm.

Put the pan over a high heat to reduce the cooking liquid by two-thirds. Add the cream and cook for a few minutes more.

To finish and serve

Whisk the chilled diced pistachio butter into the sauce, and adjust the seasoning to taste. Pass the sauce through a fine sieve directly on to the *goujonnettes*. Arrange the hot turned carrots and button mushrooms over the fish. Serve immediately.

Boeuf Stroganoff

This dish is quick to prepare and cook, and is very luxurious. *Never* overcook it! A perfect garnish would be rice pilaf, steamed potatoes or fresh pasta, the latter a favourite with Cécile de Rothschild. Taking so little time to prepare, this is an ideal dish when guests turn up without warning.

THIS RECIPE SERVES 4 PERSONS

Preparation time: 10 minutes   Cooking time: 20 minutes

750g beef fillet, trimmed	300ml double cream
60g clarified butter	2 tablespoons sweet paprika
50ml cognac	juice of ½ lemon
30g unsalted butter	salt and pepper
60g chopped shallots	75g small French gherkins (*cornichons*)
100ml dry white wine	1 tablespoon chopped fresh parsley
200ml veal or chicken stock	

Preparing the beef

Cut the fillet of beef into long and thick strips (*goujonnettes*) of approximately 10cm long and 2cm wide.

Put the clarified butter in a very hot frying pan and seal all the *goujonnettes* very quickly for about 1 minute, to lightly brown. Pour in the cognac, ignite it and then transfer the meat to a colander placed over a plate. At this stage, the meat must be very rare.

Making the sauce

In the same frying pan, melt the unsalted butter and sweat the shallots. Add the white wine and reduce the liquid by half. Add the veal or chicken stock, and let it simmer for a couple of minutes, then add the cream, paprika and lemon juice. Reduce the sauce until it lightly coats the back of a spoon. Season to taste.

Pass the sauce through a conical strainer and reheat. Put the *goujonnettes* back into the boiling sauce. Simmer the meat for 30 seconds if you want it rare and for 1–2 minutes if you prefer it medium to well done.

To serve

Add the gherkins to the meat and sauce and pour into a deep dish. Sprinkle with parsley. Serve immediately.

Paupiettes de Veau
Veal Olives

A simple veal dish such as this, was something Mother used to cook often.
A perfect garnish is some buttered spinach or potato purée.

THIS RECIPE SERVES 6 PERSONS
Preparation and cooking time: 1H hours

540g loin of veal
6 slices pork back fat, 15cm square
75g unsalted butter
1 carrot, diced
1 onion, diced
1 sprig fresh thyme
1 bay leaf
salt and pepper

Stuffing
600g pork fillet
200g pork back fat
4 slices white bread
200ml milk
5 shallots, chopped
1 garlic clove, chopped
30g unsalted butter
20g chopped fresh parsley
24 green olives, pitted and cut in
    chunks
salt and pepper

Preparing the stuffing

Finely mince the pork fillet and back fat. Remove the crusts from the
bread and soak the bread in the milk. Sweat the shallot and garlic in the
butter, then allow to cool. Mix this with the pork mince, parsley and
olives. Squeeze out a little of the milk from the bread and mix the bread
with the rest of the stuffing. Season with salt and pepper to taste.

Preparing the *paupiettes*

Cut six thin slices from the veal loin, about 10cm square, and place
individually between pieces of clingfilm. Beat out until very thin and the
squares have increased to a size of about 15cm. Arrange the veal squares
on a tray and divide the stuffing equally between them, placing it in the
centre of each square. Roll the veal over the stuffing, creating a log shape.

Wrap these logs in the back fat slices and tie with string to avoid unwrapping during cooking.

Cooking and serving

Melt half the butter in a casserole dish, and lightly colour the carrot, onion and the *paupiettes* over a medium heat. While cooking, turn the *paupiettes* and the vegetables every few minutes to achieve a lovely golden brown colour. Add the thyme and bay leaf, and continue cooking like this for about 20 minutes. Remove the *paupiettes* from the pan and keep hot.

Add 200ml water to the pan and reduce by half over a high heat. Strain the sauce through a fine sieve into a clean pan, bring back to the boil and stir in the remaining butter, cut into dice. Season to taste with salt and pepper.

Arrange the *paupiettes* on hot plates, and pour over the sauce. Serve immediately, with accompaniments of choice.

Note: To simplify the dish, the minced pork fillet and back fat stuffing can be replaced by 800g sausagemeat from the butcher, with just the green olives, shallot, garlic, parsley and seasoning to be added. This will take less time to prepare and cook, only an hour.

Coq au Vin à la Bourguignonne
Chicken Casseroled in Red Wine

This dish is typical of the Burgundy/Beaujolais area, and it tastes even better when reheated. Cockerel combs are often included, but they are not easy to find, and not to the liking of everyone. In the past, people used to keep the blood from the bird, mix it with a little vinegar to avoid coagulation, then add it to the sauce at the last minute to give more body and thicken the sauce . . . but that was in the good old days! A full-bodied wine, like a Pommard, will be the perfect accompaniment.

THIS RECIPE SERVES 6 PERSONS
Preparation time: 30 minutes, plus 12 hours' marinating
Cooking time: approximately 1 hour

1 cockerel or large free-range chicken, about 1.8–2kg in weight, cut into 8 pieces
750ml red Burgundy wine
1 large onion, cut in chunks
1 large carrot, cut in chunks
1 *bouquet garni*
3 garlic cloves
salt and pepper

50g clarified butter
30g plain flour, browned a little in the oven
300ml chicken stock
the liver from the bird, plus an extra chicken liver
6 slices French bread, lightly fried in 3 tablespoons vegetable oil
1 tablespoon chopped fresh parsley

Garnishes
24 small white onions
80g unsalted butter
a pinch of caster sugar
250g button mushrooms
1 x 200g piece unsmoked bacon, blanched and then cut into *lardons* (little chunks)
30g clarified butter

Marinating the chicken

Place the pieces of chicken in a large bowl with the red wine, onion, carrot, *bouquet garni* and garlic. Cover the bowl with clingfilm and let it marinate for up to 12 hours in the refrigerator.

Cooking the chicken

Remove the chicken pieces from the marinade, pat them dry and season with salt and pepper. Heat the clarified butter in a frying pan, add the chicken pieces, and sauté them on all sides on a medium heat until they have a nice hazelnut colour. Place in a casserole dish.

Put the onion and carrot chunks into the frying pan and sweat them over a medium heat. Add to the casserole, sprinkle with the browned flour and stir with a wooden spatula, on a medium heat, for a couple of minutes. Add the marinade with the *bouquet garni* and the garlic, and bring to the boil, stirring from time to time with a wooden spatula until it reaches boiling point. Reduce the heat slightly to a simmer, and skim the top. Add the chicken stock, cover the casserole with its lid, and simmer on top of the stove or cook in the oven at 180°C/350°F for an hour. Check with the point of a knife that the chicken pieces are tender in the middle.

Cooking the garnishes

Put the small onions in a small pan with 30g of the unsalted butter and melt over a low heat. Sprinkle them with a pinch of sugar and cook until they reach a light hazelnut colour and are lightly cooked. Reserve in a bowl.

Melt the remaining unsalted butter in a small frying pan, add the mushrooms, and toss them over a medium heat until any liquid has evaporated. Reserve with the onions.

Place the clarified butter in a hot frying pan, add the *lardons* and toss them until they have a good colour. Drain and discard the fat, and add to the bowl containing the onions and mushrooms. Keep warm.

To finish and serve

Pass the two livers through a fine sieve.

Remove the chicken pieces from the casserole dish, place in another pan, cover with a damp cloth and keep at room temperature. Reduce the cooking liquid to the texture of a light sauce, or until it very lightly covers the back of a spoon. Remove from the heat, and whisk in the purée of raw livers. Pass the sauce immediately through a sieve. Pour the sauce over the chicken pieces and keep on a low heat (maximum temperature 80°C/175°F).

Add the mushrooms, onions and bacon to the chicken and heat together for about 5 minutes. Do not let it boil. Pour into a big tureen, place the *croûtons* on top, sprinkle with the chopped parsley, and serve with small boiled new potatoes.

Estouffade de Lièvre Quercinois
Hare Casserole

This is one of the recipes that we introduced when we came to London, and which we have finally persuaded the British to enjoy! It will be easier to ask your butcher to skin and draw the hare and to cut it into portions. Also, give him a small airtight container, and ask him to keep the blood from the throat and around the lungs, as well as the liver.

THIS RECIPE SERVES 6 PERSONS
Preparation time: 20 minutes, plus 12 hours' marinating
Cooking time: about 1 hour, 20 minutes

1 young hare, about 2.5–3kg in weight, skinned and drawn, and cut into pieces	1 tablespoon wine vinegar
	4 tablespoons Armagnac
	1 bottle red Bordeaux wine
300g carrots, cut in chunks	salt and pepper
12 medium shallots	300ml veal or chicken stock
1 *bouquet garni*	300g Californian prunes
3 garlic cloves, crushed	150g caster sugar
10 black peppercorns, crushed	zest of 1 orange
3 tablespoons olive oil	30g unsalted butter, cold and diced

Marinating the hare

Put the hare pieces into a bowl with the carrots and whole shallots. Add the *bouquet garni*, garlic, crushed peppercorns, 1 tablespoon olive oil, the vinegar, half the Armagnac and the red wine. Cover with clingfilm and leave in the refrigerator to marinate for 12 hours.

Cooking the hare

Drain the marinating bowl into a colander placed over a large bowl. Remove the hare pieces, pat them dry and season with salt and pepper. In a frying pan, heat the remaining olive oil, add the hare pieces, and sauté on all sides over a medium heat until they have a nice hazelnut colour. Place the hare pieces in a casserole, with the exception of the back, which you should reserve on a plate.

Put the carrot chunks, shallots and *bouquet garni* into the frying pan and sweat over a medium heat. Add to the hare casserole, pour in the remaining Armagnac and ignite. Add the marinade to the casserole and bring to the boil. Then add the veal or chicken stock, and bring to simmering point (no more than 90°C/195°F), stirring from time to time with a wooden spatula. Skim the top if necessary. Cover and continue to cook on top of the stove at the same temperature for 1 hour, 20 minutes. Add the back of the hare after 30 minutes. Check with the point of a sharp knife that the hare pieces are tender in the middle.

Preparing the prunes

Rinse the prunes in cold water, and put them in a small pan with the sugar and orange zest. Cover with some water and poach them slowly until swollen and soft, then keep them warm.

To finish and serve

Pass the hare liver through a sieve with the blood. Remove the hare pieces, carrots and shallots from the casserole and place them in another pan. Cover with a damp cloth and keep at room temperature. Reduce the cooking liquid to the texture of a light sauce, or until it very lightly covers the back of a spoon. Remove from the heat, and whisk in the purée of raw liver and the blood. Pass the sauce immediately through a conical sieve. Pour the sauce over the hare pieces, add the drained prunes and keep on a low heat (maximum temperature 80°C/175°F).

When ready to serve, swirl the butter dice into the sauce, season with salt and pepper, and pour into a large tureen. Some mashed potatoes flavoured with fresh truffles or some salsify would complement this dish well.

Note: The stew can be cooked in the oven instead of on top of the stove. Preheat the oven to 180°C/350°/Gas 5.

Petits Légumes Provençaux Farcis
Stuffed Provençal Vegetables

These simple baked stuffed vegetables, when cooked and served in the baking Greek summer heat, led to my becoming involved with a cruise line, and enjoying over a decade of cooking on board ship!

THIS RECIPE SERVES 6 PERSONS
Preparation time: approximately 45 minutes
Cooking time: 20 minutes

6 long courgettes
400g large button mushrooms
4 large Désirée potatoes, approx.
   300g each
salt and pepper
350g unsalted butter

200g finely diced shallot
3 sprigs fresh thyme
extra virgin olive oil
200g Parmesan, finely grated
200g fresh white breadcrumbs
50g chopped fresh parsley

Preparing the vegetables

Top and tail four of the courgettes and cut across to form barrel shapes 4cm in height. Scoop out the seeds from one end of each barrel, leaving a little at the bottom to form a base.

Gently wipe the mushrooms with a damp cloth. Pick out eighteen of the best, and remove the stalks. Save the latter for the filling.

Peel the potatoes. Cut three of them straight across like the courgettes to form barrels, and scoop out the centres, not forgetting to leave the base intact. Put them in a large, heavy, flat-bottomed pan with the hollowed-out side face down. Add a pinch of salt, 200g of the butter and just cover with water. Put on a high heat until all the water has gone and the butter is starting to turn a light golden-brown colour. Remove from the heat and allow to cool. With a palette knife carefully turn each potato over and put back on the heat until the base of the potato starts to take on a light golden-brown colour. Allow to cool and then remove from the pan.

Filling the vegetables

Chop the last two courgettes into 2–3cm dice and sweat in a pan with 40g of the butter, a third of the shallot, and a sprig of thyme, until lightly cooked. Allow to cool, then discard the thyme. Fill each hollow courgette with a little of the filling.

Repeat the same process with the remaining mushrooms and stalks, using 40g butter, a third of the shallot and a sprig of thyme.

Cut the last potato into 5mm dice and repeat the process above using the remaining butter, slightly more than for the courgettes and mushrooms, the remaining shallot and thyme.

Cooking and serving

Preheat the oven to 160°C/325°F/Gas 3.

Place all the stuffed vegetables on a baking tray. Sprinkle with salt, pepper and a little olive oil. Mix together the Parmesan, breadcrumbs and chopped parsley, sprinkle over the top of the vegetables, and press down lightly. Place in the preheated oven for about 20 minutes until cooked. Finish under a hot grill for a lovely, light golden-brown top.

Notes: If Désirée potatoes cannot be found, any red potato can be used so long as they are large and uniform in shape. Désirée have the best flavour, though.

The finished raw stuffed vegetables can be prepared a day in advance if necessary, and kept in the refrigerator.

Tarte des Demoiselles Tatin
Upside-down Apple Tart

This is a classic I first learned when working with M Loyal at his *pâtisserie* in Paris. It is as much a favourite now as it was then.

THIS RECIPE SERVES 4 PERSONS
Preparation time: 20 minutes, plus 20 minutes' resting
Cooking time: 40 minutes

6 medium dessert apples, preferably
    Cox's
juice of H lemon
120g unsalted butter

200g caster sugar
plain flour
250g puff pastry (can be bought ready-
    made)

Preparing the apples and pastry

Peel, core and halve the apples. Put in a large bowl, sprinkle with lemon juice and place in the refrigerator.

Spread the butter evenly over the base of a heavy frying pan or round heatproof dish, 22cm in diameter and 5cm deep. Cover the butter evenly with the sugar, then arrange the apples, rounded side down, on the bottom of the pan.

On a lightly floured surface, roll the puff pastry out into a circle about 3mm thick. Lay the pastry over the apples, allowing an overlap of about 2 cm all around. Trim off the excess pastry with a sharp knife. Leave to rest in a cool place for at least 20 minutes.

Cooking the tart

Preheat the oven to 220°C/425°F/Gas 7.

Set the pan or dish over a fierce direct heat for 5–10 minutes until the butter and sugar are bubbling and have turned an amber colour. With a small palette knife, lift a little of the pastry away from the edges to ensure even colouring. Bake in the preheated oven for 30 minutes until the pastry has risen and is golden.

To serve

As soon as the tart is cooked, invert it quickly on to a round serving dish, taking care not to burn yourself. The pastry will now be on the bottom of the plate, with the apples on top. If any apples have slipped, push them back into place with a small knife. Serve the tart piping hot.

Note: Pears make a good alternative to the apples. In that case, I would recommend that you use Comice pears, which have a sweet taste. You must make sure, when you purchase them, that they are a touch *under-ripe.*

Index

Index

Index

Index